Mold Making, Casting & Patina

for the student sculptor

by

Bruner Felton Barrie

Adams, Barrie, Felton and Scott Publishing
Box 247, Princeton, NJ 08540

First Printing, April 1993

Library of Congress Catalog Number 91-092469
ISBN 0-9631867-0-1

Line Drawings by Barbara Johnson
Final Editing by Sue Avery
Photographs by A.B.F.S. Photographer
Book Typesetting & Design by MK Design, Skillman, NJ

Printed in the UNITED STATES OF AMERICA
Thomson-Shore, Inc., Dexter, Michigan

Adams, Barrie, Felton, & Scott Publications
New York • Boston • Princeton

I dedicate this book to my daughter, Jennifer Adams Barrie (Sunflower) for her undefined support through the trauma and the excitement of being a model and an editor. She was there from the beginning and stayed to the end, even to being the model for the moulage mold and cast. For that I can only thank her.

I would also like to acknowledge that if it were not for the following people I would never have been in a position to have accomplished this book. My late friend Alex J. Ettl, the founder of Sculpture House, the late Joe Brown, who was a fine sculptor and good man, but most of all my father George N. Barrie Jr., who through wisdom, kindness, and great compassion made the right decisions at the proper time. Thank you from the bottom of my heart.

I would also like to thank all of the sculptors, male and female, who have created a work worthy of being cast and who are using this simple manuscript to accomplish a lasting piece of art.

Sincerely,

Bruner F. Barrie

CONTENTS

INTRODUCTION

I have written this book expressly for the beginner, novice, or everyday person who would like to make a simple basic mold and cast of his or her work. I have kept the instructions to a minimum so they can be easily followed. When I began as a sculptor it was complicated, confusing, and difficult to learn, particularly from a master who didn't want to teach. I remember this and so have written these instructions to be easily comprehended and followed.

When you have completed a few molds and casts, you will tell your friends what a great mold maker and caster you are, since you will have the knowledge and experience they do not. We all do it, so have fun.

I have incorporated line drawings within the primary text so it will be easier to comprehend what I am trying to get across. At the end of each chapter I have included a step by step pictorial so you will not have to flip back and forth to get the basic procedures. I have tried to make these pictures realistic rather than fancy studio shots that you cannot relate to. I have also tried to keep the same format within each chapter so you will be familiar with the procedures, tools, and materials required with each process. Repetition is the key. I have given an overview, the basic steps, and the actual procedures that will make the mold and casts. You will have to take the time and effort to perfect your own abilities.

Although this goes against the grain, I must now write a disclaimer, since I am not actually with you to show you the procedures.

These directions are offered as a guide in the use of the materials. No guarantee, expressed or implied, is made regarding their stability or performance, since I have no control over the storage, handling, or application of these materials.

Mold making and casting will give you a great deal of pleasure and satisfaction. I hope you will experience the same joys I have over the years. I wish you the best in all that you are about to accomplish.

Bruner F. Barrie

1992

CHAPTER 1

Bas-Relief Mold

(waste mold and latex mold)

Type of Mold .... Plaster, Latex, Panel Relief
Size .... 12" x 10" x 1"
Medium of Model .... Plastilina
Time Required .... 6 Hours

BASIC CONCEPT

The bas-relief mold is a one-sided mold, made from either plaster or rubber. The shape will conform to the dimensions of the actual panel, the most common being rectangular or square. A solid plaster shell is formed over and around the entire piece to be cast by constructing a retaining wall or "fence". The plaster is poured, set, and repaired (filling in any small air pockets that may have formed while pouring the plaster to make the mold). The resulting plaster will be a solid block, except for the hollow cavity or negative indentation where the original panel was. This is a relief mold. The cavity is the negative and the subsequent cast is the positive. The interior of the negative mold will be sealed, a release agent applied, and a cast poured into this mold.

When the casting material has set up and cured, it will be removed from the mold and any necessary repairs will be made. Once the repairs are completed, the panel will be ready for a patina, which is a type of coloring. It will then be mounted or hung for display.

TIME FACTOR

This type of mold is very simple and easy to complete. The time-consuming elements are the mixing of the plaster powder and waiting for it to set-up. Allow approximately six hours for this project to be completed from start to finish.

MATERIALS REQUIRED

1. Panel to be cast.
2. Plaster for the mold and cast.
3. Water and container for the mold, cast, and cleanup.
4. Shellac, varnish to seal the panel.
5. Mold lotion or soap as a release agent.
6. Soft 100% bristle brush.
7. Wood slats, moist clay, or plastilina for fence.
8. Wood mallet to remove cast.
9. Flexible steel tool for repair of mold and cast.
10. Wire for eye hooks, sandpaper, and colors optional.

BASIC STEPS

1. Place the panel on a flat, sturdy work surface, preferably formica, with at least four inches of free space around the entire panel.
2. Construct a retaining wall or "fence" around the entire panel leaving at least one inch between the panel and the fence wall and one inch above the highest point of the panel.
3. Coat the panel and all the fence area with shellac and let dry. Coat a second time and let dry.
4. Apply a release agent such as mold lotion or green soap to the interior area of the fence and panel.
5. Pour mixed plaster into the area between the panel and the fence walls until the plaster is level with the top of the fence, and allow to dry and set hard.
6. Remove the fence when plaster is hard; remove the mold from the panel and repair any air holes in the mold.
7. Apply a sealant to the interior area of the mold; shellac.

PREPARING THE MODEL (PANEL)

Place the model (panel) face upward on a nonporous work surface, allowing at least one inch of free space around the entire perimeter for construction of the mold. A piece of this type will often be modeled on a separate workboard which may be placed directly onto the work table. If there is not enough room or free space around the workboard and the area required to make the mold fence, then a flush fitting work surface should be built up to make an even flat work area.

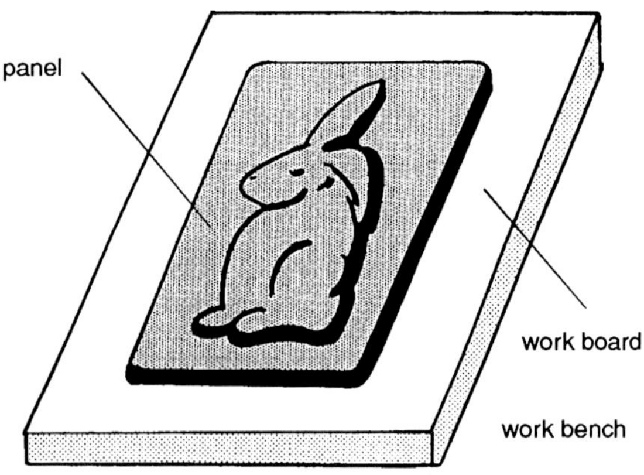

Figure 1.1. Panel on a work table.

If the panel has been modeled from plastilina (the medium under discussion) it will adhere to the work area, as will moist clay. Secure the panel firmly to the work area so it will not shift during the mold making process. Moist clay is best worked when in the leather hard state. Once the panel has been secured construct a retaining wall or fence around it.

BUILDING A RETAINING WALL (FENCE)

To create a mold, a fence or retaining wall is formed around the perimeter of the panel with enough space between the walls of the fence and the panel to form a shell when the plaster is poured into the area. The retaining wall contains the liquid plaster until it sets and hardens, forming the shell or mold. The size of the fence or retaining wall is determined by the size of the panel.

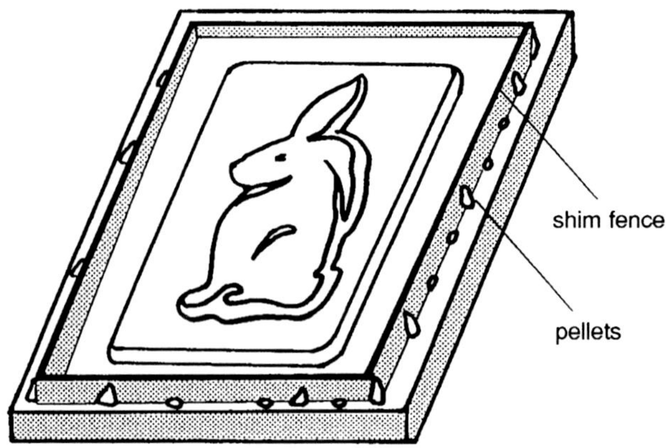

Figure 1.2. Panel with fence.

The fence should be constructed of material sturdy enough to contain the plaster. The larger the panel the heavier the material, of course.

Actual Construction: In our case the fence will be made of wooden slats purchased from a hardware store. They should be 1/8 inch thick and 1½ inches wide. Draw a line one inch from the panel around its entire perimeter to allow at least one inch between the fence wall and the panel.

Cut the wood slat sections to match the outline around the model. Make up enough pellets of clay to place one at two inch intervals around the fence wall. These pellets can be made from moist clay or plastilina.

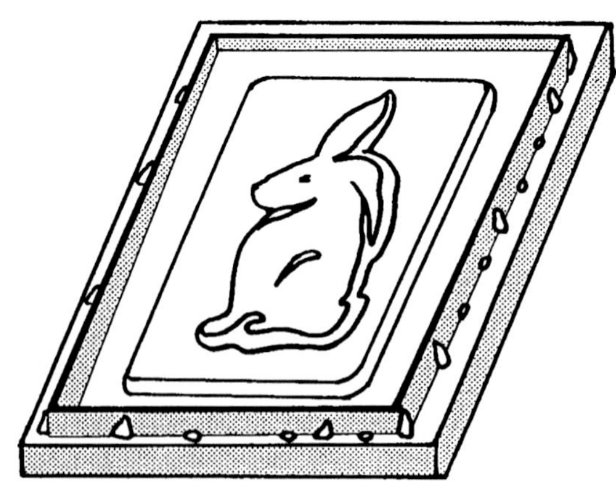

Figure 1.3. Fence construction.

Place the cut wooden slats on the outline, with the corners flush. Secure the section with pellets of clay at two-inch intervals. With a small amount of clay fill in the corner areas where there are openings, so that no liquid plaster will escape when poured. If the fence walls are too large hammer finishing nails into the ends of the wood pieces.

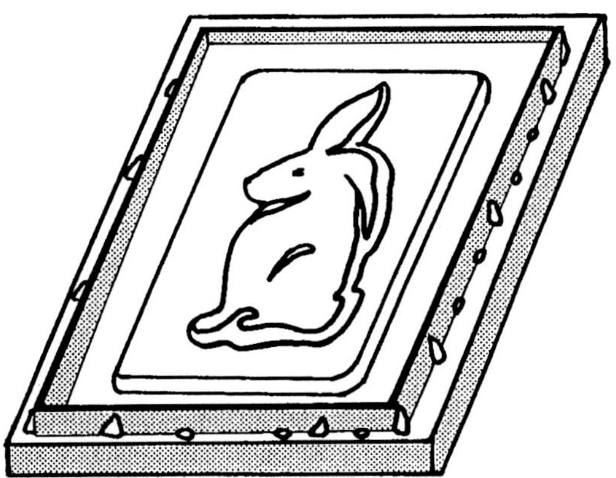

Figure 1.4. Securing corners of fence.

You will probably notice that pellets of moist or oil base clay adhere nicely to the slats and work surface. I like to use oil-based plastilina for my pellets. To seal or plug cracks or crevices I generally use moist clay since it fills in easily. The height of the fence will be determined by the highest point of the panel. The fence must be at least one inch above this highest point so the resulting mold wall will be at least that thick. Once the fence has been constructed, you are ready for the next stage, sealing the panel.

SEALING THE PANEL

When plaster is used to create a mold, the model is almost always "sealed" first, regardless of the type of material used for the model. There are exceptions to this rule, such as highly polished, nonporous stone and metal surfaces, but the plastilina model we are using must be sealed as a final step before pouring the plaster. This involves coating the model with a shellac/alcohol mixture, which separates or "seals" off the model from direct contact with the liquid plaster. Without this sealant, the plaster would adhere directly to the surface of the model, making it almost impossible to separate the two once the plaster has cured.

The sealant I most often use in this process is a mixture of one part shellac to one part alcohol. Using a paint brush, apply this shellac/alcohol mix over the entire surface of the area into which the plaster will be poured including the surface of the model, the work surface, and the inside surfaces of the fence.

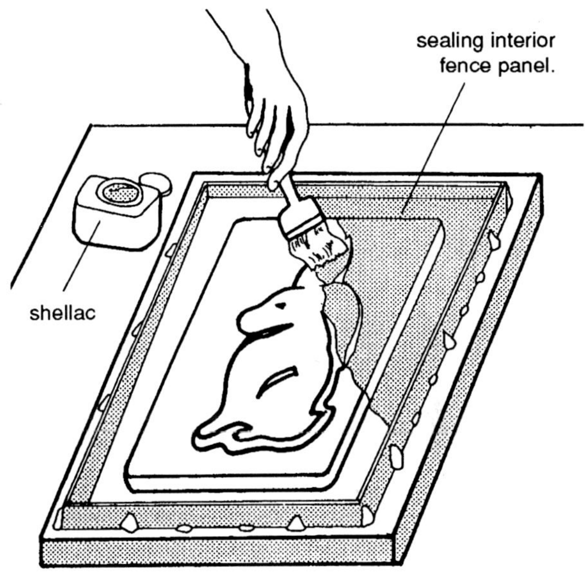

Figure 1.5. Sealing the model.

After the coating has dried, a second coat should be applied and allowed to dry. Be careful to remove any bristles that may have come loose from the brush and remained on the surface of the model, and to smooth any air pockets that may have formed during the application of the sealing mixture.

When both coats of shellac have dried, apply a final coating of mold lotion (tincture of green soap) to the entire surface that you have sealed with the shellac. This is the final step before the preparation and pouring of the plaster to form the mold. Apply the mold lotion with a brush and allow to dry. It will act as a release agent and allow for the easy separation of the mold from the model.

PREPARING AND POURING THE PLASTER

Before preparing the plaster for pouring, make sure the model and the working platform on which it is secured are level and not tipped to one side or the other. If not level, correct the situation before proceeding.

To determine how much plaster you will need, calculate the interior dimensions of the area encompassed by the fence (retaining wall). The formula for determining the volume of an area of square or rectangular shape, as in our project, is fairly simple: measure and multiply the length by the width, then multiply that sum by the height. In our example, that would be 12" x10", which equals 120", by 2", for a final sum of 240 cubic inches.

Once you have determined the number of cubic inches involved, turn to the weights and measurements section in the appendix. This will give you the correct amounts of plaster and water needed to fill that volume. In this case, it would be four pounds of plaster and three pints of water. The panel itself takes up space and you may be wondering why we did not account for this in the calculations. The reason is, you should always make more plaster than you need for the minimum requirements. If you end up with less plaster than you need to finish a project in mold making and casting, you will invariably have to start over from the beginning, not an enjoyable task I can assure you, having made this mistake a number of times myself. Plaster is a relatively inexpensive material and the small cost is good insurance against having to start all over again.

Having determined the correct amount of plaster needed refer to Appendix A for instructions on mixing the plaster if you are not familiar with the procedure. When the plaster powder and water have been mixed to a creamy texture, it is ready to be poured. Don't forget that you have a limited time in which to use the plaster in its liquid state, about 15 to 20 minutes. Now is certainly not the time for a snack!

You should now have the model and working platform level, with the model properly sealed and prepared, and a bowl or bucket of liquid plaster at the ready. It is time to begin pouring.

The secret to pouring successfully is to pour gently and avoid splashing the liquid plaster. This not only prevents the creation of a mess, which will need to be cleaned up, but it also helps to prevent air bubbles from being formed and distorting the interior surface of the mold. Do not pour the plaster directly onto the panel, but rather to the side of the panel, in the space between the panel and the fence.

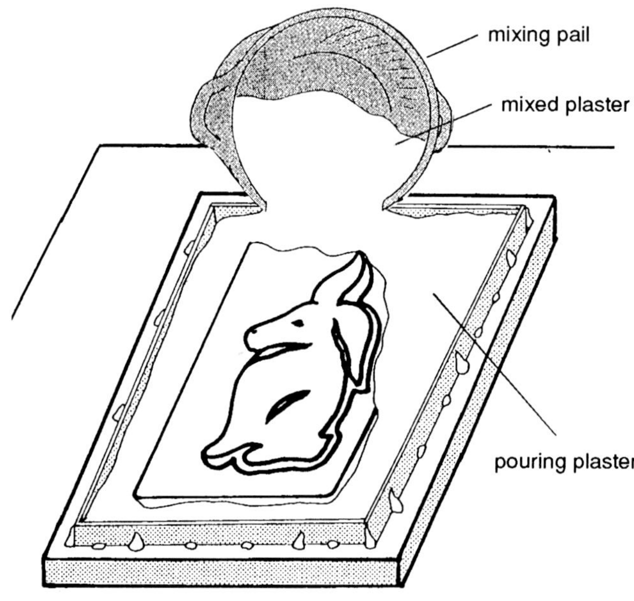

Figure 1.6. Pouring plaster.

Raise the bowl or pail of plaster slightly above the level of the fence. Pick a spot between the model and the fence, then slowly begin to pour the plaster into this area in a gentle fashion.

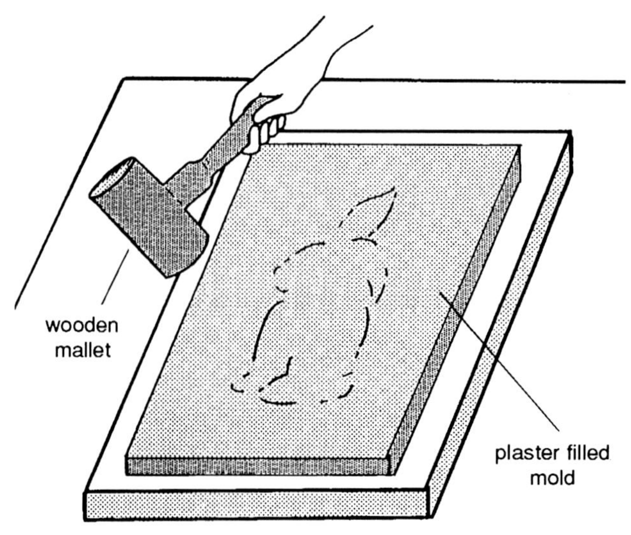

Figure 1.7. Tapping.

Continue pouring until the entire area is completely filled to a space approximately 1" higher than the highest point of the panel, to the top of the fence material. Tap the base board to release any air bubbles.

Let the plaster set a few minutes, then use a stiff straightedge or a block scraper to level off the top surface of the plaster. This top surface will become the bottom or base, of the mold once the plaster has set completely.

After about ten minutes, you may notice that the plaster is becoming warm to the touch and is beginning to harden. The warmth is part of the natural reaction process and is not in any way dangerous. In fact, once the plaster has hardened sufficiently, you may place your hand directly on the surface of the plaster (as most people do) and feel the warmth as it generates.

Once the plaster has been poured and leveled, let it sit without disturbing it for at least an hour. This will allow the material to set-up.

REMOVING THE MOLD

The mold has been formed when the plaster has set for at least one hour. The fence section should now be taken off and the model removed. After removing the fence section, lightly tap the edges of the mold. It should "pop" off of the model. Gently lift it from the work surface. If the mold fails to release and the plaster still seems cool and damp, let thc mold set and dry out for an additional hour. Repeat the process. If the mold still refuses to release, try lifting the mold (with the model still inside) off the working surface. Tap the edges of the mold against the working surface. If the model still does not release, then you must simply dig the plastilina model out of the mold using a sharp-edged steel tool, being careful not to damage the interior surface of the mold in the process. The model will usually release from the mold on the first or second attempt.

CLEANING THE MOLD

When the panel has been successfully removed from the mold, there will most likely be some residue of plastilina adhering to the plaster. This residue must be removed prior to casting the panel. This is easily done by using a sharp steel tool to gently scrape the clay material out. Be very careful not to damage the interior surface of the mold. After the bulk of this excess material has been removed, you may use soap and water to clean out the remaining material.

When the mold has been completely cleaned, inspect the interior surface for damage and air pockets. Any defects must be repaired before the mold can be used. A certain amount of touch-up or repair work is to be expected in the construction of most molds. Use a small amount of plaster that has been added to the appropriate (normal) amount of water and allowed to partially set without mixing. The plaster should be used while still wet and workable.

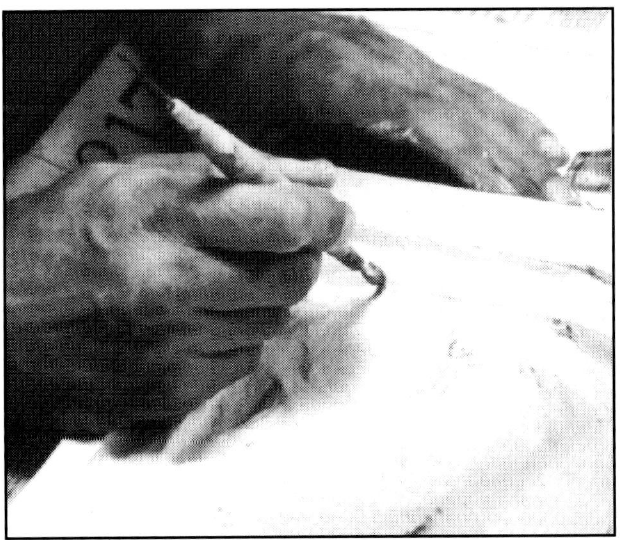

Figure 1.8. Repairing air holes.

Place the plaster in any air pockets or hole defects with a flexible pallet tool. Then smooth to the original contour of the inner mold with a damp cloth. All imperfections and defects should be inspected and repaired to the best of your ability before continuing. A perfect cast is only produced by a mold that has a perfect casting (interior) surface.

CASTING THE PANEL

When the entire inside surface of the mold has been cleaned, repaired, and smoothed, it must be treated and sealed before the actual casting process can begin. Thus the casting material, in this case the plaster, will not fuse with the porous surface of the mold, also constructed from plaster.

The plaster mold will be so treated as to make it nonabsorbent. This includes submerging the mold in water, a step often neglected by many novice and intermediate grade mold makers and casters. It might seem that such a step would prove destructive to the mold, but certain chemical reactions take place during the setting and curing process that impart characteristics to the plaster, enabling it to withstand a complete water saturation without damage of deterioration.

The first step of the sealing process, is to brush a separator or release agent onto the interior of the mold.

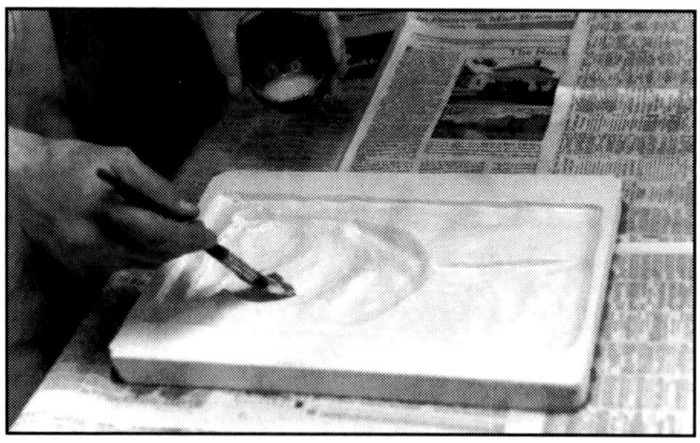

Figure 1.9. Soaping the mold.

The release agent we will be using is mold lotion or tincture of green soap. This brushing application should be kept up continuously for about 25 minutes, as the dry plaster of the mold is very absorbent. A soft bristle brush is usually preferred for this work. Again you must be careful to remove any bristles that have loosened and remained on the interior surface of the mold.

Lather up the interior of the mold, reaching all cracks, crevices, and hard to reach areas. (The casting material will find its way to all areas, if poured correctly.) After the solution appears to have been totally absorbed, remove any excess froth or foam and liquid from the mold surface, especially in the joints and recesses. Any soap left in the mold will attack whatever freshly poured plaster or gypsum product is used for the cast and therefore must be removed.

Let the mold dry thoroughly, then brush a small amount of olive oil or baby oil onto the interior of the mold until a dull sheen or luster appears. Try a small drop of water on the surface. If the water does not bead up, like water on a newly waxed car, more soaping and/or mold lotion is required. No water should be absorbed into the mold surface.

Now the most unusual step occurs, one that I am still amazed at. The prepared mold is totally submersed in a container of clean water for approximately 15 to 20 minutes, or until it is entirely saturated. The set plaster of the mold will not deteriorate or be damaged, but must totally absorb the water so the freshly poured plaster of the cast will not adhere to the mold. If the mold is even slightly dry, it will absorb the water of the cast material. This will cause air bubbles and some plaster will adhere to the mold interior and ruin the cast.

After the mold has soaked for the requisite length of time, the excess water is drained and the cast poured. Many times an instructor has telephoned me to complain that a cast will not release from the mold. Every time it is because the mold was not soaked prior to pouring the casting material. Soaking is an essential for a good, clean cast.

Once the interior of the mold has been cleaned, repaired, and soaked, it is ready to receive the casting material.

PREPARING THE CASTING MATERIAL

We will be using casting plaster to make our cast, the same material used in the making of the mold. This material is the most suitable for both the mold and the cast, providing a good long lasting mold and a strong and effective casting material. There are other plaster or gypsum materials that may be a little harder, such as hydrocal and hydrostone, but the strength in these products will not be needed for our purposes and they are somewhat more difficult to use. Trust me.

We will be using Pristine White Casting Plaster. There are other types of plasters; plaster of paris can be bought in a hardware store. However, I cannot recommend these since the plaster grade, generally used for construction and plaster board, is not the professional grade required for casting sculptured pieces. Mix the casting plaster as you did the plaster for the mold, in a sifting motion with the plaster powder added to the water. The mixture should be thicker than heavy cream, but still flowing.

Before mixing and pouring the plaster, take the basic measurements of the mold: length times width times depth, minus about 10% for the mold area. Refer to the area-equals-volume chart in Appendix F to determine how much dry plaster powder and water will be needed. I recommend you mix at least 20% more plaster than is necessary. Throwing away a few pounds of plaster is better than having a mold that is not completely filled.

Mix the plaster in a flexible rubber or aluminum bowl, adding the plaster to the water, sifting it through the fingers so a smooth lump-free mixture is achieved. Do not be timid in placing the plaster in the water. Grab a handful and sprinkle it in a circular motion, until a mound of about 1 inch develops above the water line. Be sure to place the dry plaster powder container close to the mixing bowl since dropped powder will cause a mess. I suggest that the plastic bag be folded completely back so the hand can easily grasp the powder. Refer to Appendix A for mixing procedures.

After the plaster powder has been added to the water to a peak of about 1 inch above the water line, let it sit for approximately 3 to 4 minutes. This will allow the plaster to absorb the water.

Next, carefully lower the hand to the bottom of the container and with fingers spread slightly, gently mix the plaster to a smooth heavy cream texture. The mixing should be done gently, scraping the sides of the container and folding the plaster into a smooth consistency free of lumps. Do not allow any air to get into the plaster mixture,

Before pouring, lift the container of plaster and tap it lightly so that any air bubbles will rise to the surface and can be scraped away.

POURING THE CAST

Pour the liquid plaster into the mold from the sides.

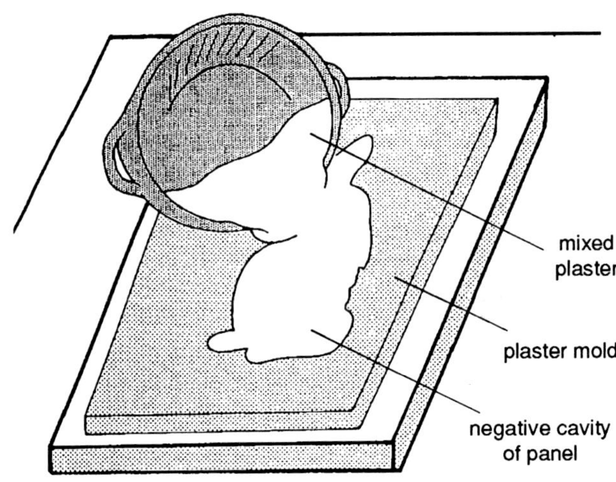

Figure 1.10. Pouring the cast.

Fill the mold with the casting material without spattering or allowing excess air to get into the cast. Pouring from the side allows the plaster to fill the mold with a natural flow and to take its natural perimeter within the mold and rise evenly to the top. If there is too much plaster, level it off with the block scraper or a straight-edge tool, making a level and even cast to the mold.

In the areas where the plaster may not have flowed properly, take a pointed tool and probe. This will help the plaster to fill up the entire cavity of the mold without any air bubbles or gaps, including right angles and crevices. Additional plaster can be added if needed.

Next, the mold should be lifted and tapped with a mallet so any air bubbles that might have been trapped can escape. The air bubbles will rise to the surface. Smooth the surface with a block scraper or straight-edge tool.

INSERTING EYE HOOKS

Each panel should have two eye hooks or hanging devices inserted while the plaster is still wet. Since the plaster has a water base, any material that will corrode or rust should not be used. I suggest a strand of aluminum wire. Eye hooks are easy to make and insert. I advise that the hooks be constructed before the cast is poured. The size of the wire depends on the weight of the panel. We will be using 1/16 inch wire, which is pliable enough to bend with the fingers or with needle nose pliers.

Cut two strands of wire long enough to double over, creating a loop and leaving ends long enough to entwine together and insert into the plaster cast to support the panel when hung.

Cut the wire with the sharp edge of a knife hit with a hammer, with household scissors, or wire cutters.

After the lengths are cut, fold them over, leaving a loop at the closed end and twisting the open ends around one another. The soft wire may also be wrapped around the end of the needle nose pliers to form the loop. Make the loop large enough to accommodate placement over a nailhead for hanging. Take your fingers or pliers and bend the loop portion to a 90 degree angle from its horizontal plane.

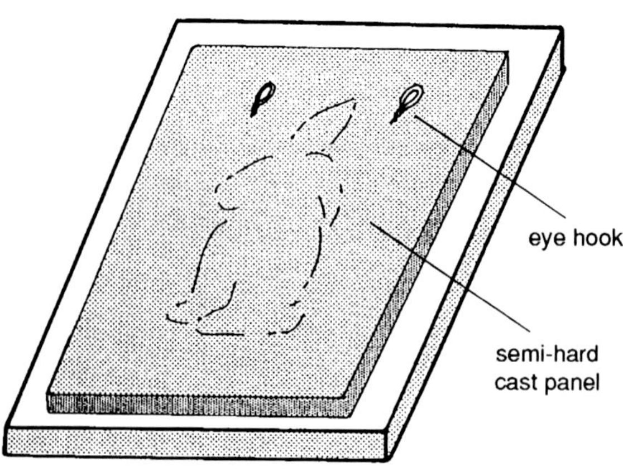

Figure 1.11. Eye hooks.

Push the twisted ends into the wet plaster on the back of the panel to about 1/8 inch in depth. Make sure the ends are inserted at equal distances from top and sides so your piece will hang evenly. Cover the inserted wire with a small amount of fresh plaster, then smooth the plaster even or flush with the back of the panel. If the plaster is becoming too stiff, use a damp cloth to smooth the surface or use the stiff edge of the block scraper. Only the loop ends should protrude from the panel. When the plaster is set and cured, the panel will have installed hanging devices.

I suggest you determine the placement of the hooks prior to pouring the plaster to ensure that they are even and do not extend above the top of the panel. Minor adjustments to the loop can be made after the plaster has set, but take care not to break the loops free from the panel when doing so.

This is the most common way to attach hanging devices. Other methods can also be used such as drilling the set plaster or even gluing hangers to the back of the panel.

REMOVING THE CAST PANEL (de-molding)

When the plaster has been poured and the eye hooks are properly inserted and smoothed, the plaster is left to set-up for at least one hour. As the plaster begins to set, it will become warm to the touch. By placing the palm of your hand lightly on the back of the panel, you can feel the reaction of the plaster with the water as it sets up. This generally occurs about 15 minutes after the plaster has been mixed and poured.

When the plaster has totally cooled, set, and cured (allow at least one hour) it is time to remove the panel from the mold. If there are no dramatic under-cuts to restrict the removal and if the sealing process and release were completed properly, tap the sides of the mold lightly with a wooden mallet. This will jar the panel loose from the mold. Do not hit the sides so hard that the mold is damaged.

Place some cloth or pieces of newspaper down to make a "bed" large enough to cushion it as it falls out of the mold. Push some cloth or newspaper into a hammock or "pillow" at one end of the "bed." Turn the mold **gently** over onto the pillow area. With the pull of gravity, your panel should fall out of the mold onto the bed.

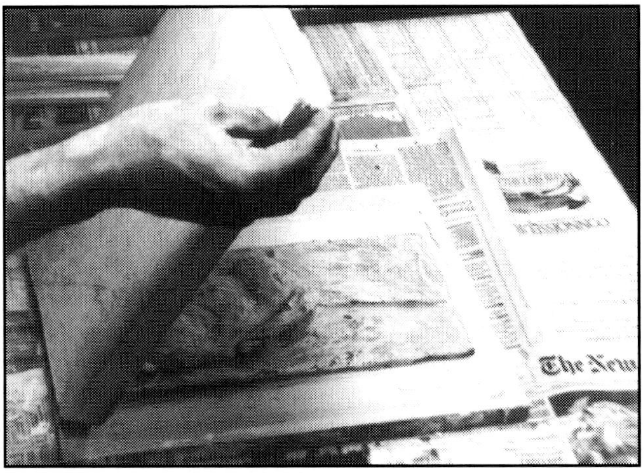

Figure 1.12. Removing the cast.

With your hand under the panel, guide its descent and landing. If by chance the panel does not drop completely out of the mold, additional tapping on the sides and top may be required. You may also want to raise the sides of the mold and tap them on the work surface. If you are still unsuccessful take a small cup of water and pour it into the cracks between the mold and the cast. If you remove the panel this way, let it dry for another hour thoroughly. In humid areas this may take longer.

If the panel still does not release from the mold, the mold must be chipped away, piece by piece to expose the cast. Do this **very slowly and gently**, so the cast will not be harmed.

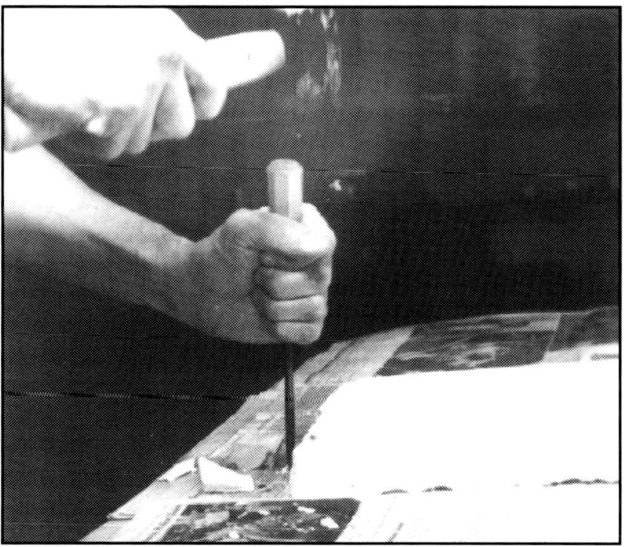

Figure 1.13. Chipping away the mold.

PATINA OF THE PLASTER PANEL

The final step before placing the panel is to apply a patina or coloring as desired. When working with plaster or gypsum-based materials that are porous, any type of coloring may be used: shoe polish, acrylics, oil based paints, even food coloring. Whatever effect is desired, it can be obtained through any of these applications. I suggest you experiment on a small piece of set plaster before decorating the final panel. I have cast and decorated about 50 rectangular samples, recording the process of each so I can duplicate it as needed.

Patina is somewhat of an art in itself and I have written an entire chapter on the subject. Refer to Chapter 8 for more detailed information.

Now that you have finished your sculpture, having made a mold and cast and colored your panel, you may want to hang your piece. In deciding where consider background lighting, and color coordination with surrounding objects. But always remember, the piece was created, cast, and finished by you. Your appreciation and acceptance are first and foremost. After all, you are the sculptor.

PICTORIAL OVERVIEW

Relief Mold of a Panel, Basic Steps

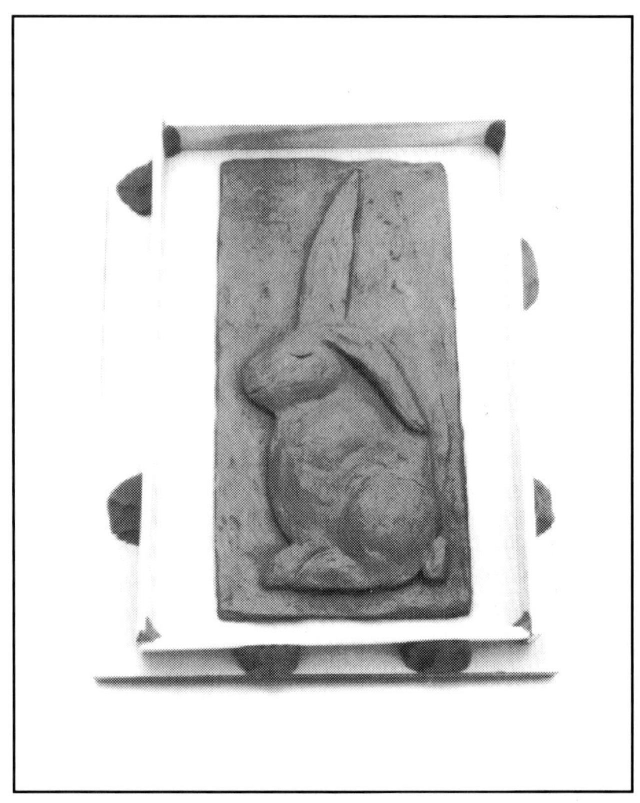

2. Panel, secured fence and clay support pallets.

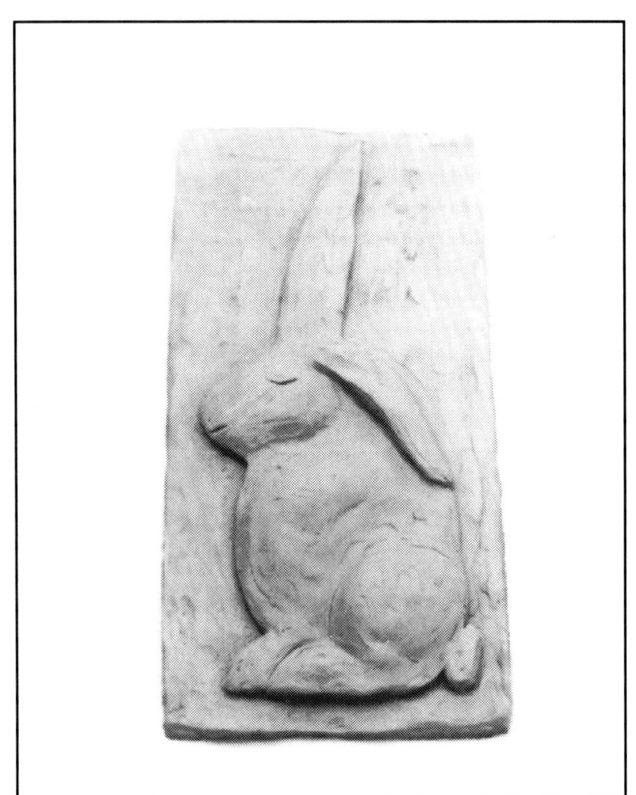

1. Panel on work surface.

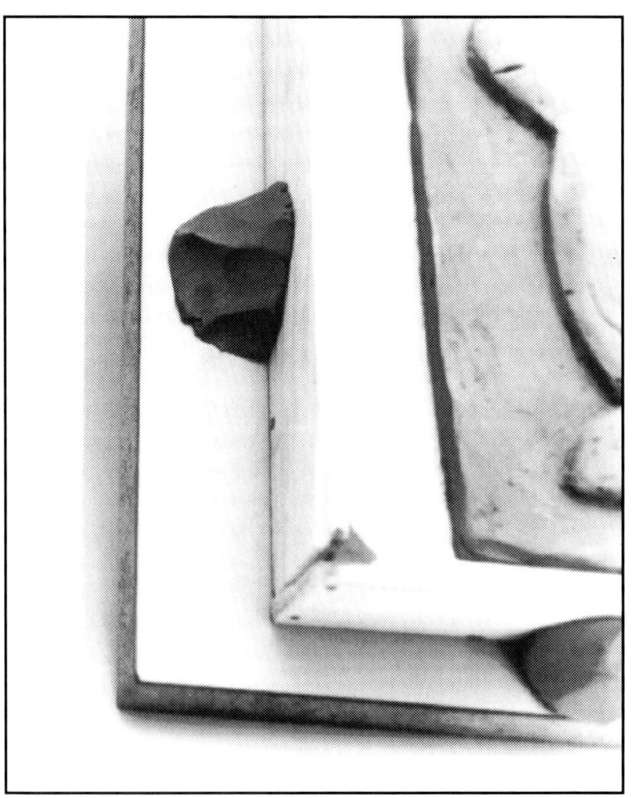

3. Close up of support pellets.

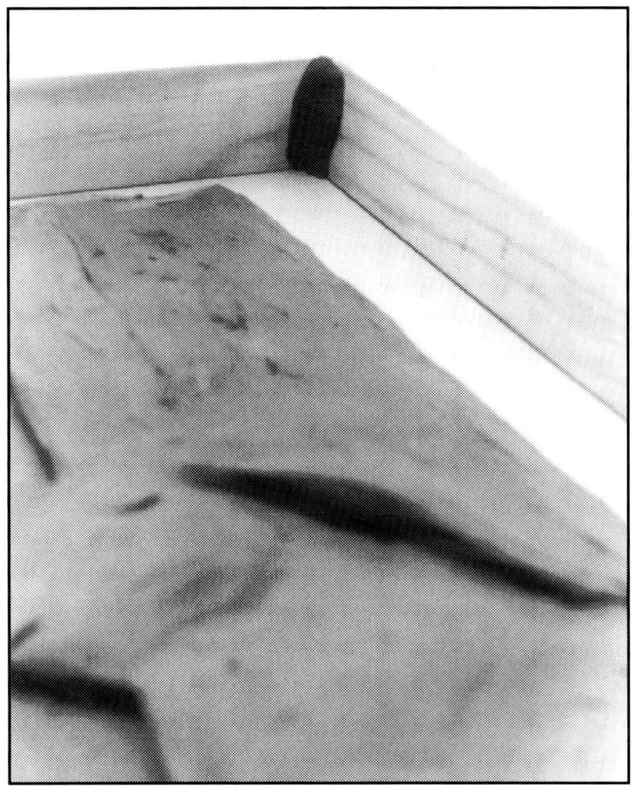

4. Inside securing of fence at joints.

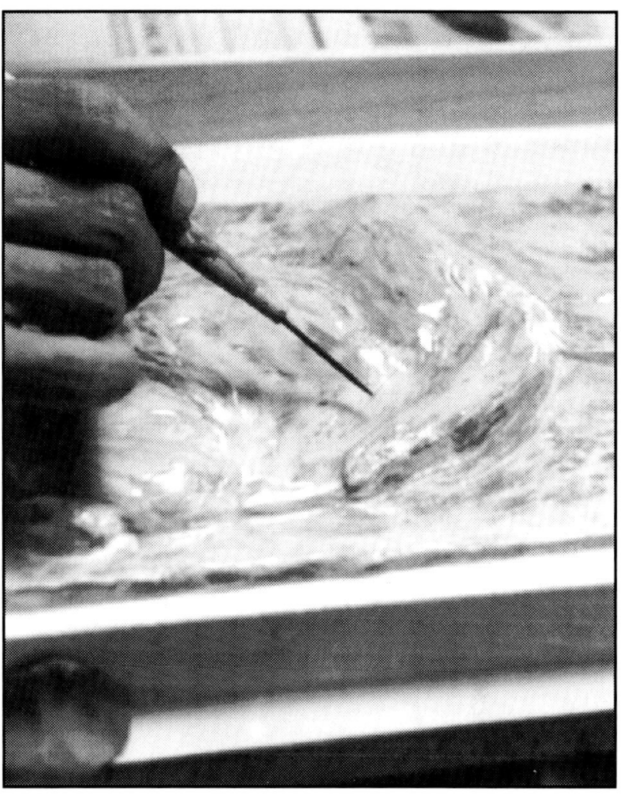

6. Removing air bubbles.

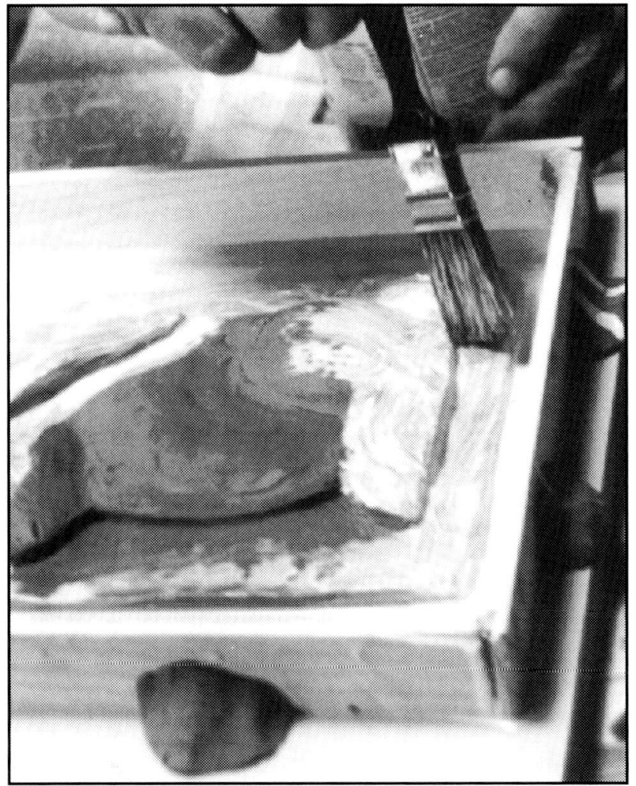

5. Sealing panel and fence support with shellac.

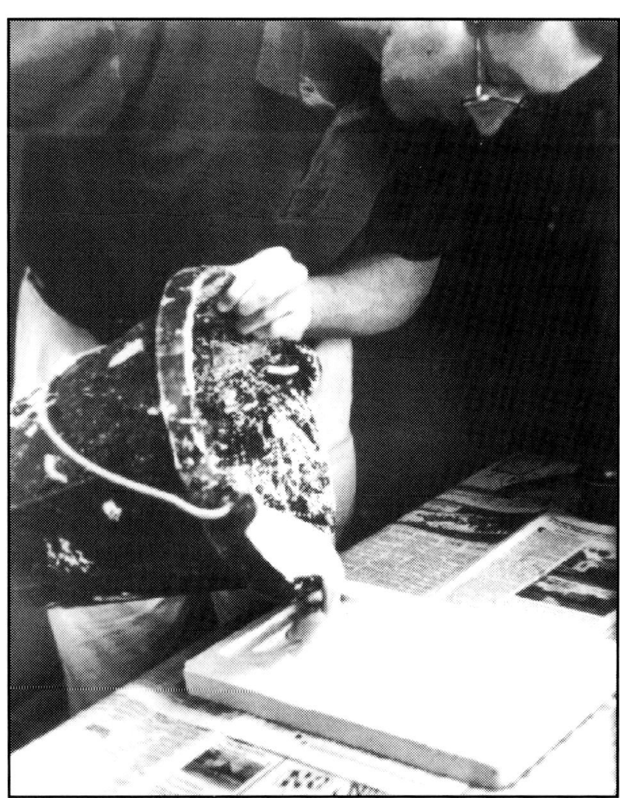

7. Pouring plaster mold in fence.

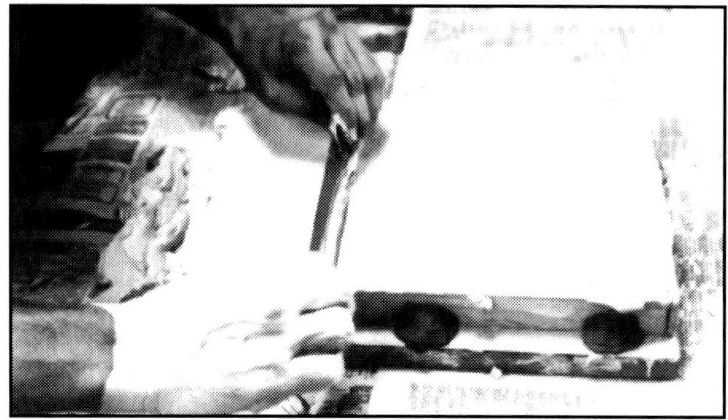

8. Leveling plaster mold.

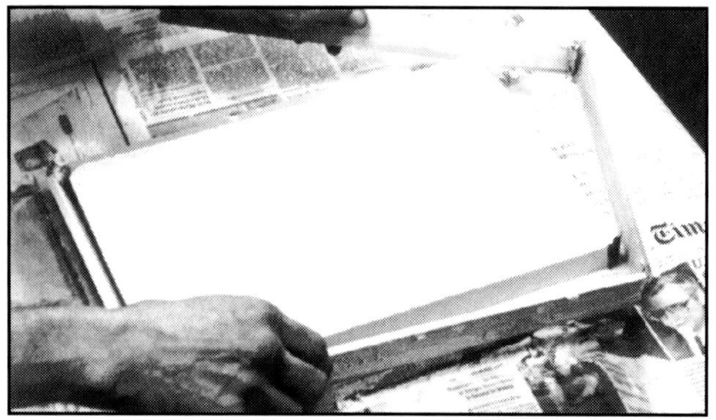

9. Removing fence after plaster mother mold has set.

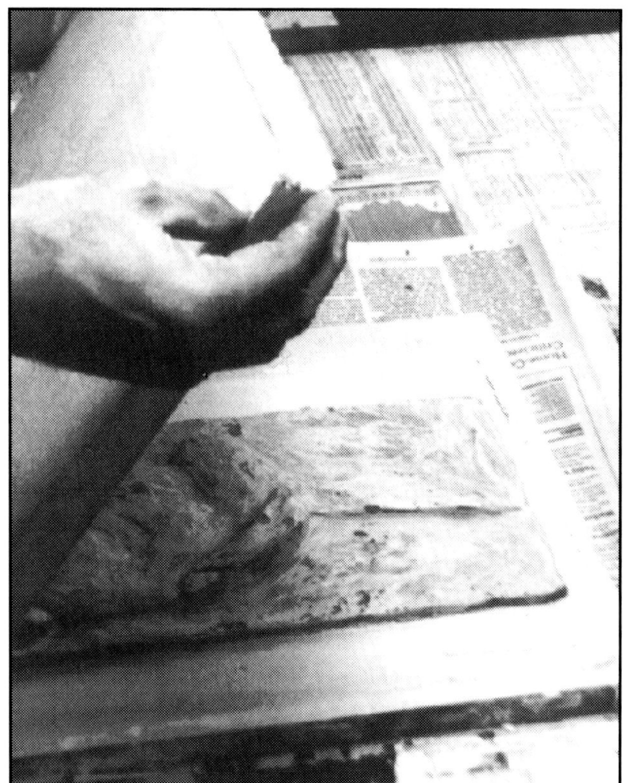

10. Removing mold from panel.

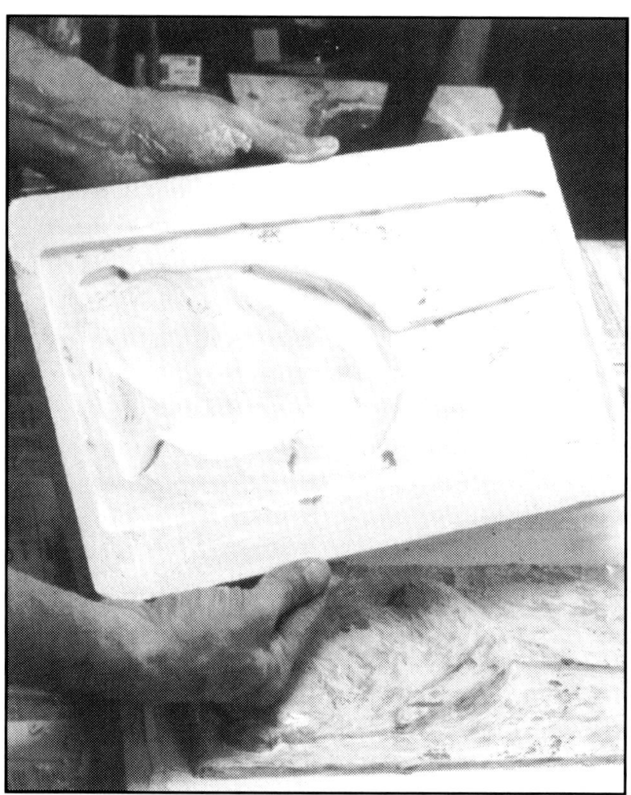

11. Mold after being removed

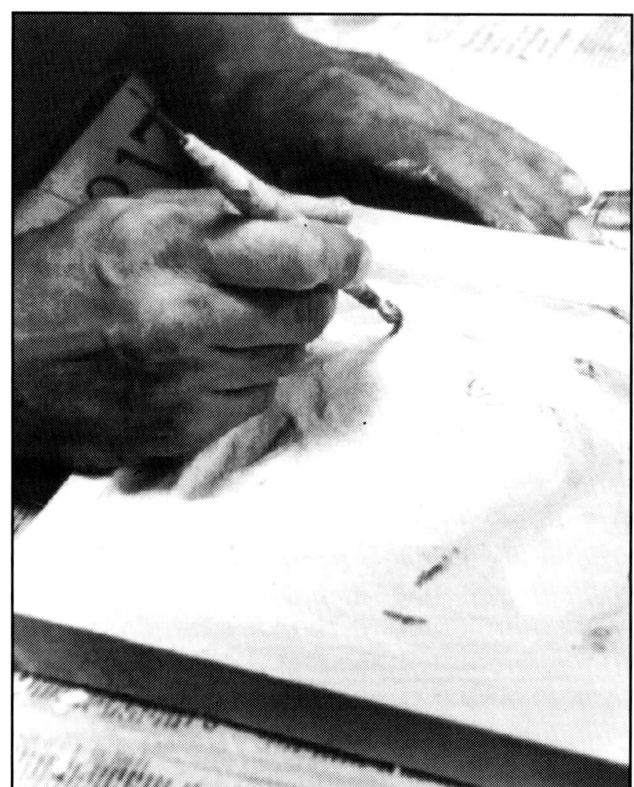

12. Repairing mold, air bubbles.

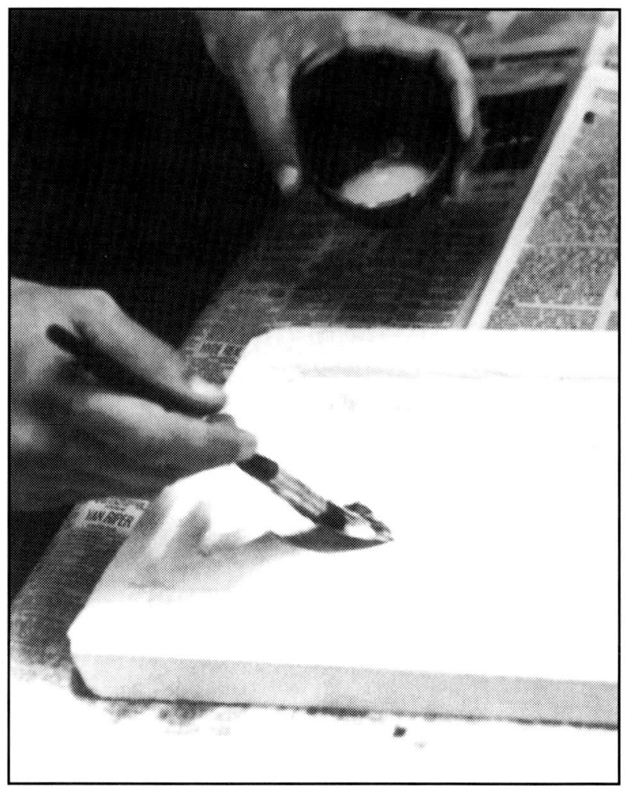

13. Sealing the mold for casting.

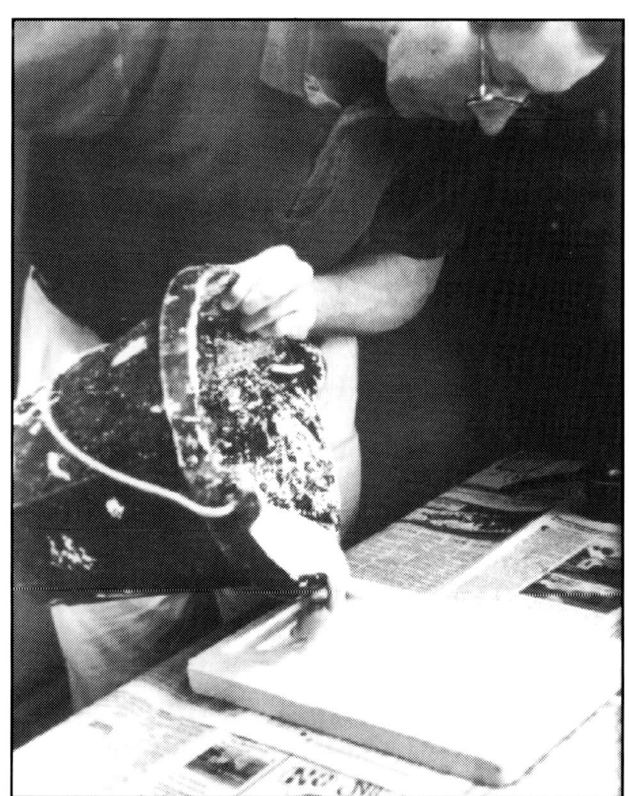

14. Pouring the cast.

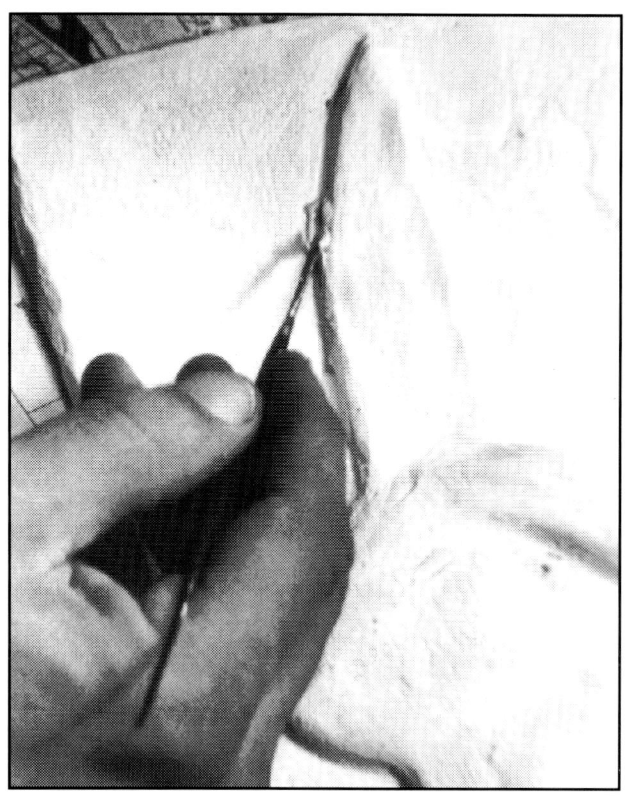

15. Repairing finished cast.

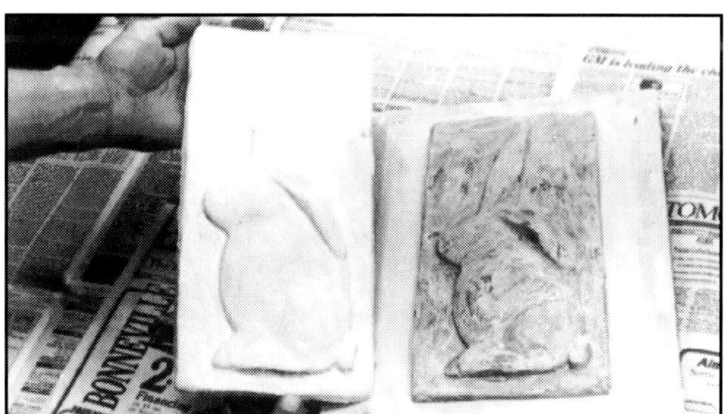

16. Mold and panel.

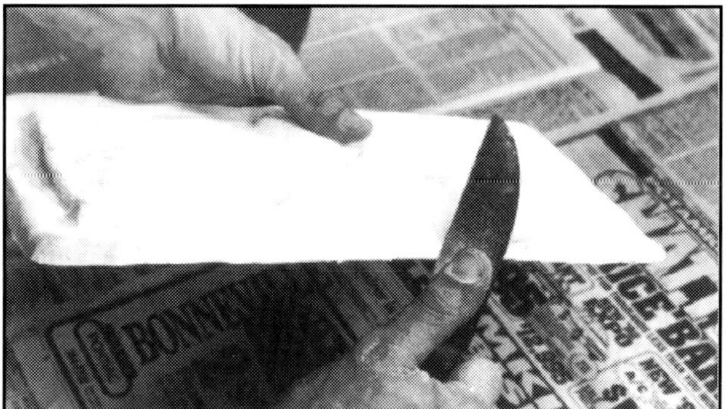

17. Trimming cast after being removed from mold.

LATEX RUBBER MOLD OF A PANEL

Place the panel facing upward on a nonporous work surface, usually the same work board the panel or relief was molded on. Seal the piece and at least two inches around the perimeter of the model with shellac or clear varnish and let dry.

After it has dried, brush on approximately 20 coats of latex rubber. Let each coat dry **completely** before applying the next coat. No release agent is necessary between the model and the rubber. After 8 to 12 coats of pure rubber have been applied, add paste maker to the rubber at a ratio of two parts rubber to one part paste maker by volume (2:1).

Build up the rubber until it is about 1/8 inch thick. When the rubber has been built up properly and dried, build a retaining fence around the area where the rubber has been applied. The fence can be placed onto the rubber if necessary. There should be at least one inch between the fence and the model on all sides. When the fence has been erected, seal the interior areas with shellac and when dry, apply a thin coat of release to the fence area and the rubber.

Mix a fresh batch of plaster and pour the liquid plaster into the retaining area of the fence. Fill the box or retaining area of the fence level with liquid plaster and scape with a block scraper to even off. Let the plaster set for at least one hour or until hard. Remove the fence material, remove the rubber from the model, and clean the interior areas, replace the rubber mold back into the plaster mother mold and cast a new batch of plaster in the rubber mold supported by the plaster mother mold. Tap any air bubbles loose and scrape the top level. Let the plaster set until hard, then invert the mold and remove the cast.

Repair any air bubbles or damage that may have occurred while pouring. Finish with a patina and display. If eyes hooks for hanging are desired place them while the plaster is still semi-wet, but not in a liquid state. Be sure to place the eye hooks even and far enough from the top of the piece so they will not show when the plaque is hung.

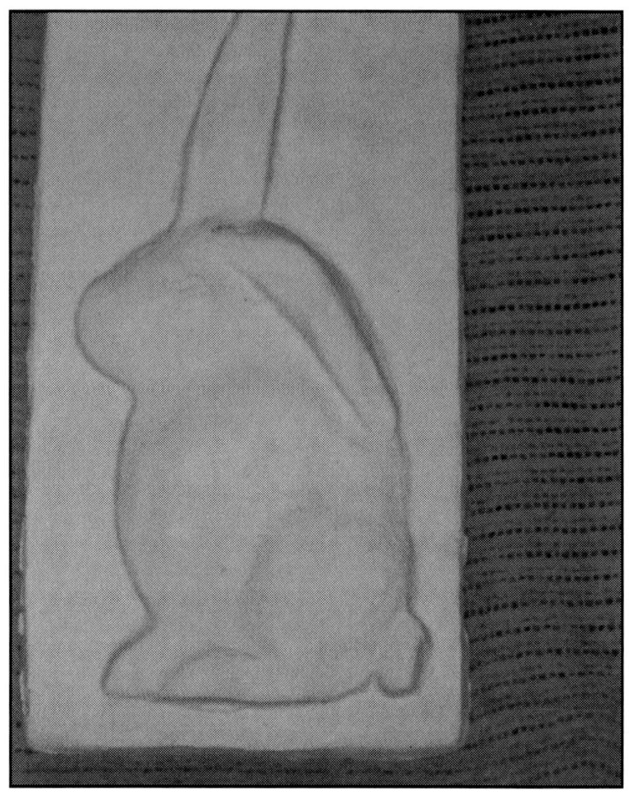

1. Panel to be cast.

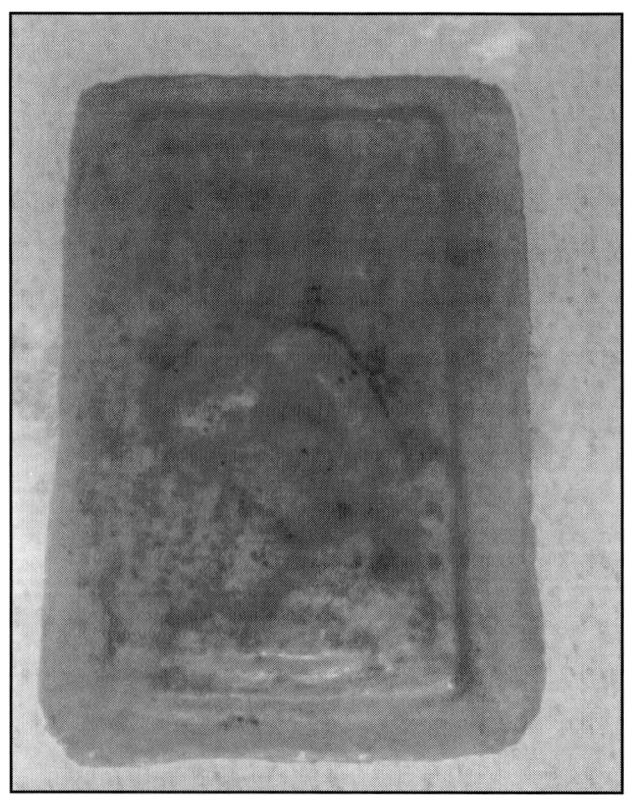

2. Latex covered panel.
Latex extending 1 1/2 inches outward

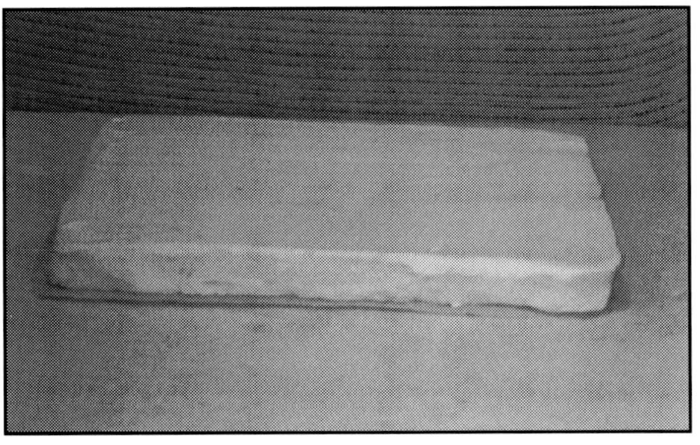

3. Plaster mother mold over latex and panel.

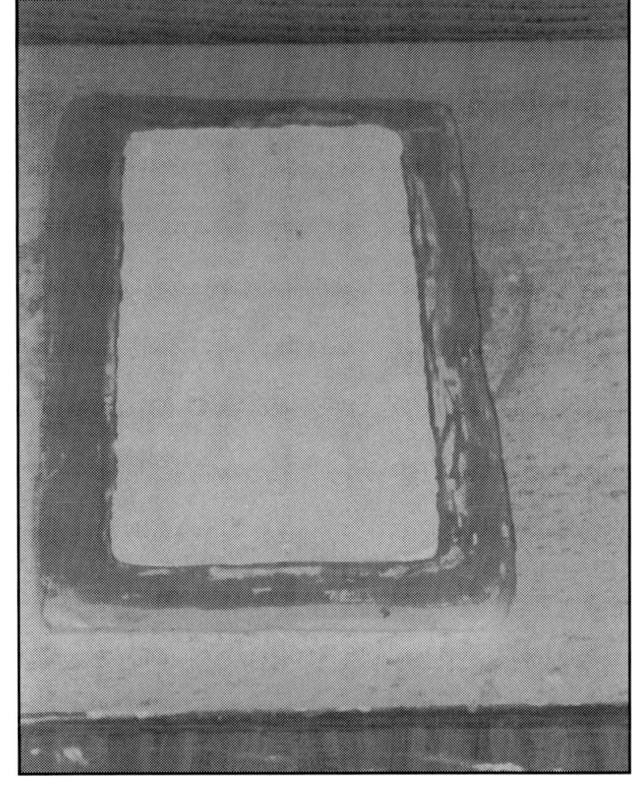

5. Cast latex panel in mother mold.

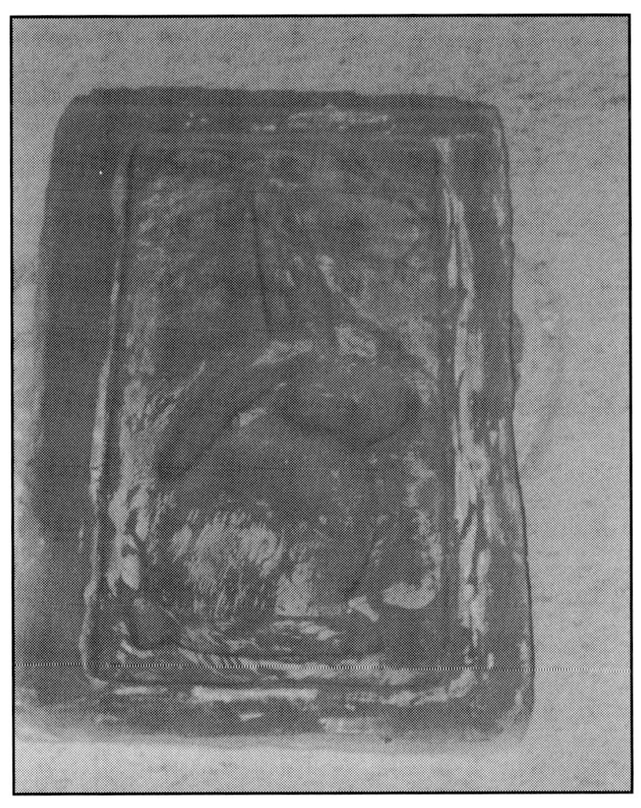

4. Latex negative in mother mold, ready for casting.

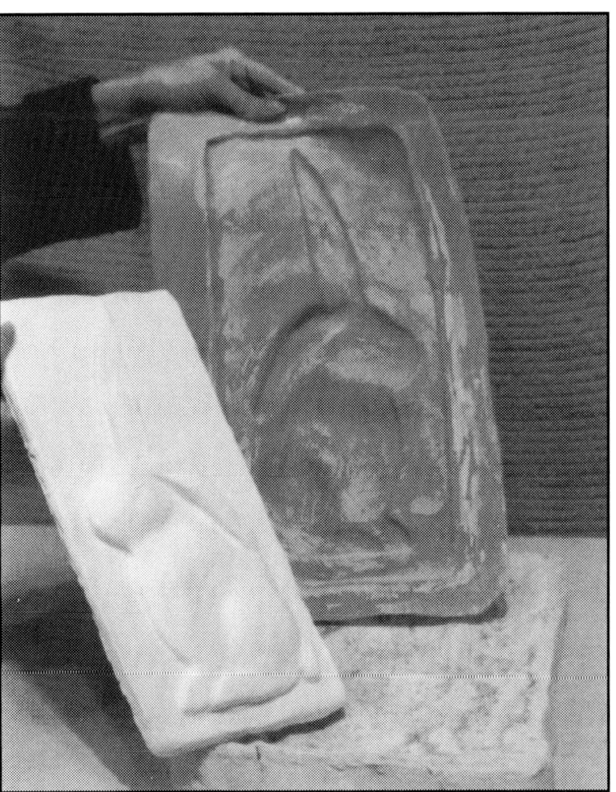

6. Casting of panel, latex mold, and plaster mother mold.

CHAPTER 2

Plaster Waste Mold

(Head)

Type of Mold .... Plaster
Size & Type of Mold .... Life Size Head and Bust
Medium of Model .... Plastilina
Time Required .... Beginner, 9 hours

CONCEPT

The basic concept in making a plaster waste mold is to gain a single cast or likeness. The mold will be destroyed with the model in the process of retrieving this single cast. The piece will be finished in greater detail then used as a master model. A rubber mold for multiple castings will be made from the master model and casts drawn from it. When the mold deteriorates, another mold can be made from the master model. Thus all details are preserved. The finished cast may also be covered with patina and mounted for display.

The waste mold will be made in two separate halves of solid casting plaster (multiple piece waste molds can also be made, but we will be dealing with only a two piece mold). The model will be divided into two sides, front and back, with the seam or dividing line the least conspicuous part. A shim or diving fence will divide the mold in half. The front of the mold will be constructed first. The fence will then be removed and the second or back half of the mold will be made.

When the two halves have set and dried, they will then be removed from the model, cleaned, repaired, and the interior of the cavities sealed and coated with a release agent. The two halves will then be placed back together and secured. Mix the casting material, and leave to set-up. The outer shell of the mold is then removed by chipping the shell away with a hammer and chisel. You will know when you are coming close to the cast and will not damage it by chipping, because the initial coat of plaster will have been colored with a water base pigment, in this case the plaster bluing.

When all pieces of the mold have been removed, the cast is ready for cleaning, repair, and patina or coloring.

TIME FACTOR

The beginner should allow about 9 hours from start to finish. This includes about 5 hours of drying and set-up time, which can be used as free time.

TOOLS AND MATERIALS

It is always good to have more than enough tools and materials. Unfortunately beginning mold makers can't always accumulate as much. There fore, I will keep the list of tools and materials to the bare essentials.

1. Model to be cast.
2. 2, 25-lb. containers of plaster powder.
3. 1 pt. of shellac.
4. 1 pt. of alcohol.
5. 1 qt. of mold lotion or green soap.
6. ¼ lb. bluing for the initial plaster coat.
7. 1 roll, shim or fence material.
8. 6" stiff block scraper.
9. 2 soft bristle brushes.
10. 1, 1½-lb. wooden mallet.
11. 1, 1" width flat steel chisel.
12. 1, 5" diameter small mixing bowl.
13. 4 to 5 lbs. of clay, moist or oil, for plugging holes.
14. 1, 3 gal. large mixing bowl.
15. Water for clean-up.
16. 1 flexible steel tool, pallet type.
17. 1 steel hook tool.

18. 1 sheet 400 grit, wet-dry finishing paper.
19. Measuring cup.
20. 1 newspaper, daily type.
21. Rubber bands or twine, heavy enough to secure mold.
22. Patina material for coloring if desired.
23. Base for display if desired, large enough to extend beyond the model, usually two inches around entire perimeter.

BASIC STEPS

1. Place the shim or separating fence material, dividing the model in half front and back. Do this so the least noticeable seam line will be visible.
2. Seal the entire model and fence with shellac and let dry.
3. Apply a release agent.
4. Construct the first half of the mold, by placing a damp newspaper over the other half to prevent plaster from spattering over it.
5. Use colored or tinted blue plaster for the initial coat. Complete the next two coats with white plaster, inserting support rods.
6. Remove the fence or shim after the plaster has set. Make key grooves and insert plug at top of model. Seal the face of the new plaster wall and plug.
7. Apply a release agent to the exposed mold area that has been sealed.
8. Remove newspaper and construct second half or back of the mold. Use colored blue plaster for the initial coat as with the first half. Complete the mold with two coats of white plaster, inserting support rods.
9. Remove the two halves of the mold when set. Clean and repair inncr surface of both halves.
10. Seal and soap interior surface of the dried and repaired mold.
11. Allow both halves of the mold to soak in water for about 15 minutes.
12. Remove from water and drain excess water.
13. Secure the two halves together with key grooves locking. Use heavy rubber bands or twine to hold the mold securely together.
14. Prepare casting material and pour the cast. Let the mold set-up for at least 1 hour.
15. Remove the cast be chipping away the outer plaster shell with a mallet and chisel.
16. When all the white plaster has been removed, **gently** remove the blue plaster. Leave delicate areas such as the eyes, under the nose, and under the chin until last.
17. Remove the last of the blue plaster to expose the entire cast.
18. Repair any air holes or chip marks with plaster. Remove seam line of the mold.
19. When the cast is dry, patina or color and mount for display as desired.

PREPARING THE MODEL

DIVIDING THE MODEL

When modeling a head and bust, either in moist clay, plastilina, plaster, or wax over an armature or free form, remember to create a base sufficient to support the weight of the piece. Too often the sculptor does not apply the modeling material far enough down to the base of the supporting armature and the weight of the material causes the model to fall over or tilt, an occurrence seldom due to the design or efficiency of the armature. (Armature: is the internal structure or skeleton that holds the modeling material in basic geometric form prior to finishing a piece of sculpture).

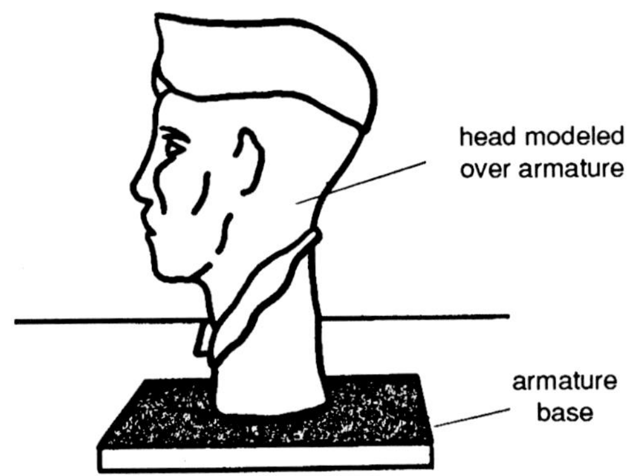

Figure 2.1. Placing the model.

You have modeled your head and bust. It must now be divided into two halves, front and back. The dividing line should separate the face (the front) from the back.

Two methods of separation can be used. One leaves one ear in the front portion of the mold and the other ear in the back. The other leaves both ears in the front portion of the mold, with the back of the head a smaller portion . We will be using the former method, leaving one ear in each half of the mold. I feel it is easier to remove the mold and clay with this method. Either way is acceptable, however; the individual mold maker can determine through experience which he or she prefers. Regardless of the method used, the model should be so divided that the seam line, when the cast is made, is in the area least offensive and easiest to clean. It would therefore stand to reason you would not divide the model down the middle of the face, and have to clean and repair the seam line in the most noticeable area.

PLACING THE SHIM OR FENCE

(24 inches of material required)

When the dividing line has been decided on, divide the model with a shim or a fence. The fence can be made of moist clay, plastilina, or metal (aluminum or brass). To make a clay shim, roll the clay out on a flat surface to a ¼ inch thickness. Cut the strips 1½ inches wide and to a usable length. These lengths are inserted into the model along the dividing line.

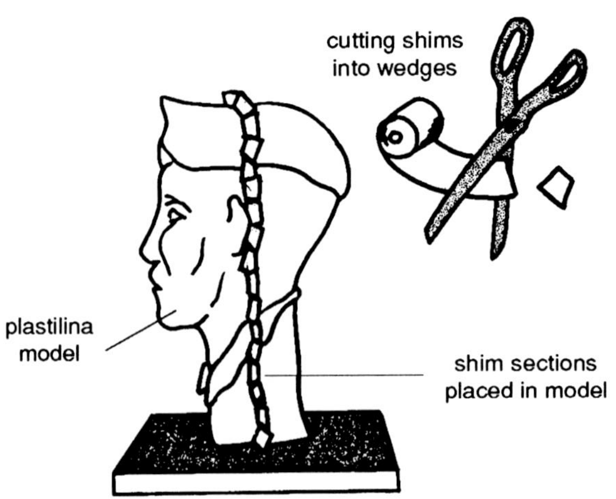

Figure 2.2. Constructing the fence.

Moist clay or plastilina shims are usually used with hard surface models made of stone, plaster, or wood, which are not soft enough to have pieces of metal inserted into them. Since we are working with a soft material, we will be using an aluminum shim. Metal shim material can be purchased in aluminum or brass rolls approximately 20 feet long and 1½ inches wide, and of a thickness that can easily be cut and shaped.

We will be using an aluminum shim. It is non-corrosive and will not react to the water in the plaster, which the brass has a tendency to do. The shim is cut into wedge shapes for insertion into the plastilina model allowing for a 1 inch protrusion at the top. The shim may also be cup to the exact contour of the model when necessary.

After the wedges are cut, they are inserted directly into the model to a depth of ½ inch. They will overlap one another to form an even, solid wall. Begin at the top center of the model and work the left and right sides alternately, pushing the wedges into the model right down to the baseboard.

Be sure to leave no gaps when placing the shim. There should be no openings for plaster to leak through. A little practice may be required, but an even solid fence is not hard to accomplish. When the full length of the shim fence is in place, it should be level and even. There should be a protrusion of only 1 inch above the entire surface of the model.

If moist clay or plastilina is used, apply it in the same manner, securing it with pellets of the same material.

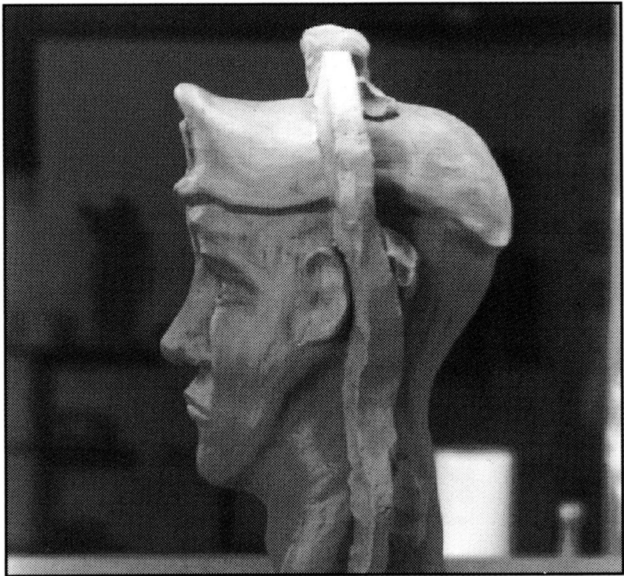

Figure 2.3. Pellets on shim.

This will hold it in place, so the model will not collapse when the first half of the mold is made.

SEALING THE MODEL

When the shim or dividing wall has been properly placed and is even, apply a coat of shellac, thinned or reduced with equal amounts of alcohol (1:1), to the entire surface of both the model and the fence wall. This combination of shellac and alcohol will not leave a residue buildup on the model and in the nooks and crevices.

For the product we are discussing, mix 1 pint of alcohol with 1 pint of shellac in a quart container. Make sure the quart container is sealed tight when not in use.

It is best to apply the mixture to the model in a gridlike manner, covering the areas as follows: front upper left, front upper right, front lower left, front lower right, back upper right, back upper left, back lower left, and back lower right. The entire model should now be coated.

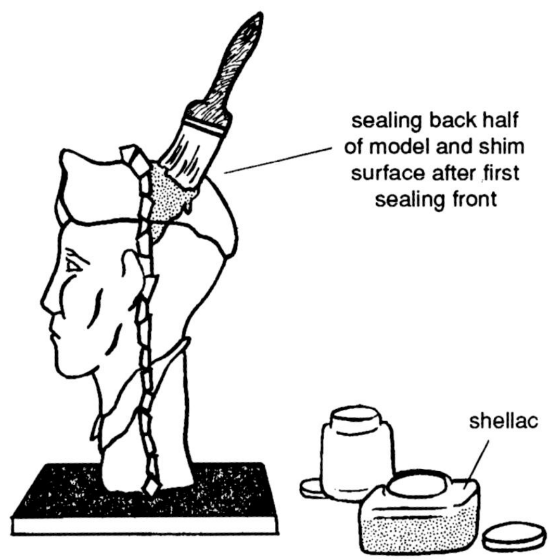

Figure 2.4. Applying shellac.

Apply one thin coat to the model and shim fence area and let dry. Then apply another thin coat and let dry. Be sure to cover all areas that will be coming into contact with the plaster of the mold. This includes the shim fence and a 2 inch area from the base of the model. The mold will also occupy this space. Quite often this base area is forgotten and the mold sticks to the baseboard. When applying the shellac mixture, angle your view so the wet gloss reflection glances off the surface. Thus you can be sure that all areas are covered.

Using the grid procedure, you will not miss any of the areas, especially with the second coat, which is harder to see when applying. Do not apply the shellac mixture so heavily that it will run or drip. Destroy any air bubbles with the tip of a pin or pointed object so there is a smooth surface.

MAKING THE MOLD

FIRST COAT

Now the shim or fence is in place. The entire model has been sealed and we are ready to begin making the first half of the plaster mold. We will begin with the front or face side of the model. However, before beginning there are a few necessary steps to undertake. First, we must cover the back half of the model with damp newspaper to prevent plaster from splattering on it. Dampen ordinary newsprint, such as your daily paper, with enough water to make it pliable, but not dripping wet.

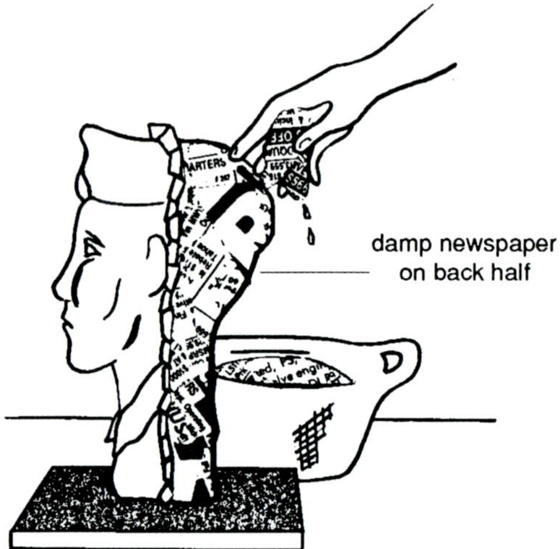

Figure 2.5. Applying newspapers.

Layer single, small pieces over the exposed back of the model, fence, or base. Other types of paper may be used, thin wrapping paper or empty grocery bags. However, ordinary newspaper is usually the most accessible and easiest to handle and will stand up to the water nicely. Remember, the newspaper is only a protection device. It will be removed and discarded after the first half of the mold is completed.

Next, apply a release agent, mold lotion or liquid green soap mixture, to the front half of the model using a soft bristle brush 1 inch wide. Let dry. By careful dabbing, be sure to get in all the grooves and crevices, especially the ear and eye sockets, since you do not want the mold to stick in these areas. However, do not let the separating agent build up in these areas either. Remove all air bubbles and froth. Wet soap will have an effect on the poured plaster, so make sure the release material has dried properly before applying the plaster. The fence and base area should also be treated with a release agent.

MIXING THE PLASTER

When making a waste mold, one must color the first coat of plaster that is applied to the model. This initial coat will be a little thinner and colored blue: thinner because it will be picking up the most minute details. Subsequent coats will be thicker white plaster. After the cast has been poured, the mold will then be removed by chipping away with the mallet and chisel. As the outer white layers of plaster are chipped away and the inner layer of colored plaster is reached, the blue plaster acts as a warning to the mold maker. Beware, you are getting too close to the model and should take extra care in removal of the mold itself.

To prepare the color coat of plaster, add a water soluble pigment to the water used for mixing the plaster batch. We will be using plaster bluing, mixed into the water until it is a deep royal blue. When the plaster powder is added to the water, the strength of the color will be diluted. We want to be sure our first coat is dark enough to be noticeable when the mold is removed. Other colors may be used: yellow ochre, red iron oxide, or even food coloring, but they all tend to become too "thin" for my taste and I do not recommend them. Mix enough blued plaster to make a coating ¼ inch thick over the entire model surface. Our model is 14" high, 6" wide, and has a depth of 3". Use the ratio to weight formula for plaster powder and water found in Appendix A.

When the bluing has been added to the water and dissolved, add the proper amount of plaster powder, sifting it through the fingers and spreading it over the surface of the water in a circular motion. The plaster powder should be added to the water, not the water to the powder. Let the powder sink to the bottom and build up on its own. Let it absorb the water before mixing it in. Wait about 3 minutes after the plaster has been added to the water, and a small mound or peak is visible an inch above the water line.

Now, slide one hand down the side of the pail and gently agitate from the bottom with your fingers spread. The plaster and water begin to mix slowly; use the palm of your hand to scrape the sides of the container. Fold the mixture into itself until it reaches a smooth consistency. Continue doing so until the plaster has thickened to the point where you can make an indentation on the surface. It should be about, or just greater than, the consistency of heavy cream. The plaster is now ready to be applied.

APPLYING THE PLASTER

Have a container of clean water and a few hand towels nearby for easy cleanup. For our application, we will be using what is called a "backhand four finger flick." I have tried all other methods — underhand, side arm, spoon throw, and overhand. All I can say is, the age-old standard backhand flick is the only way to go.

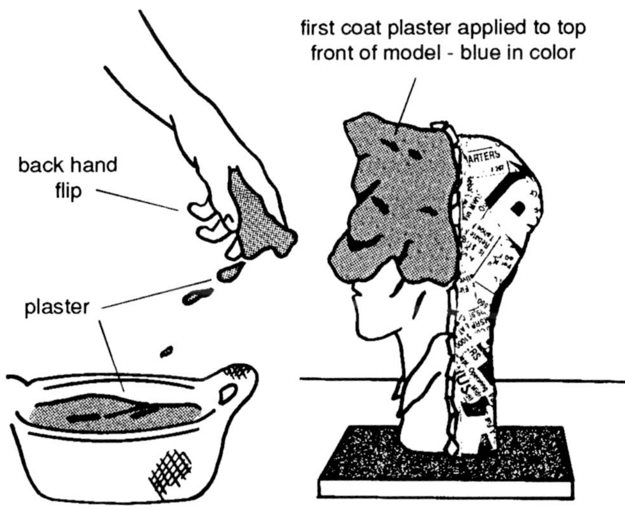

Figure 2.6. Backhand flick.

To "flick" the plaster, grasp a small amount of the mixture with your first three or four fingers; index, middle, ring, and pinky. With an upward motion flick the plaster underhanded onto the exposed front area of the model. Begin with the top center and work downward left to right. Cover the entire front area and work down to the base model. As the plaster will be flowing, you can blow it into the hard to reach areas, spreading it with quick short puffs. This technique is similar to that of blowing out birthday candles.

I suggest you draw a line around the base area a distance about 1 inch from the model. This will give you a guide as to how much plaster to use for the mold and its approximate thickness and will also maintain a proper thickness when cleaning the work area. When starting out in mold making, it is not uncommon to apply the plaster before it has thickened enough to stay in place. The plaster is generally applied when it is still too thin and flowing and it will flow or slide down the side of the model and onto the base area. If this happens, scrape the plaster up with the block scraper and reapply it to the model.

In applying the first coat be sure to get the plaster into all the areas of the model. Otherwise air pockets will form leaving gaps which will cause growths or pimple-like formations on the cast. To avoid these pockets, especially in the eyes, ears, and nostrils, use the technique mentioned before: Pretend you are blowing out birthday candles. The flicked wet plaster will then fill those hard to get at areas. Don't blow too hard or you might blow the plaster completely off the model. As the plaster thickens, level a flat area at the top of the mold

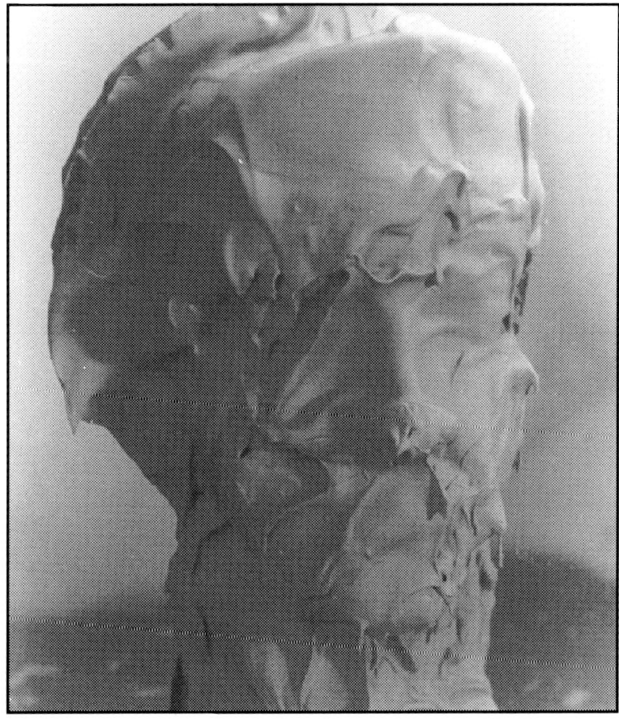

Figure 2.7. First coat, blue.

(figure 2-7). This will provide a flat surface to support the mold when it is inverted for pouring. This leveling can be done with the block scraper.

After the first coat has been applied, clean the base area around the model with the block scraper and discard excess plaster. Do not throw plaster down the drain; it will eventually clog the system. Save it until it is hard and throw it into the garbage can.

SECOND COAT

After the first coat has dried, apply a coat of release to this first layer. Rinse out the mixing container with clean water, prepare a new batch of regular white casting plaster, and apply it to the model. This will assist in easy removal of the final mold. The plaster for this coat can be somewhat thicker.

Apply the second coat in the same manner as the first, with the backhand flick, beginning with the top center and working downward. **DO NOT** smooth the plaster between coats; the new coats will adhere better. If the surface seems too smooth, rough it up a little with your fingers or a steel tool, but don't go overboard. When the second coat has been applied, clean the base and work area. Your mold should now be at least 1/2 to 3/4 inch thick along the entire outer surface, with greater density around the eye and ear areas. The plaster should be all white.

After the second coat we will apply a third and final coat. This is not always necessary, especially when attaching support rods, but I tend towards the old school methods and will always advise a third coat. Our mold will be 1 inch thick on completion. A heavier, thicker mold is not necessarily stronger or better. At times it can be more cumbersome and harder to handle. So don't get the idea that thicker is better.

ATTACHING SUPPORT RODS

Although not always necessary, if they are to be used, support rods or irons should be placed during the second coat. They should be of a noncorrosive material such as almaloy or aluminum wire. We will be using 1/4 inch thick aluminum wire for this medium size mold. Aluminum wire can also be used in the cast to add strength. The support rods should be cut to the proper length and shaped to the contour of the piece before making the mold. Placed on the outer and upper quadrants of the mold, they are secured during application of the second coat. The rods are crossed at the upper and outer sections, touching one another at intersecting points (Figure 2.8).

Apply a small additional dab of plaster at these joints to secure the rods to one another and to the mold sides. These rods bond the mold together and protect against the suction caused by the separation of the mold from the model. On smaller or less complicated molds, these additional supports may not be required.

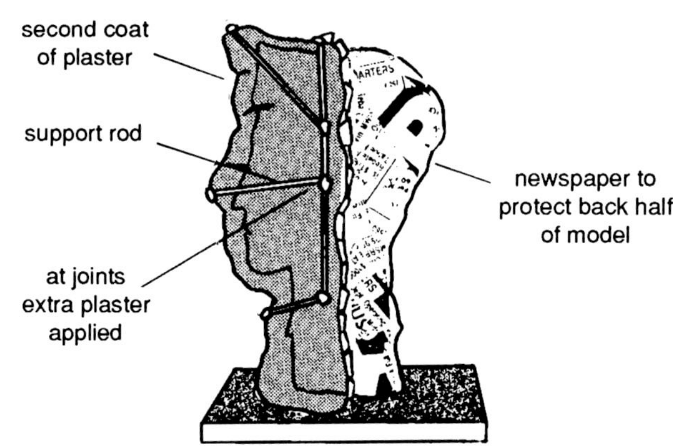

Figure 2.8. Second coat support rods.

THIRD COAT

The third and final coat will be applied with another new batch of white plaster using the flicking method as before. Cover the entire mold and base area with new plaster as before. Start with the top center and work downward and outward. You will be covering the support rods and forming a smooth solid outer coating. With the last coat, smooth the surface plaster with the fingers or a wet cloth and level the top with a straight edge or block scraper.

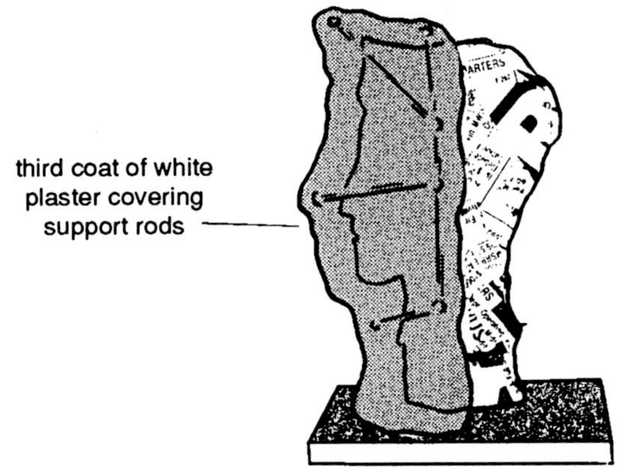

Figure 2.9. Third and final coat.

Scrape the base of the mold clean and the surrounding work area as well. The plaster at the top of the shim or fence will be level with a thickness of about 1 inch. The first half of the mold is now complete and should be left to set and dry for at least one hour.

BACK OF MOLD

PREPARATION

When the first half of the mold has set for at least 1 hour and is dry, it is time to prepare the back or second half. First, remove the fence or shim from the plaster and model, leaving the exposed walls of the plaster on the first half of the mold. We must now make **key grooves** and **countersunk notches** in the wall of the front plaster mold (Figure 2.10) to

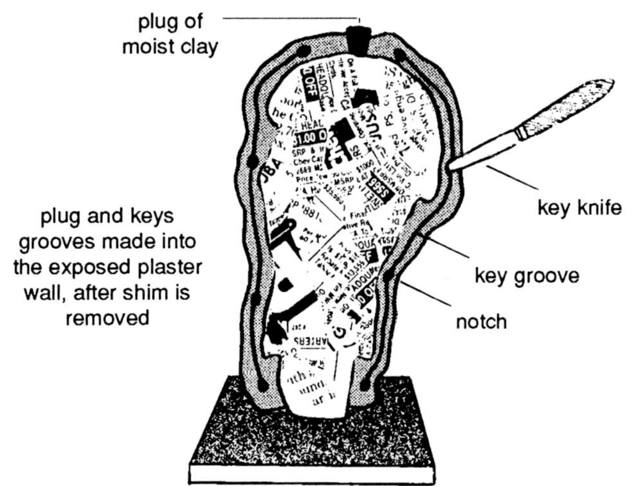

Figure 2.10. Key grooves.

ensure that the two halves will attach back together exactly. There will thus be no movement of the two halves when the plaster of the cast is poured. To make the key notches, take the point of the knife and twist in a corkscrew motion so there is a circular indentation about 1/4 inch deep.

You may also use a hook knife or small hook-end steel tool for this. The notches, located at the four outer sectors of the mold, upper left, upper right, lower left and lower right, should now be connected along the mold wall by a small groove or channel leading to the base of the model. This is called a key groove and is about 1/8 inch deep and made by scraping with a small steel hooked tool. Leave the damp newspaper on the model during this scraping so shavings of plaster will not fall on the model surface.

When you have completed the notches and key grooves, lightly dust them with a dry soft bristle brush and blow excess plaster away until the mold is dust clean. You can then remove the newspaper by folding it inward to contain any particles of loose plaster; discard it as trash.

We now place a plug or wedge of clay at the top of the model. Make a wedge shape approximately 2 inches long, ¼ inch thick at the top, and 1 1/4 inches wide, tapering to 1/8 inch at the bottom (Figure 2.11). This wedge should be placed on the top center of the model and mold wall, so the wedge is the model and the wall of the mold and protruding ¼ inch above the top of the fence or shim.

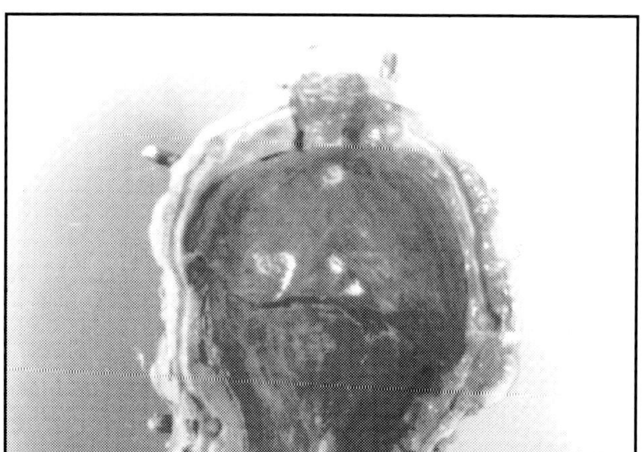

Figure 2.11. Plug

Now is the time to seal or treat the plug and the exposed area of the plaster wall, so the two halves will release easily without fusing together. This is done with the one-to-one shellac and alcohol mixture, again using two thin coats. When the last coat has dried thoroughly, apply a frothy coat of mold lotion or green soap to the entire area of the fence and model with a soft bristle brush and let dry. The entire model area, shim, and 2 inches from the mold should be coated so that any flung plaster will not adhere to the surface of the first half of the mold.

FIRST COAT BACK HALF

The second half of the mold will be constructed exactly like the first half. I will briefly go over the basic steps but the directions are the same as for the first half.

First mix a new batch of plaster and apply to the model after a release has been brushed on and let dry. Leave the surface rough and apply a second coat of white plaster. Attach preshaped support aluminum rods with "blobs" of plaster at the intersecting points. Add a third coat of fresh white plaster and smooth onto the entire surface.

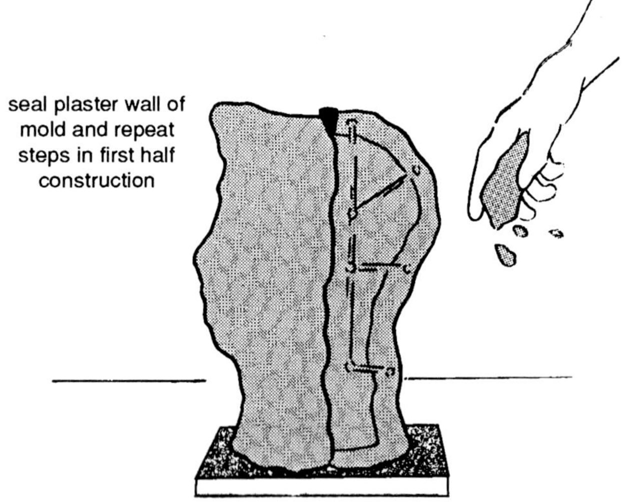

Figure 2.12. Applying second coat of plaster on back.

Cover the rods completely and clean the work area after each coat. Level the first coat of plaster even with the top surface of the wall, except where the plug extends above the shim. After the plaster has been applied to the entire back half of the mold, let it dry or set for at least 1 hour. You should now have over the entire model, a solid plaster shell approximately 1 inch thick and entirely white.

REMOVING THE MODEL

After the plaster has completely setup, we are ready to separate the two halves and remove the model from the mold. If the model has been sculpted in moist clay, plastilina, or wax, you may soak the entire mold in hot water to soften the interior modeling material, making for an easier release. This is not entirely necessary and if not easily accomplished, can be bypassed.

PLUG REMOVAL

The first step in separating the mold is to remove the clay plug at the top center. Since the material is either moist clay or plastilina, it can simply be dug out with a steel tool. When the plug has been completely removed, pour warm water into the opening. Water not absorbed by the plaster of the mold will drain out at the bottom. Be prepared for this excess.

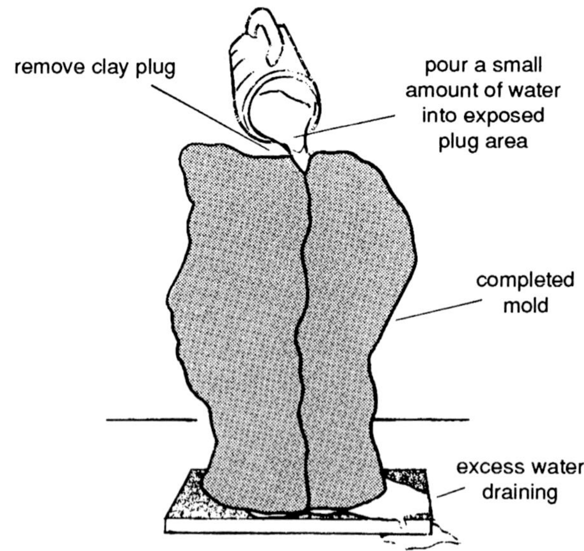

Figure 2.13. Separating mold from model.

We must now wedge or pry the two halves apart. There will be a natural suction holding the halves together despite the releases, soaking, and water. To pry the halves apart use a mallet and flat chisel, staring at the top and working alternately on the left and right at about every 3 inches. Insert the blade of the chisel at the seam or separating line by lightly tapping with the mallet. Go down both sides of the mold in this manner, trying to just slightly open the mold with gentle pressure, pushing back and forth with the chisel and pouring small amounts of water into the mold at the same time.

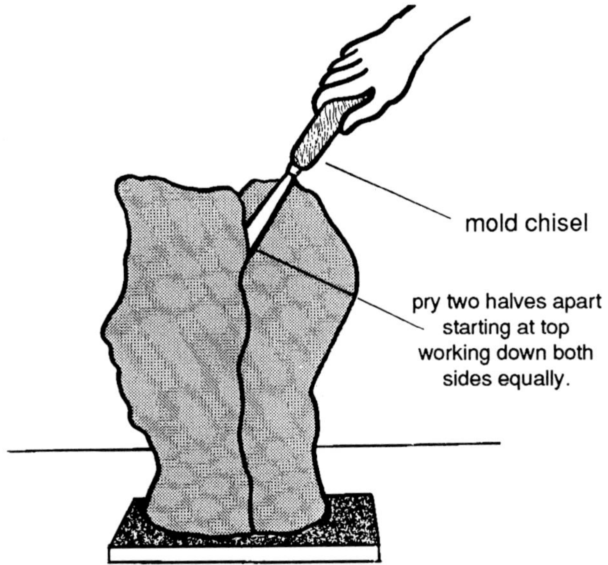

Figure 2.14. Separating two halves.

Do not insert the chisel too far into the mold or it will damage the interior walls. If desired, small "V" shaped wooden wedges can be hammered into the openings to facilitate opening the mold. I generally use these only with larger, more difficult, molds. Pour water during the entire process as needed. When the opening is wide enough, place your fingers in the opening and gently pull the two halves apart. Again, work from the top and proceed downward left to right. The smaller or back half of the mold generally comes free first; rarely do the two halves pop off cleanly together. When half of the mold has been removed, catch your breath, set it aside well out of the way, and remove the other half. Be firm with the removal and not timid. The mold should be strong enough to take the pressure. Pieces of the model may be left in the interior of the mold, but this is to be expected. Once removed, the two halves must be cleaned, inspected, and repaired as necessary.

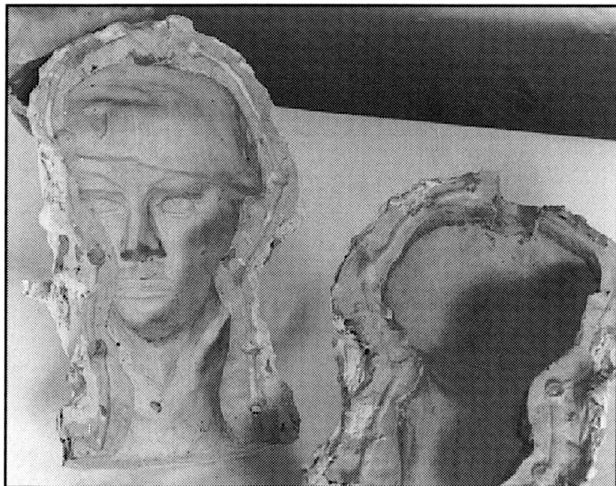

Figure 2.15. Separated halves.

CLEANING AND REPAIRING THE MOLD

CLEANING

You have now successfully made and removed the mold without breaking any of the sections, let us hope. There may be spots where the plaster was not applied thickly enough and repair is necessary. This will be discussed later. Meanwhile, the interior must be cleaned of any modeling material that may have been left while separating the two halves. This usually occurs in difficult areas such as eyes, ears, hair, and sharp angles. The material can be removed with the edge of the steel plaster tool or its point as necessary. Work as delicately as an archeologist removing dirt from an artifact. Be careful not to damage the interior of the mold. Take time to clean the mold thoroughly; the resulting cast will be a reflection of you.

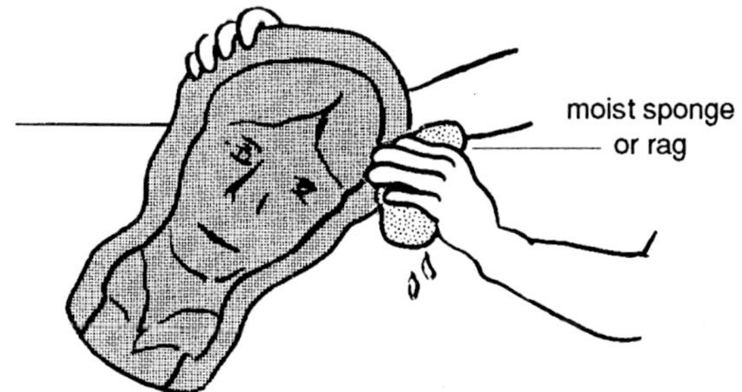

Figure 2.16. Clean and repair mold interior, seal, soak and soap.

REPAIRING THE MOLD

Now that the entire surface has been cleaned, go over the inner surface of both halves and inspect for any deformities or possible air bubbles. Use a flexible steel pallet tool to take fresh plaster and fill in these areas. Mix a small amount of plaster in a rubber mixing bowl which can easily be hand held. Repair the holes and smooth with a damp cloth. When dry, sand with wet dry paper in the dry state.

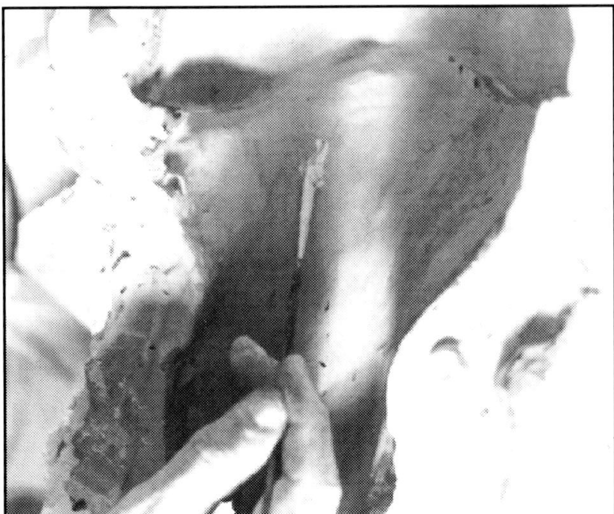

Figure 2.17. Repairing air holes.

Dust the interior with a dry fine bristle brush to remove any excess plaster dust. Do a final inspection, going over every inch of the interior of both halves. When both of the interior molds have been cleaned and repaired to your approval, we will begin preparing the mold for casting.

PREPARING THE MOLD FOR CASTING

The two halves must be treated before the casting material is poured. As with the panel, we will apply a solution of mold lotion with a soft bristle brush. Brush liberally for about 20 minutes until the entire surface area has been saturated with solution. Be sure to include all hard to reach areas such as eye sockets and crevices. Remove any froth or foaming. Then let both halves dry for approximately 15 minutes.

Next, soak each half of the mold by submerging in clean water for 20 minutes. This will ensure complete saturation of the mold so your casting material will not adhere to the molds walls. When completely soaked, remove the two halves from the water and let them drip dry.

Apply a small amount of olive oil to the entire surface of both halves of the mold. The result will be a dull shine or luster. A small amount of water placed on the mold should bead up, like water beading up on a newly waxed car. If the water **does not** bead up but absorbs into the mold, additional soaping with mold lotion will be required and the mold should be soaked again.

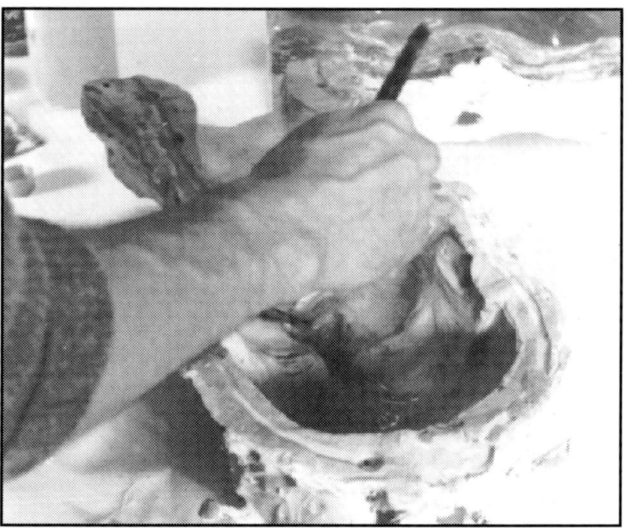

Figure 2.18. Soaping mold interior.

Once the mold has been prepared in this fashion, you are now ready to secure the two halves together for the pouring of the casting material. Place the halves back together so the key grooves and countersunk notches line up and lock with one another.

Secure the mold halves together with heavy rubber bands or thick twine. You may also use bungy cord, which can be purchased at your local hardware store. Remember to buy the proper length, approximately 25% larger than the diameter of the mold area. The rubber bands should be about 1 inch thick and long enough to go around the diameter of the mold easily but still hold tightly. The pressure of the poured plaster will force the halves apart if they are not securely fastened. Heavy rubber bands can generally be purchased at a hardware store and sometimes at a stationery store. You may also use a section of a tire inner tube, available in gas stations and some bicycle shops. You can also use heavy twine incorporating an ordinary slip knot. Place the bands or twine near the top, center, and lower sections of the mold. To ensure a tight fit, you can place wedges of wood in a few places between the mold and rope and tap them down. Be sure you have tied the rope as tight as possible (Figure 2.19).

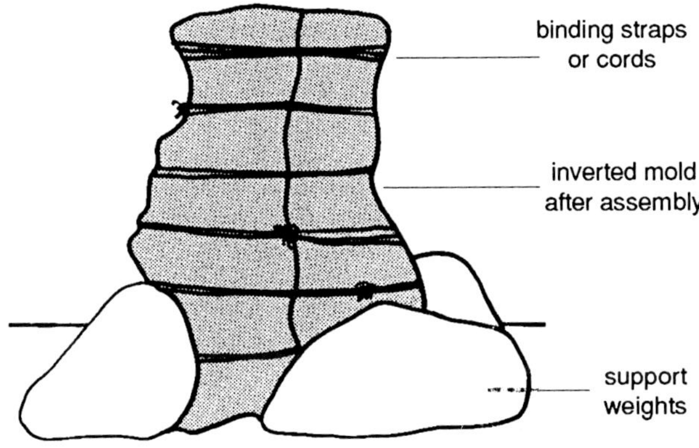

Figure 2.19. Secured mold.

MIXING THE CASTING MATERIAL

Once the mold has been prepared and secured, mix a new batch of plaster to pour the cast. Make sure you mix enough material. Hollow castings with this walls can be made, but the process is difficult and is taught in advanced classes. For our part, we will be casting solid pieces.

To find the amount of material needed for your casting, refer to the chart of weights, mixture, and formulas in the mixing plaster section.

The casting material is pristine white casting plaster. Mix it with the water as you did for the mold. Before mixing the material to be poured, invert the secured mold so the top with the flat level area is solidly and evenly placed on the work surface (Figure 2.20). Remember that the plaster in its container must be lifted above the top opening of the mold to be poured. If the mold is 15 inches high and it is on a workbench that is three feet high and your height is 5 feet 10 inches you will be lifting a heavy load well above waist level in a difficult position. I suggest that the mold be placed on the floor for pouring. Use braces or supports of some type to secure the mold and prevent it from accidentally falling over. You will be using both hands for the pouring. Make sure the opening is level before pouring the casting material.

POURING THE CAST

When the mold has been sealed, soaked, secured, and inverted, and the casting material has been mixed to the smooth flowing consistency of heavy cream, it is time to pour the cast. Rather than simply dumping the entire amount of casting material into the mold, we will be using a more precise method to achieve a good solid cast and ensure that it will be free of air bubbles and air pockets. First, pour enough casting material into the mold to fill it one quarter full. Tilt the mold to a 45 degree angle. Now gently pour the casting material down one side of the mold, not straight into the center of the open cavity. Place your container of casting material down on the floor, pick up the mold, and pour the casting material from the mold **back into** the container. Rotate or turn the mold clockwise, so the casting material coats the entire surface of the interior as it is being poured back into the mixing container. Repeat this process again to ensure that all nooks and crannies have been coated with plaster.

Now, place the inverted mold back on the floor and **in one motion** fill it entirely with plaster right to the top. Pour the plaster down the sides if possible since you want to avoid air mixing with it. Be gentle, but from the first pouring to the completion, there should be no hesitation or timidness since the plaster will begin setting up and should be completely poured while still in its flowing state. After the mold has been filled, inspect the seam line for leaks. If there are areas where plaster is escaping, plug these areas with pieces of plastilina or moist clay to stop the flow of plaster. If necessary, fill the mold with additional plaster. This is very common so don't think you have a problem.

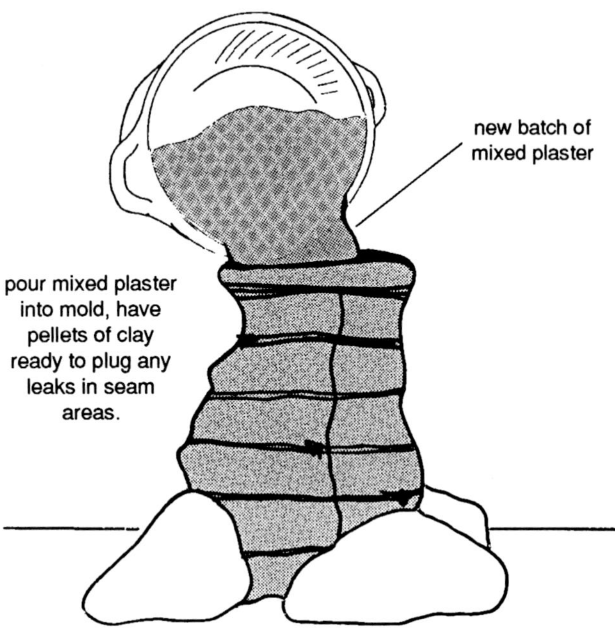

Figure 2.20. Pouring plaster.

When the mold has been filled, lightly tap the sides to jar any air bubbles that may have been formed. These bubbles will rise to the top; scrape them off with the block scraper. Once the cast has been poured, tapped, and leveled, let it sit for at least 1 hour before removing the mold.

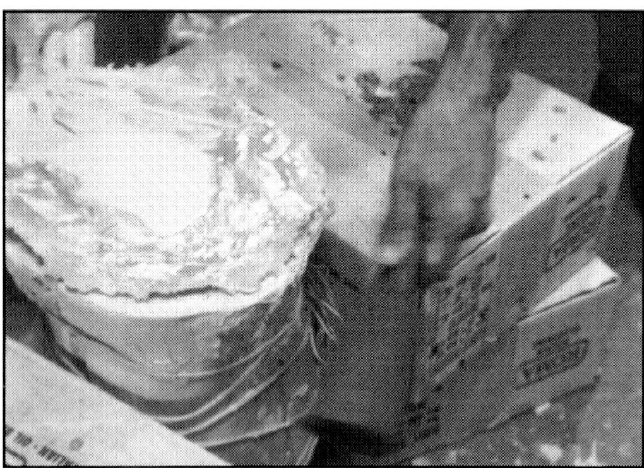

Figure 2.21. Tapping the mold.

REMOVING THE MOLD

This aspect of mold making and casting is probably the most rewarding and exciting. After the plaster has set for at least 1 hour, remove the rubber bands or twine and the chipping process can begin.

Using the mallet and flat chisel, begin at the back top center of the mold and start to chip away the surface. This should be done **lightly**. Remove one layer at a time, working from top to bottom, on both the front and back if you wish. Plaster chips may fly occasionally, so eye protection is recommended. The mold pieces should be cleaned up as they fall to the work area.

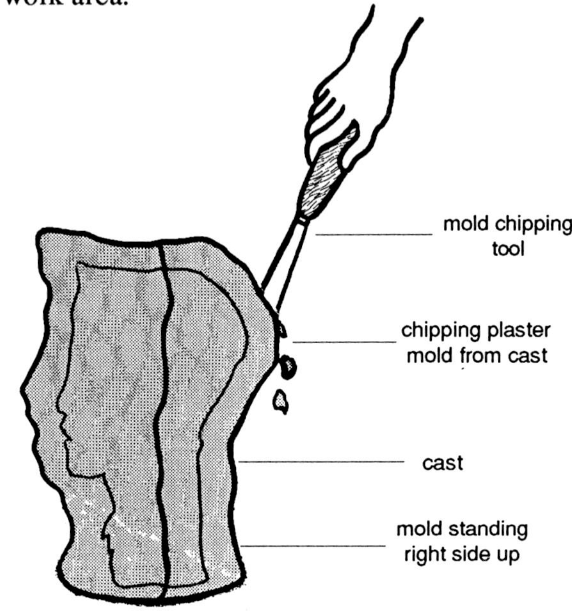

Figure 2.22. Chipping away mold.

Remove all the plaster down to the blue layer, leaving delicate areas around the eyes, under the nose, the ear, and under the chin until last. These are the most susceptible to damage and the plaster

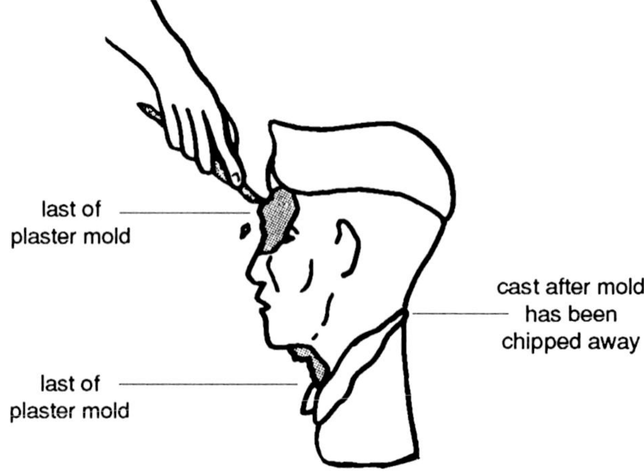

Figure 2.23. Delicately chip away eye and nose area.

around them should be removed with the utmost care. A 1/8 inch flat chisel and a light mallet are good instruments for this. Use light, delicate tapping. Proceed with **caution** since you don't want these fine areas damaged in any way.

The blue or colored layer of plaster is directly next to the cast and is the final coat to be removed. When all the plaster has been removed, inspect the cast for any defects or abnormalities that may have occurred during the mold making or casting procedures.

REPAIRING THE CAST

Once all the plaster has been removed, you will have a plaster cast in the round and the exact likeness of the original model. With great luck, the cast will have come out perfectly without any imperfections. In all likelihood, however, this will not be the case and repairs will be necessary. This is normal so don't worry about it. The most common defects are air pockets, formed when the plaster does not adhere directly against the model. If not corrected, these pockets will fill with plaster in the casting, causing a lump or pimple formation on the cast. They can easily be removed by scraping with a steel tool or sanding with dry or wet dry abrasive paper. Smooth the raised areas, working even with the natural original lines of the model. These lumps generally occur in the hair line, eye sockets, and ears where the plaster has the most difficulty in adhering.

When the cast is being poured, small air pockets sometimes form where the plaster does not fully penetrate the hollow cavity of the mold. These air holes or cavities will cause missing areas in the cast, usually in joints or around right angles of the mold and most commonly at the end of the chin where the cast plaster has not filled the mold. To repair these cavities or holes, mix a small batch of fresh plaster and apply a small amount at a time with a flexible steel pallet tool. The moisture of the plaster will be absorbed almost immediately by the plaster of the cast.

After drying, smooth the filled areas with a damp cloth or sand with a dry or wet dry abrasive paper.

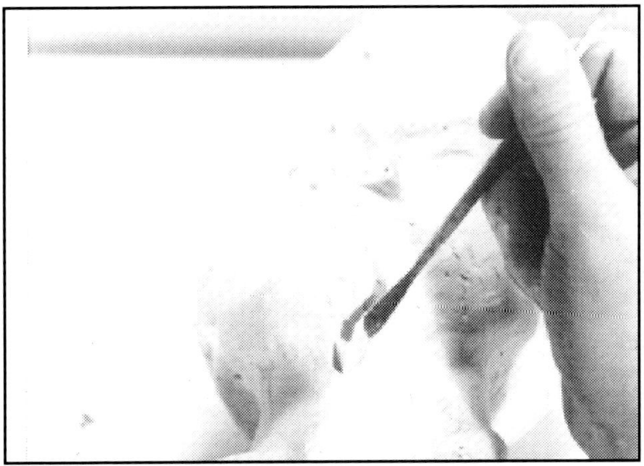

Figure 2.25. Repairing air bubbles.

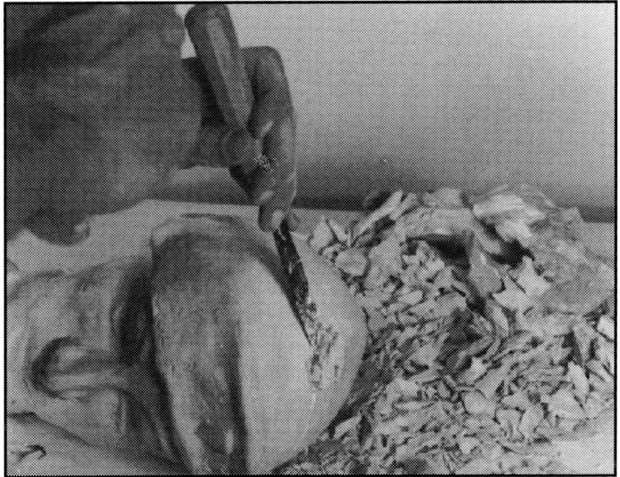

Figure 2.26. Removing seam line.

When all appendages and holes have been cleaned and repaired, you must next smooth the seam line where the two halves of the mold join. This can be done with a steel tool, lightly scraping and then sanding with extra fine 500 grit sand paper or wet dry paper. The seam line should conform to the original contours of the cast and model.

Now your cast is completed, except for options such as patina, coloring, and mounting.

Since patina and mounting are distinct craft trades, and require comprehensive and detailed explanations, I have prepared separate chapters on each. For patina and coloring, refer to Chapter 8; for mounting on a base refer to Chapter 9.

PICTORIAL OVERVIEW

Waste Mold of the Full Head and Neck

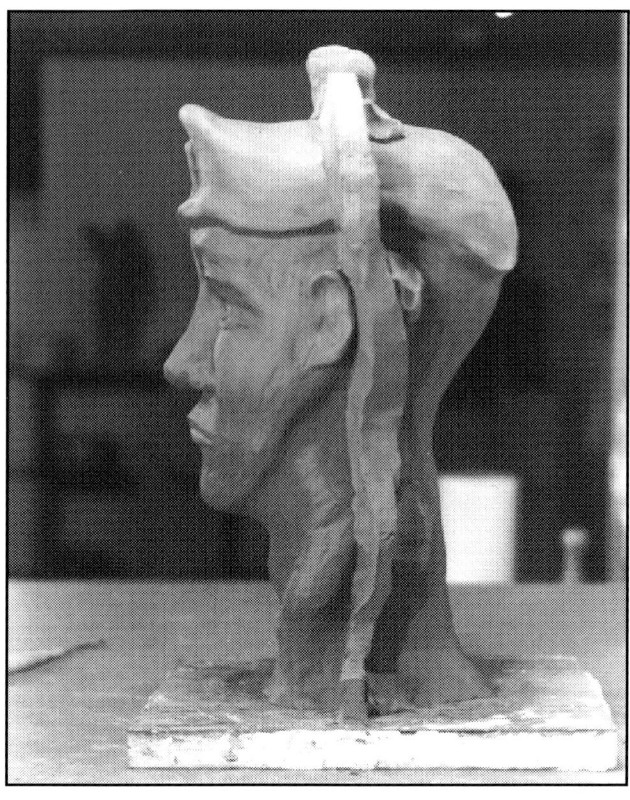

2. Shim placed around the model separating the front from back. Pellets holding the shim in place.

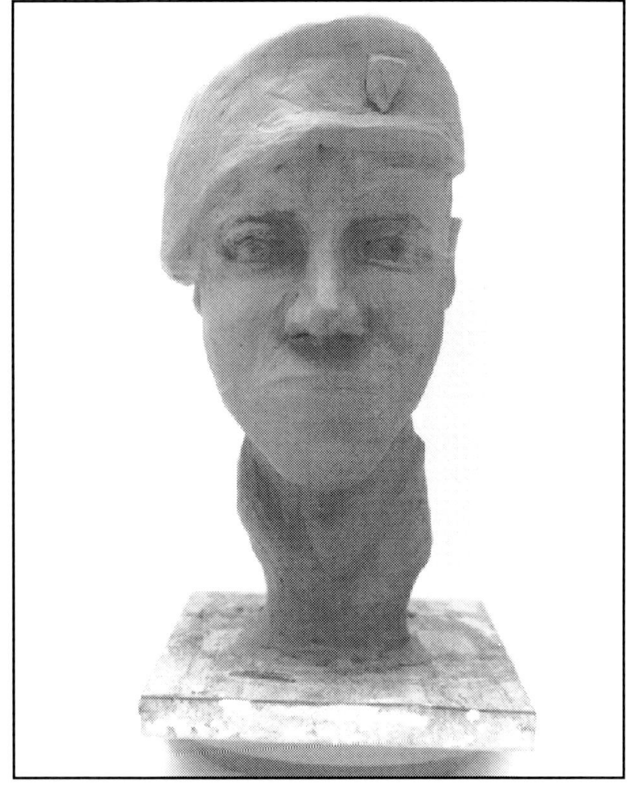

1. Model placed ready for the mold to be made

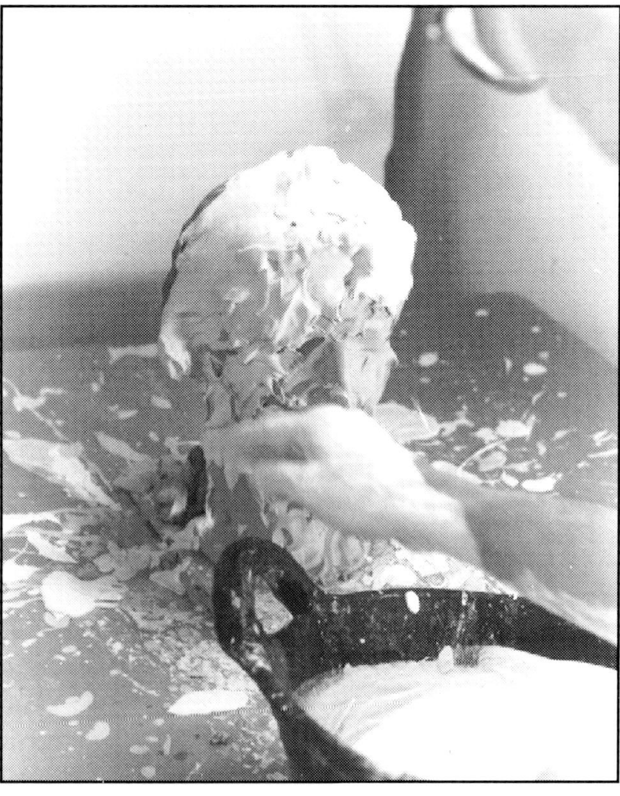

3. First coat of plaster being applied with the back hand flip. Blue plaster being used for the first coat only.

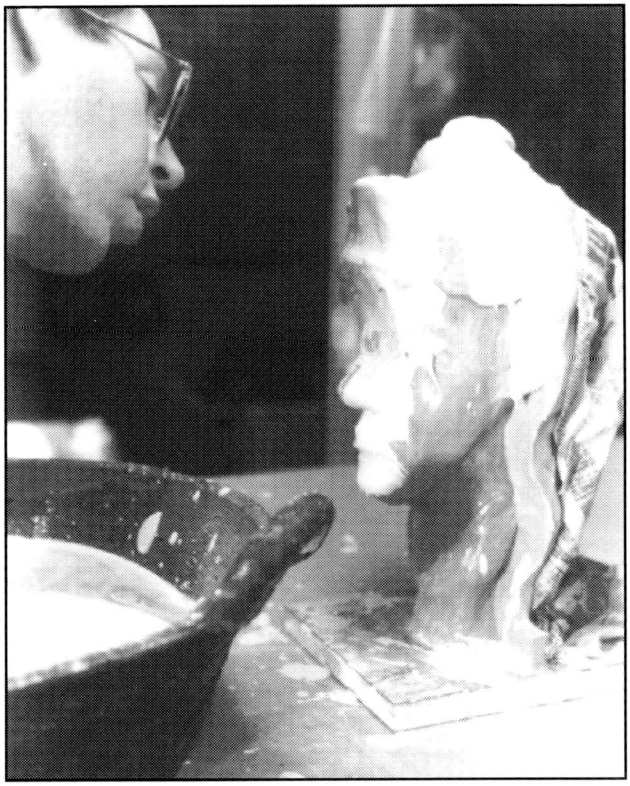

4. Blowing plaster into the hard to reach areas.

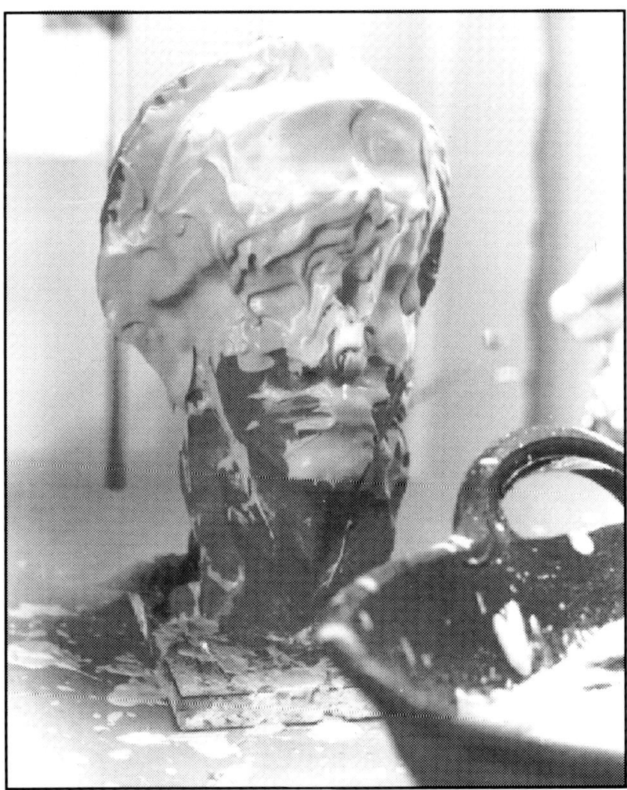

5. First coat of plaster being applied from the top down.

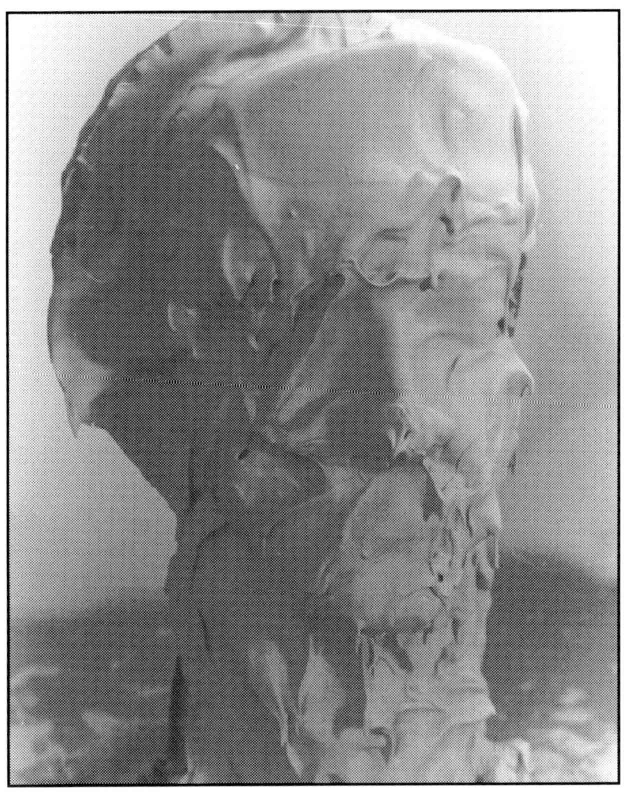

6. Complete first coat of plaster over entire front of model.

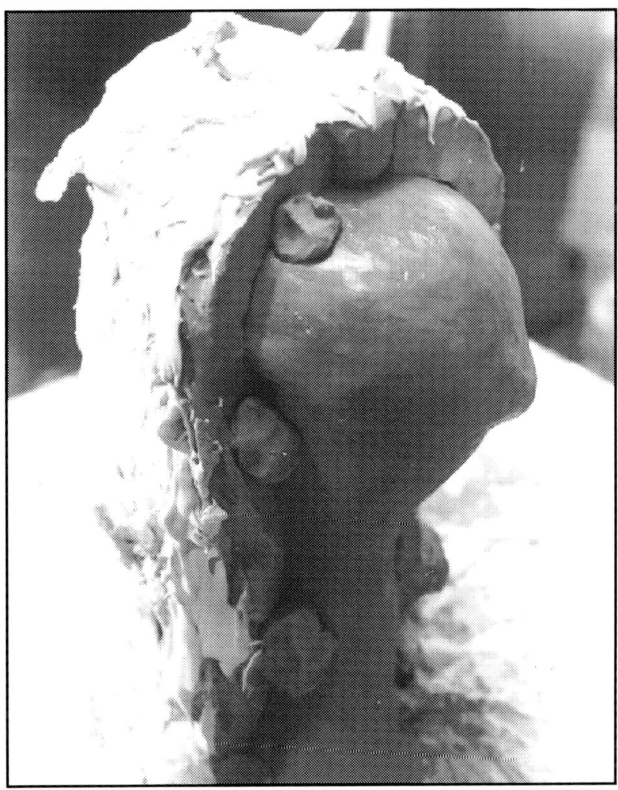

7. Front half of the mold completed. Leaving the back exposed.

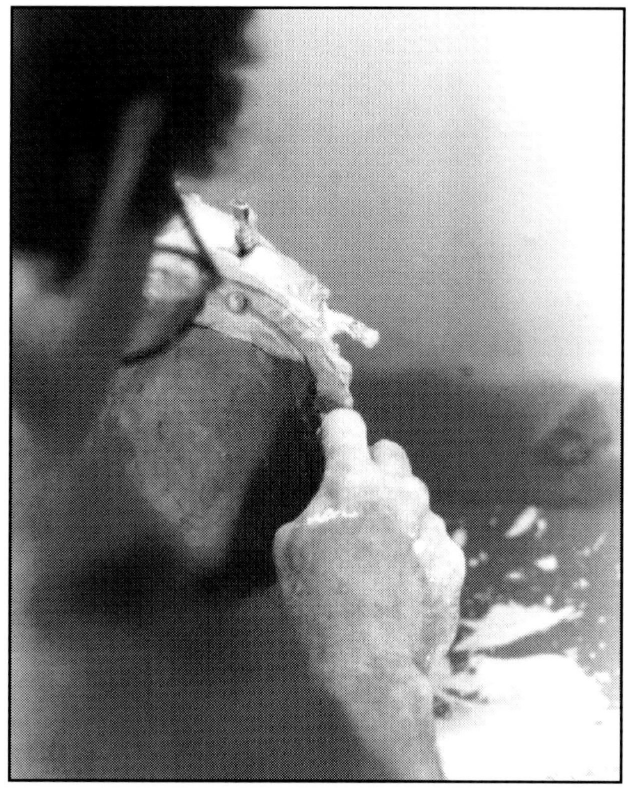

8. Cutting key grooves and notches in set plaster after the removal of the clay shim.

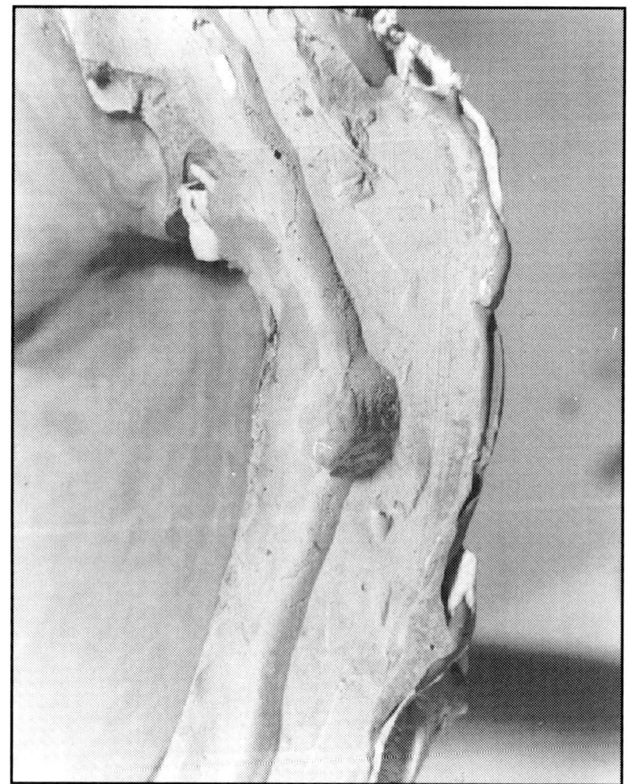

9. Close up of the keys made in the set exposed area of the mold.

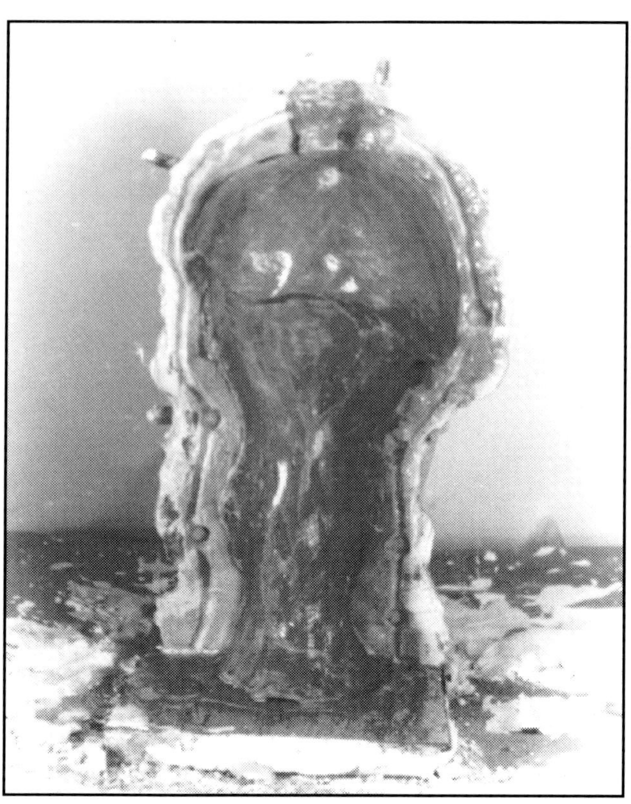

10. Shellacked back half of the model prior to making the second half of the mold.

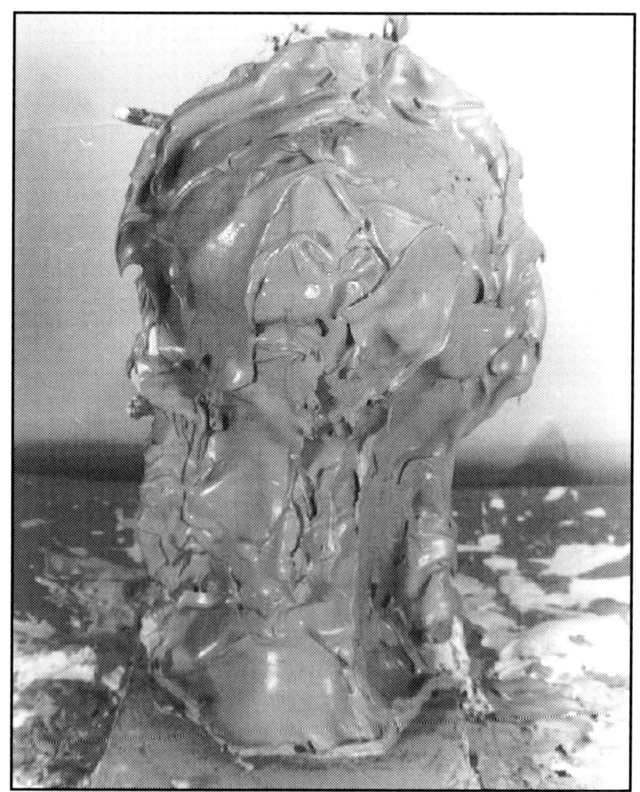

11. Back half of the mold's first coat after plaster has been sealed and parting agent applied.

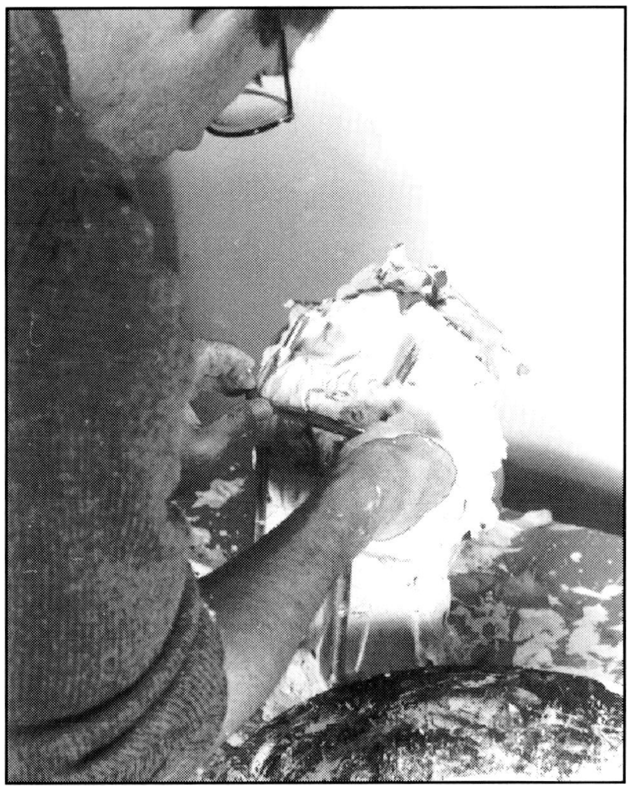

12. Inserting support rods to the back half of the mold.

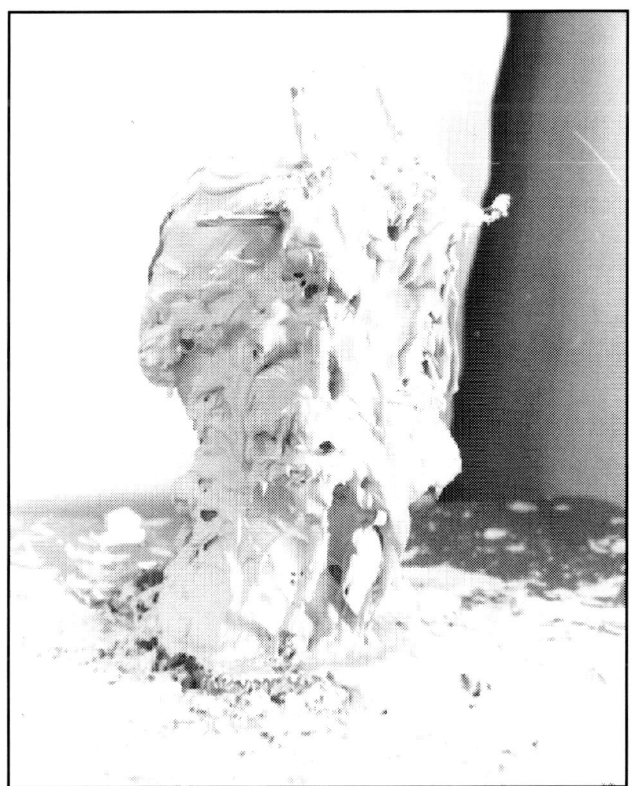

13. Completed mold with rods attached.

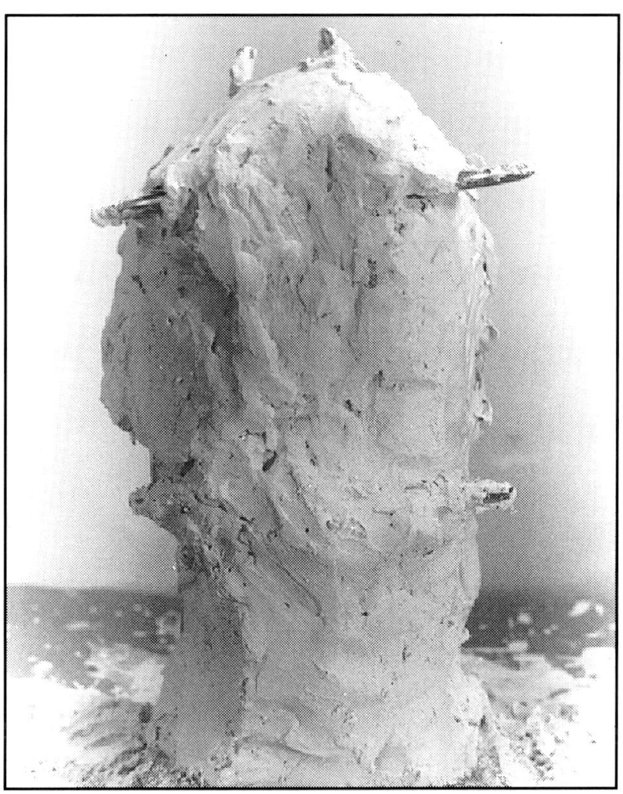

14. Complete mold with rods attached and final third coat of plaster applied.

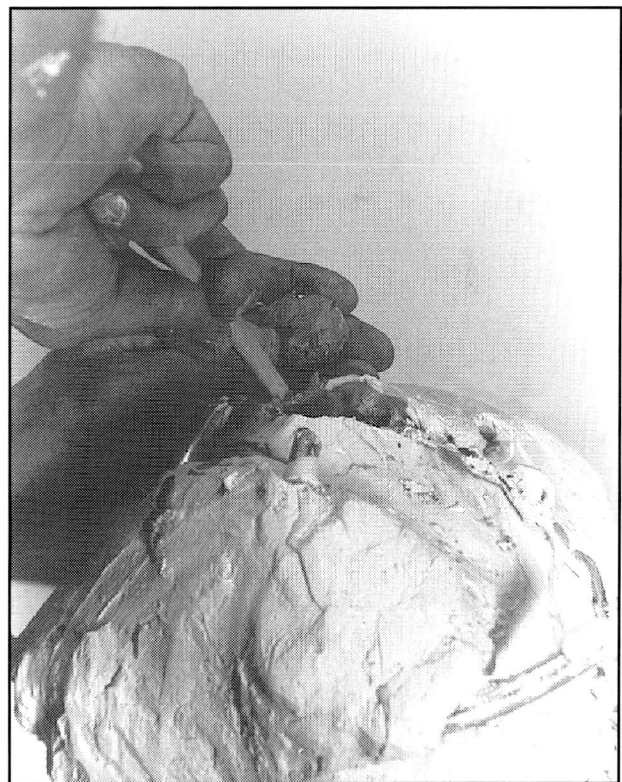

15. Removing the clay plug after plaster has set for one hour.

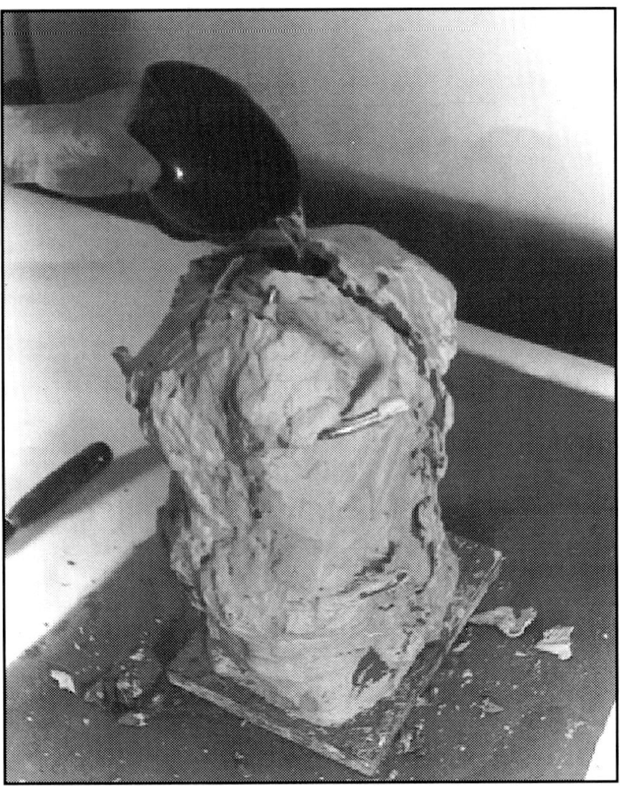

16. Pouring water into the open plus area to assist in separation of the plaster halves.

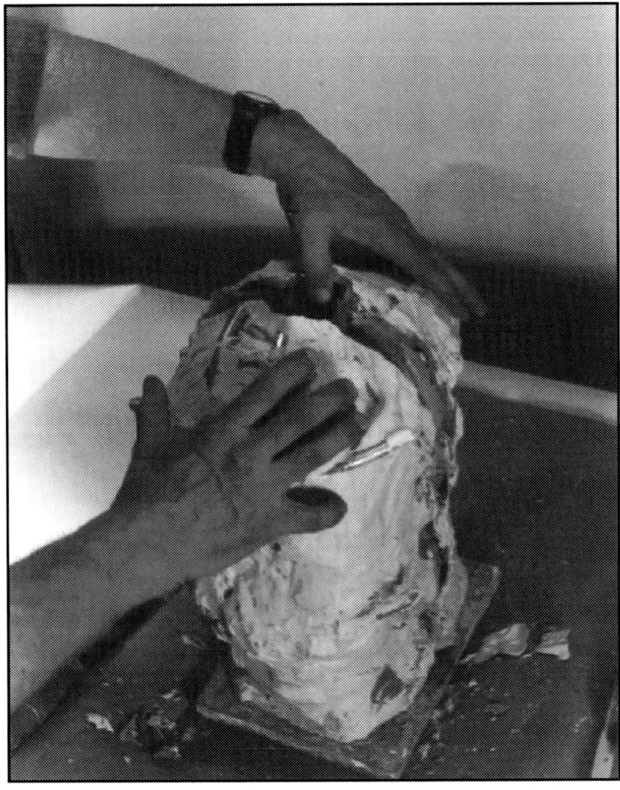

17. Separating the front and back sections of the mold.

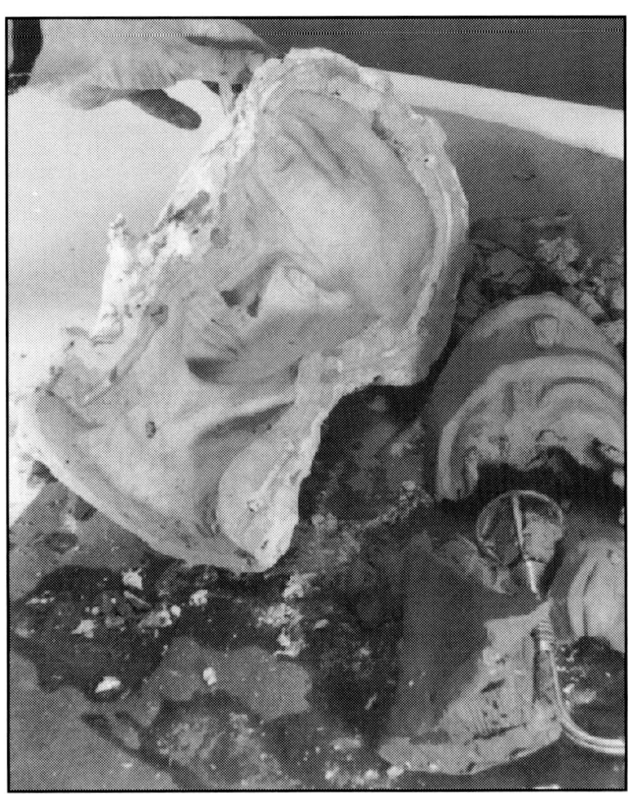

18. Front half of the mold with the remains of the model after being removed from the mold.

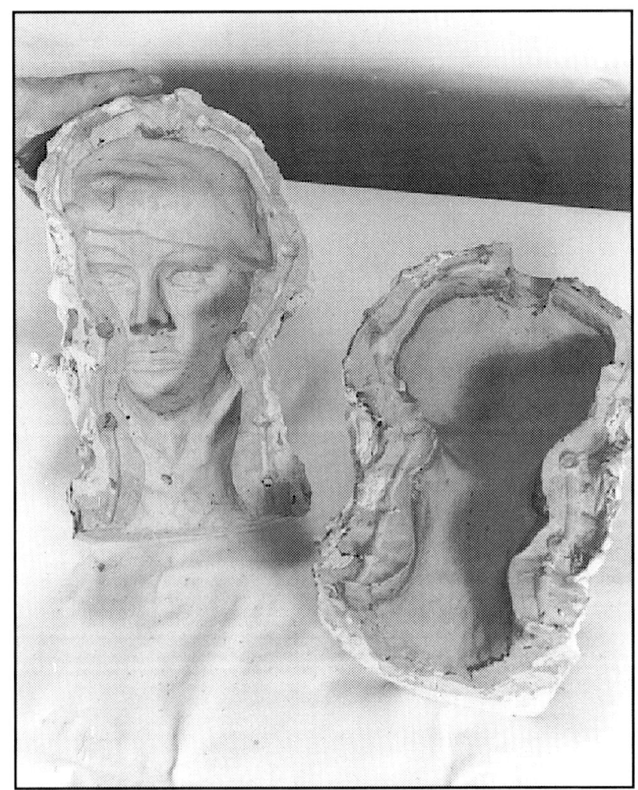

19. Front and back halves of the mold after removal of the model.

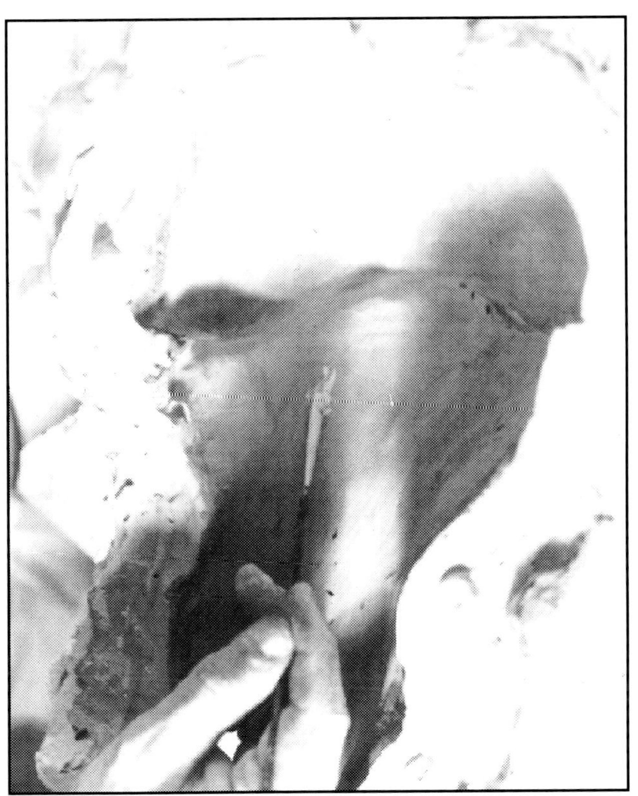

20. Patching air bubbles in the interior surface of the mold so a smooth cast can be made.

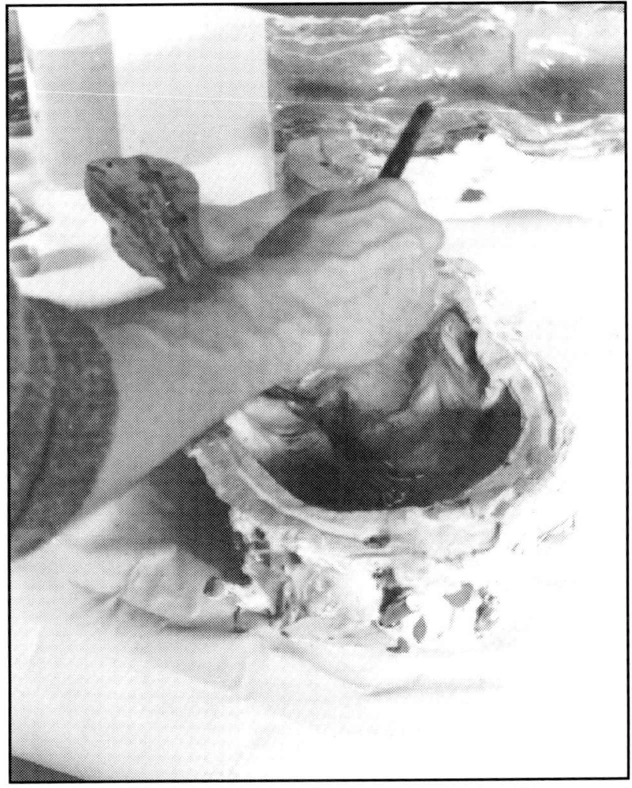

21. Soaping the interior of the mold for at least twenty minutes, in preparation for casting.

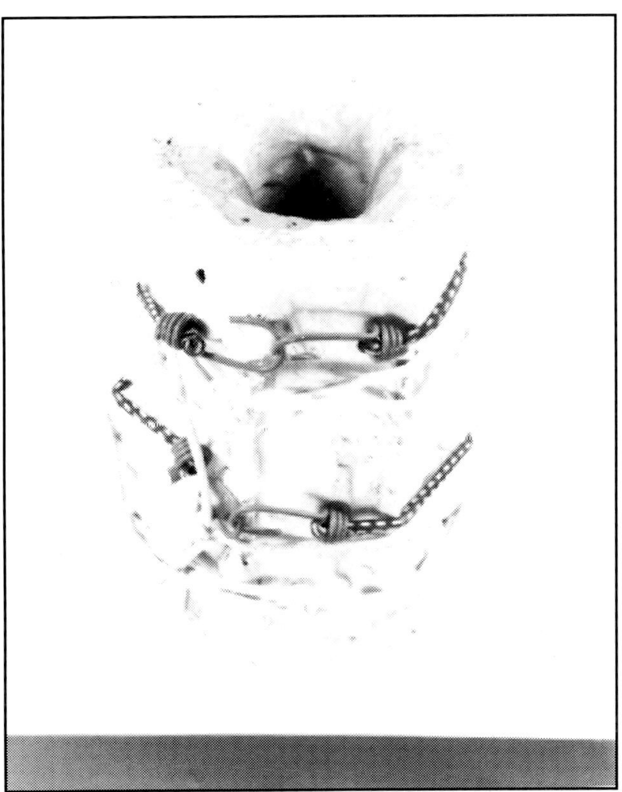

22. Completed mold with securing straps and inverted for casting to be poured.

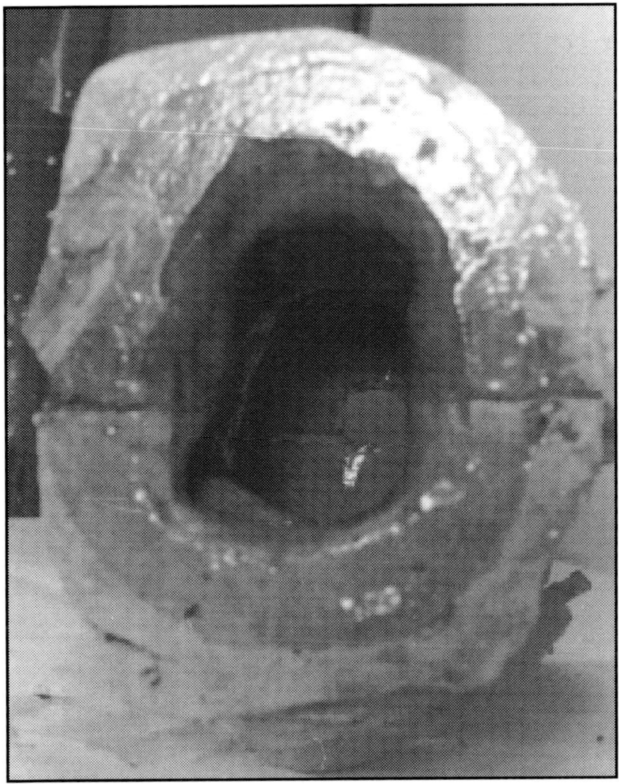

23. Front view of the mold after being shellacked and sealed ready for casting plaster to be poured.

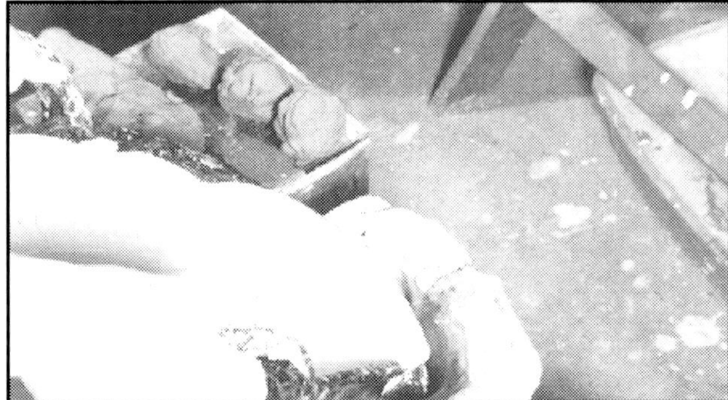

24. Pouring the casting material into the prepared mold.

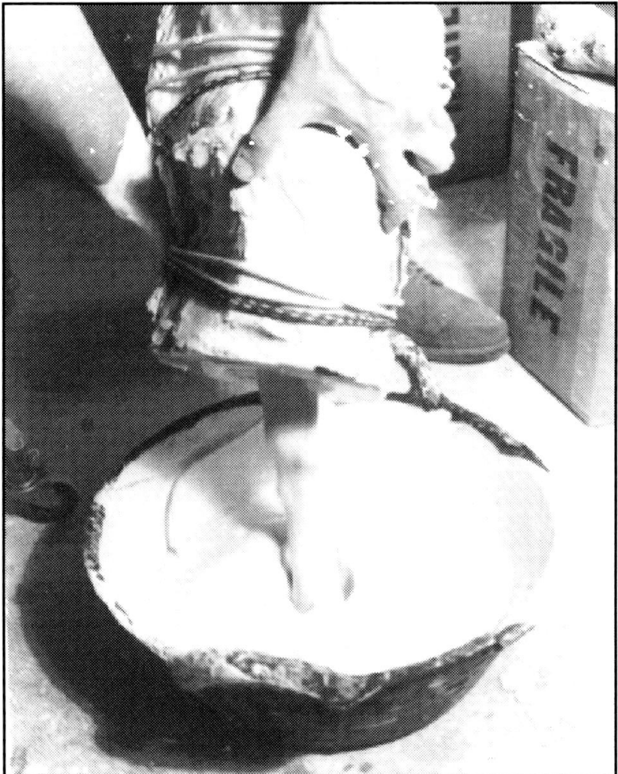

25. Removing the first pouring of plaster to coat the interior of the mold.

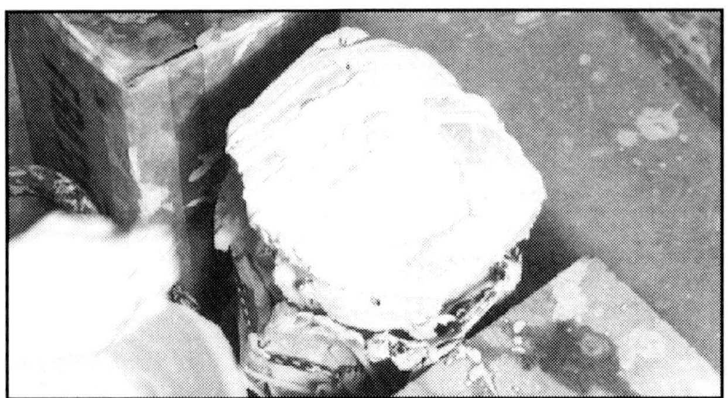

26. Filled mold with casting plaster mold should be tapped to remove air bubbles formed in the pouring.

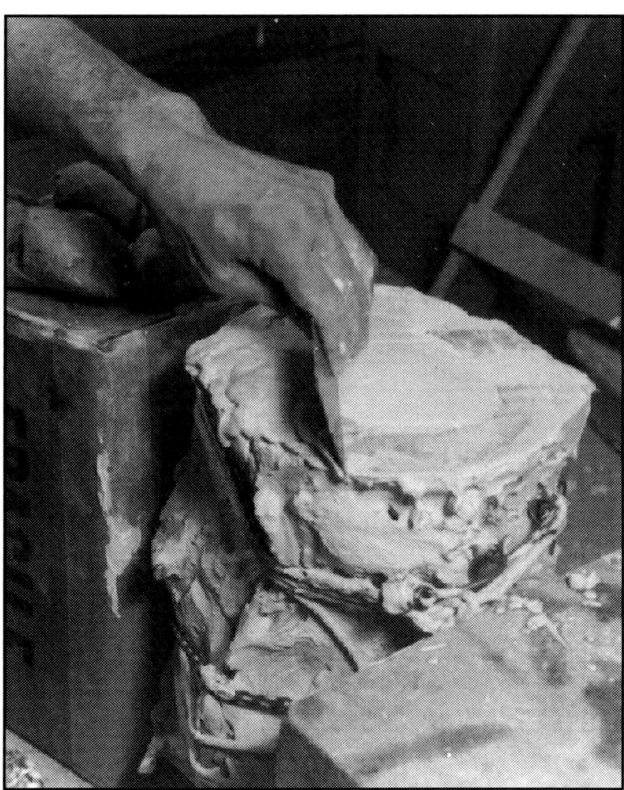

27. Leveling the top of the mold after casting plaster has been poured.

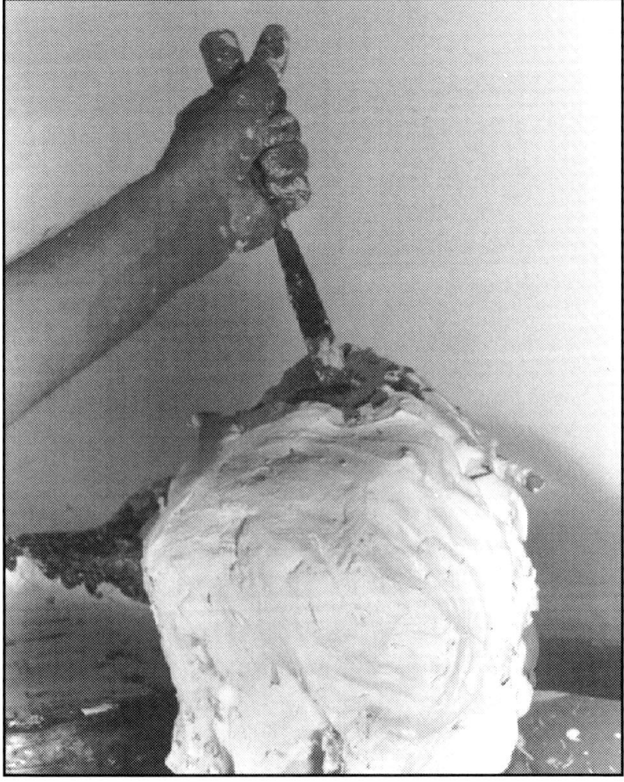

28. Removing plug from mold after casting has set.

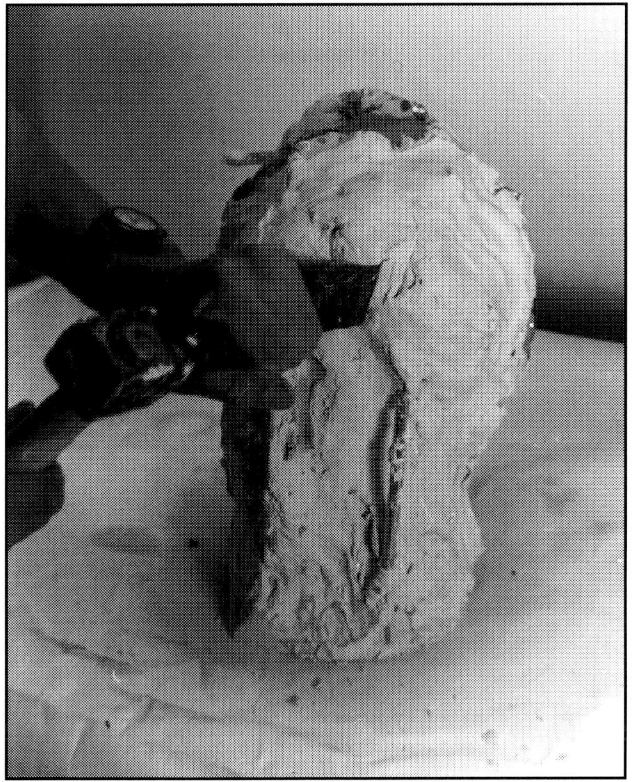

29. Chipping away the first and second layers of the mold after casting has been poured and set.

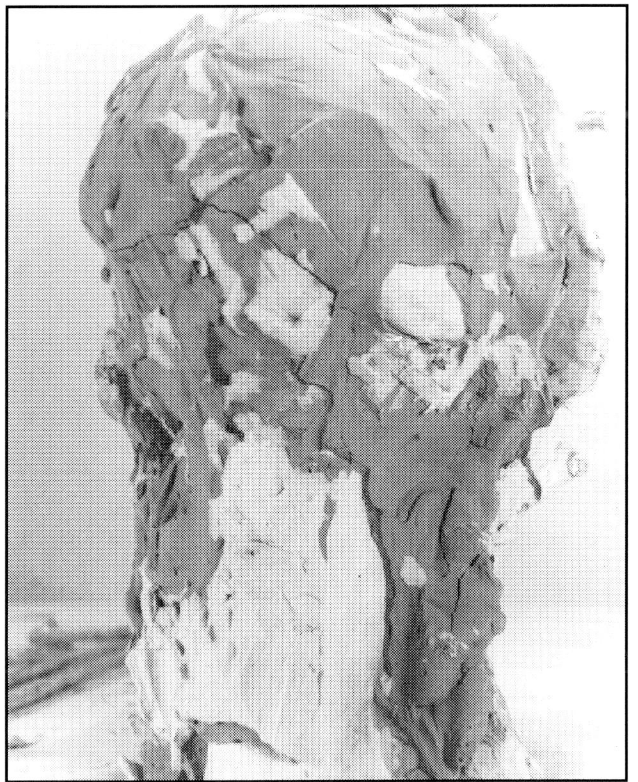

30. Last layer of the mold being removed (blue coat of plaster showing we are close to model).

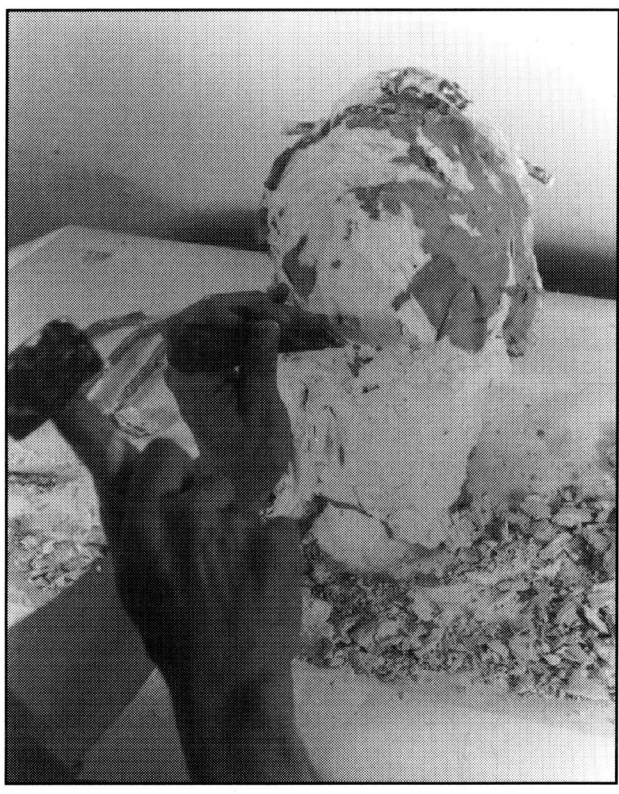

31. Final removal of the plaster mold exposing the cast.

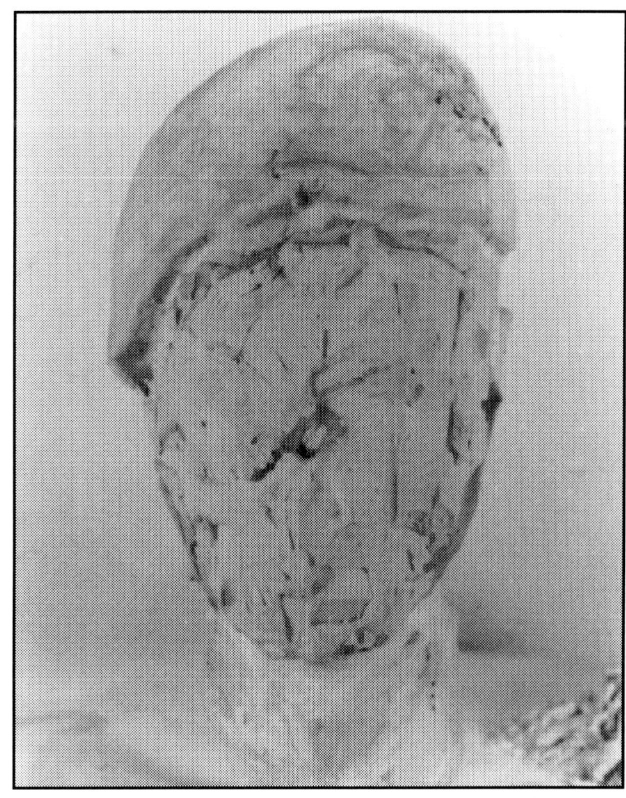

32. Plaster bluing on the last section of the mold being removed around facial area. The most delicate.

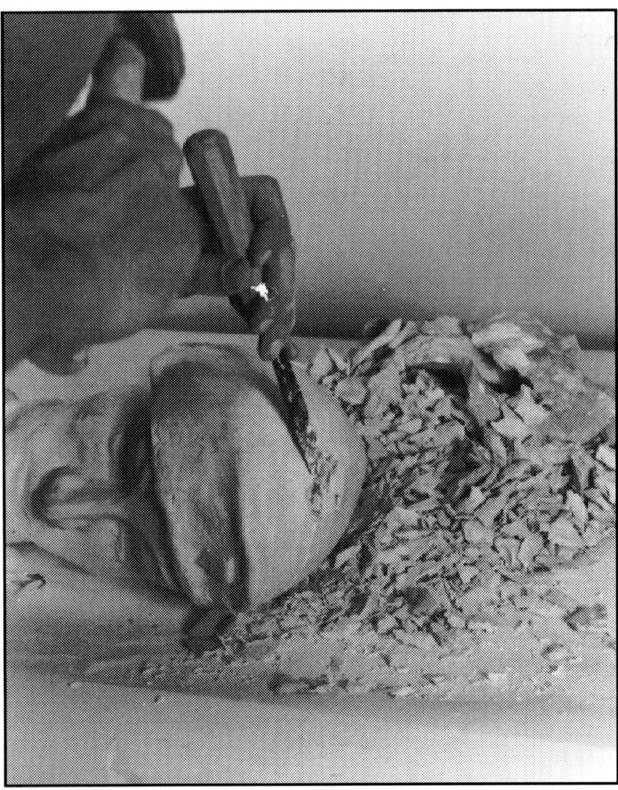

33. Removing plug area and seam line where the mold joined.

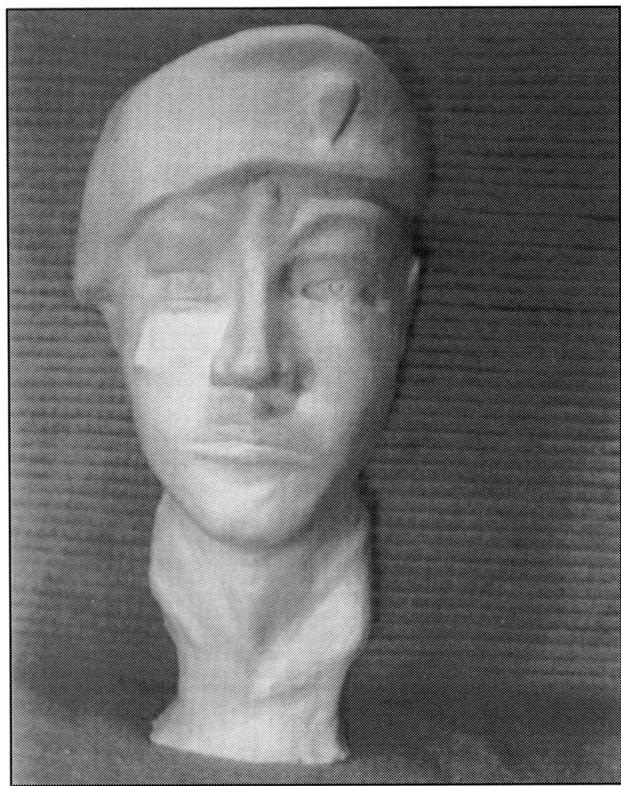

34. Finished casting of the model after mold has been removed cast finished with sanding and repair.

CHAPTER 3

LATEX RUBBER MOLD

(Life Size Head)

A latex rubber mold is probably the easiest to make of the durable rubber molds, although the actual construction generally takes longer.

Layer after layer of rubber must be applied to build up the proper thickness and each layer or coat must dry before the next coat can be applied. Latex rubber is the natural rubber sap from the rubber tree suspended in a water and ammonia base. The normal storage or shelf life of latex rubber, when stored in an air tight container with a foil lined lid is about nine months. Store the material in a cool dark place. Exposed to light, the rubber will take on a pink tint. This will not in any way affect its strength or working characteristics but psychologically, the user may not feel right about the different color.

Latex rubber is air drying. Apply thin layers one at a time and allow each to dry thoroughly. Allow 1 hour of drying time between each coat. Do not let the material puddle since a thin skin will form and self seal, preventing the interior surface from drying. This is a very common mistake and should be avoided. It most often occurs in the eye sockets and at angles and joints, where the material has been applied too thickly. Separators will generally not be necessary with most of the traditional sculpture mediums. However, the latex will absorb into porous materials such as plaster, wood, fabric, styrofoam, cardboard, and other paper-based materials and they should be sealed prior to application of the latex.

Latex rubber will also react to petroleum and sulphur-based materials, such as most of the professional grade plastilinas commonly used in sculpture. These must also be sealed so there will not be a reaction. Sealing is usually done with two thin coats of alcohol mixed with shellac in a 1 to 1 ratio. Then, using a fine bristle brush, apply the latex. Keep the brush in mold lotion of water so the latex will no set-up and can easily be combed from the brush when you are finished. Wet latex can be washed with water in its liquid state and when cured, can easily be peeled from any surface. You will always end up with small droplets of rubber on different areas of the work surface. It is rather fun to peel these off!

Keep track of coats you apply. A filler can be added to the latex after about 16 coats. This will save time and rubber but remember you will be applying about 20 coats altogether in order to make a durable mold that should last 20 years.

To store the finished rubber mold over long periods, keep it in a cool place preferably with the plaster mother mold around it for support. Some sculptors keep a plaster cast in the rubber to ensure that the rubber keeps its shape.

Casting into the latex should be done with low heat materials such as gypsum based products (plaster), cement, or cast stone products that do not have a large thermal output. I do not recommend casting resins, wax, or metals into latex molds, since the odds are great that the rubber will be damaged. Some mold makers disagree and so use these products. If you want to try, do a test run first and please don't complain if it doesn't come out to your satisfaction.

Deterioration will set in after about 500 casts of pristine white casting plaster have been made. Depending on how the mold was made and if there are extremely delicate areas and an abrasive material of casting is used, this may occur sooner. Do not allow the latex to freeze because of its latex content. If it freezes it will most likely effect the performance of the material. The water content may cause the material to shrink a little so when making the mold, it is a good idea to have an apron at the base of the model to absorb the moisture and prevent loss of detail.

A release agent is not usually required when casting the proper materials into a latex mold, but I mist the interior of the mold just prior to pouring the casting material.

TIME FACTOR

The beginner should allow about 24 hours from start to finish. This includes drying time between coats, which is a large part of the time. I have allowed for less than 1 hour drying time between coats since you will probably cheat anyway. Please note that the drying time may vary depending on humidity, dampness, and room temperature. In some cases, drying time between coats may be as long as 5 hours.

TOOLS AND MATERIALS

1. Model.
2. 1 qt. liquid latex.
3. 1 lb. paste maker or filler.
4. 5 lbs. moist clay for shims.
5. 1 key knife.
6. 2, 25-lb. boxes of plaster for mother mold.
7. 25 lbs. plaster for casting.
8. 1, 6-inch block scraper
9. 1 qt. mold lotion or liquid green soap.
10. 1, 3½-gal. rubber mix pail.
11. 1, 3-inch small mixing retouching pail.
12. 1 flexible steel tool.
13. 1, 1-inch applicator brush.
14. Patina colors, display base if desired *(optional)*.

PREPARING THE MODEL

Any model with a porous surface, petroleum or sulphur base must be sealed prior to applying the latex. Nonporous surfaces such as marble, alabaster, vitrified ceramic, or sealed wood need not be sealed. To seal models, use two thin coats of alcohol mixed with shellac 1 to 1. The shellac, if applied by itself or too heavily, might become too thick and cause loss of detail.

With the sealant, cover the entire model and an area extending about 3 inches from the base area of the model, creating a type of flange.

The more accomplished will now insert a 3 to 4 inch cardboard shim in the back of the head and neck area, going in about ¾ of an inch. We will be using a thin piece of cardboard, cut to the exact contour of the area where the shim will be placed. Commercial shims will not be wide enough to suit our purposes. Cardboard inserts may be made of dry cleaning or shirt cardboard, or of oak tag or manila folder. The piece must be at least 3 to 4 inches wide. Cut the material to conform with the contours of the model and insert the shim directly into the piece.

If the model is cast plaster, scrape or scribe a trough in the plaster and place the cardboard in the groove. This shim will create a type of flange, so the rubber will not shift when the cast is poured. With larger molds such as a head, this happens quite often if the flange is not built up. On smaller pieces it is not necessary.

After the model has been completely covered with sealant, check to make sure there is no build up in corners or crevices. If any air bubbles have formed, prick them with a pin point and smooth the area.

Cover the entire model, shim, and a 2 to 3 inch area beyond the base with two coats of shellac and alcohol mixed 1 to 1. I like to mark this base area with a grease pencil, just to have a general idea of the area to be coated with rubber.

When the sealing agent has dried thoroughly, no other release is necessary before applying the latex rubber.

APPLYING THE RUBBER

The application of latex rubber is very simple. Take a fine bristle brush and wash it in mold lotion or a watered down solution of liquid green soap. This will prevent the rubber from coagulating in the brush and the brush will be easier to clean when you are finished. Between coats, during the mold making process, store the brush in the mold lotion, water, or soap solution. Drying time between coats is about 60 to 90 minutes, but can be speeded up by blowing with an electric fan.

Apply the rubber in thin coats, one over the other, with each coat drying before applying the next. The first coats will be clear and dry to the touch. As the rubber thickens, it will become a shade of light brown and will snap back when the edge is pulled. The rubber must be applied in this fashion and not poured as a solid, since the outer layer of rubber will form a skin and seal itself.

When applying the rubber, the first four coats are most important. They will be picking up the greatest amount of detail of the model, whereas additional coats are applied more for the strength of the mold.

Take the brush and remove any excess liquid with a cloth; dip it into the rubber trying not to create air bubbles. When mixing the rubber, stir the material gently and slowly. **Do not shake** the container. If you pour the rubber from the gallon container into a wide mouth container, do this **slowly down the sides**. Do not splash the rubber into the container allowing air to get in. The rubber generally does **not** have to be stirred and can be used directly from its container.

Prick with a pin point and smooth any air bubbles that do form when applying the rubber. Apply one thin coat of rubber to the entire model extending outward at the base for at least 3 inches in all directions. Remove any old rubber from the brush and container opening, so these hardened pieces will not be incorporated into the mold coats.

When working with latex, no release agent is required when it is applied over a model properly sealed with shellac. When applying over copper or brass, use a clear acrylic sealant. We are making a glove or coat type of mold in this application.

After the entire model and base area have been covered with a thin coat of rubber, let this dry for at least 1 hour to 90 minutes, or until the rubber snaps back when pulled. These first thin coats will generally have a milky color. When dry, the rubber will adhere to itself. Don't be too concerned if the drying time is longer than specified, but do not apply another coat until the prior coat has thoroughly dried or the rubber will form a thin film and seal itself over the damp interior.

Apply at least 16 coats of rubber over the entire model and base area in this fashion, letting each coat dry before applying the next. When the 16 coats have been applied and dried, we will begin using a mixture of rubber and filler. This will save the amount of pure rubber being used and give greater strength to the mold.

MIXING AND APPLYING THE FILLER

Paste maker has been developed as a natural cotton flock material. It is light in weight and can be mixed with latex rubber to give a greater density of volume, while adding strength to the supporting layers of a latex mold. The mixing ratio is two parts of paste maker filler to three parts of latex rubber (2 to 3). Mix the paste maker filler with the rubber in small quantities to form a medium thick paste. Apply this mixture over the entire area of the model and base as with the previous coats and let dry. The paste maker can also be mixed by eye, but remember to mix the filler into the rubber and not to get the mixture so thick that it will not go on smoothly. Apply 4 to 6 coats of the rubber and filler mixture, until the rubber is about ¼ inch thick evenly spread over the entire mold area. Let the rubber dry **thoroughly** between coats. We will now make a plaster mother mold over the rubber so it will not lose its shape when the cast is made.

PLASTER MOTHER MOLD

First divide the rubber covered model into two halves, front and back, with moist clay or plastilina shim, 1 inch high and 1/8 inch thick, supported with pellets at approximately 1 inch intervals against the back wall of the shim and against the rubber. On the smooth front side of the shim, cut tapered locking keys, using the hook tool or key knife. Place these keys every 4 inches along the shim for the entire length of the shim. This will ensure that the plaster mold will not shift when pouring the casting material. Apply two coats of shellac to the face or front of the shim with the key grooves, letting the first coat dry thoroughly before applying the second.

After the second coat of shellac covering the shim surface has dried, place damp newspaper over the back half of the model.

Mix a batch of white casting plaster and using the flicking motion, make the first half of the plaster mold, starting at the top and working downward. The plaster should be up to the top of the shim, about 1 inch thick, and distributed evenly over the entire area of the mold. Refer to the weights and measure charts in Appendix F, for the proper amounts of plaster powder and water and for the proper mixing procedure.

Insert support irons or rods at the completion of the plaster build-up. This will aid in separating the two halves when the mold is completed.

After the plaster has set for at least 1 hour, remove the shim exposing the plaster wall of the mother mold. Seal this wall area and about 3 inches into the top of the plaster mold with two coats of shellac letting each coat dry before applying the next. Now apply a thin coat of release to the wall are and the other side of the rubber that is now exposed. Prepare another batch of fresh plaster and make the second half of the plaster mother mold as you did the first half. Again, attach support rods near the completion of the second half.

MAKING THE CAST

When the plaster mother mold has set for at least 1 hour, it can be removed from the rubber with a mallet and chisel and the rubber can then be removed from the model. To do this we must first take a sharp knife, an Exact-O type, make a cut in the rubber through to the cardboard beginning at the center back of the beck and cutting upward to the top center of the head. This cut will include the flange area at the base of the model.

After the cut has been made, gently pull the rubber from the model. It will have elasticity and will regain its shape after being removed. It will also be inside out. At this point, clean the rubber with warm water so none of the modeling material remains inside the mold. Flip it right side out and place it back inside the mother plaster mold, fitting it securely flush to the interior of the mold.

With heavy rubber bands or twine secure the plaster halves together, locking the key grooves, and mix a new batch of plaster for casting. Use the weights and measures chart to determine the amounts required. Pour the prepared plaster into the mold and tap up any air bubbles from the surface; let the plaster set for at least 1 hour. No release agent is necessary when using cement or gypsum based (plaster) products.

When the plaster cast has set for at least 1 hour, remove the bands or twine. The mother mold can then be separated from the rubber and the rubber pulled from the cast in the same manner as from the model. Leave the cast for at least 4 hours to cure.

Now, clean any seam lines left on the cast where the rubber was cut in the back of the model. Repair air bubbles with plaster and smooth and sand rough areas. Then patina or color the cast and mount as desired.

NOTE:

To store the rubber mold, clean and dry it, then replace it in the mother mold. Place some type of support in the hollow cavity to help retain its shape.

For longer periods of storage, I recommend filling the mold with fine white sand. For shorter periods foam packing or cloth strips can be used.

PICTORIAL OVERVIEW

Latex Rubber Mold (Life Size Head)

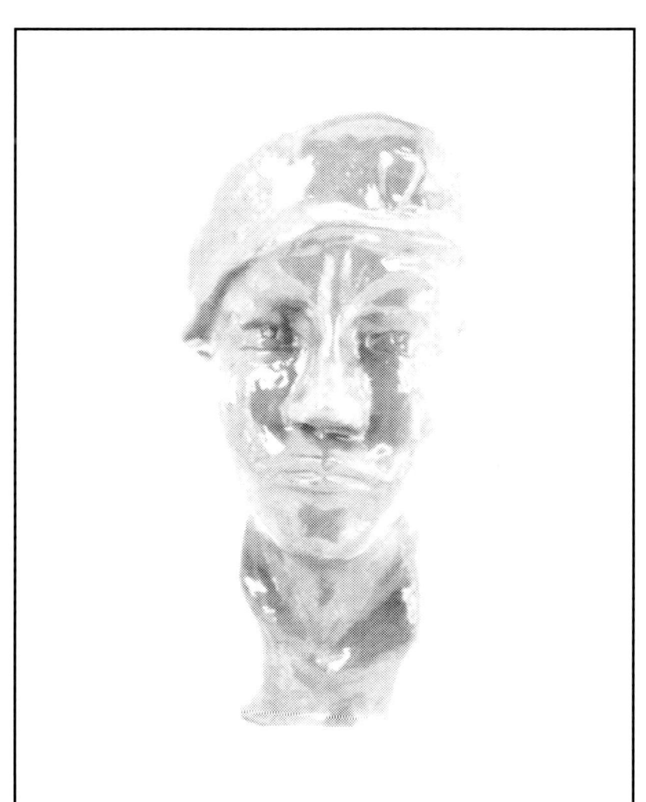

1. Original model.

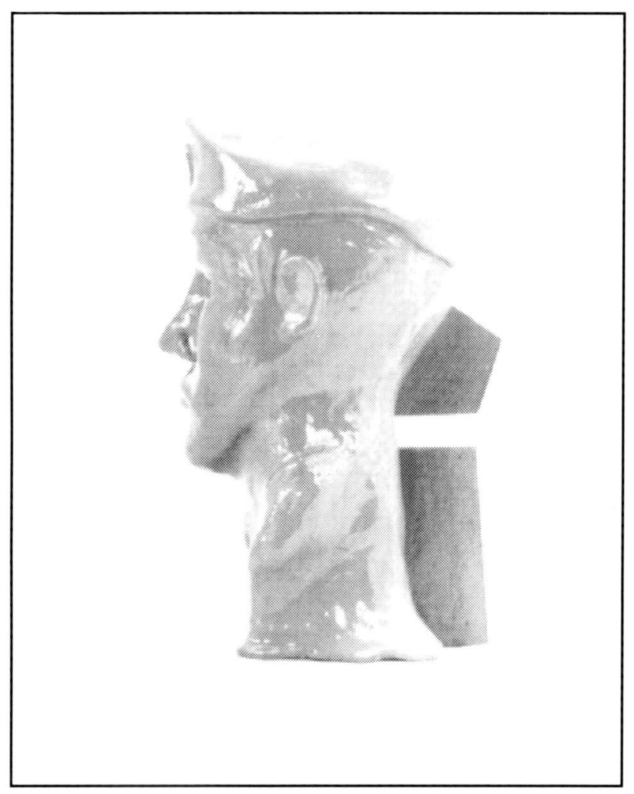

2. Model with cardboard shim inserted.

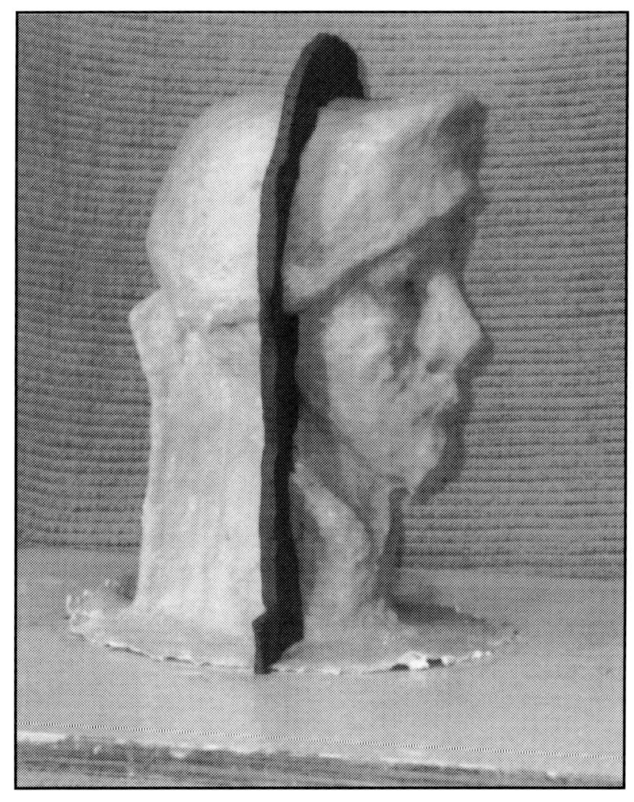

3. Model covered with latex, with separating clay shim for mother mold.

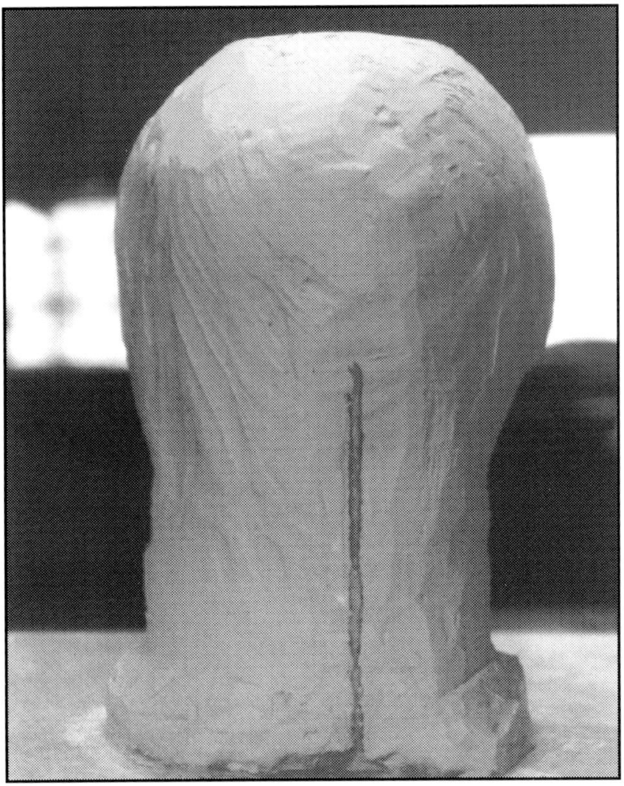

4. Back of mother mold with flange exposed.

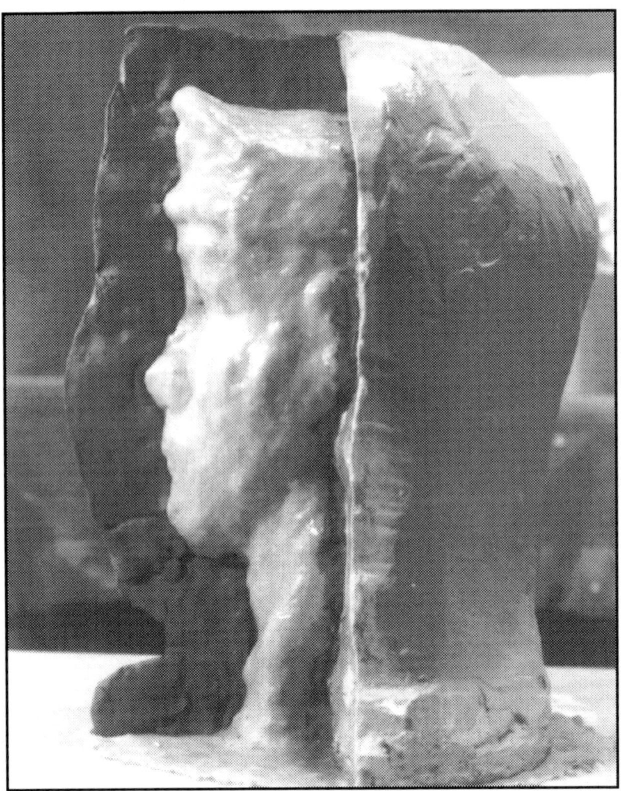

5. Back half of mother mold with shim separating front sections, side view.

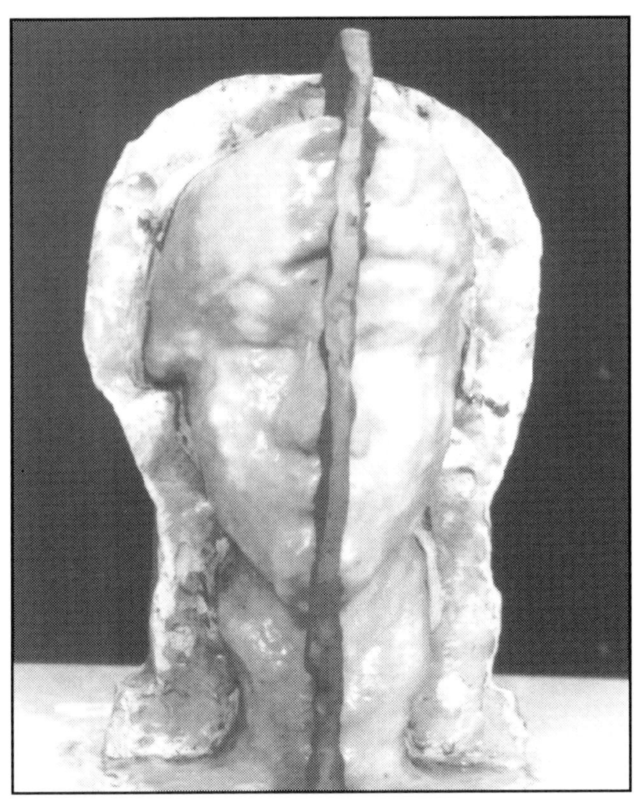

6. Shim separating front section, front view.

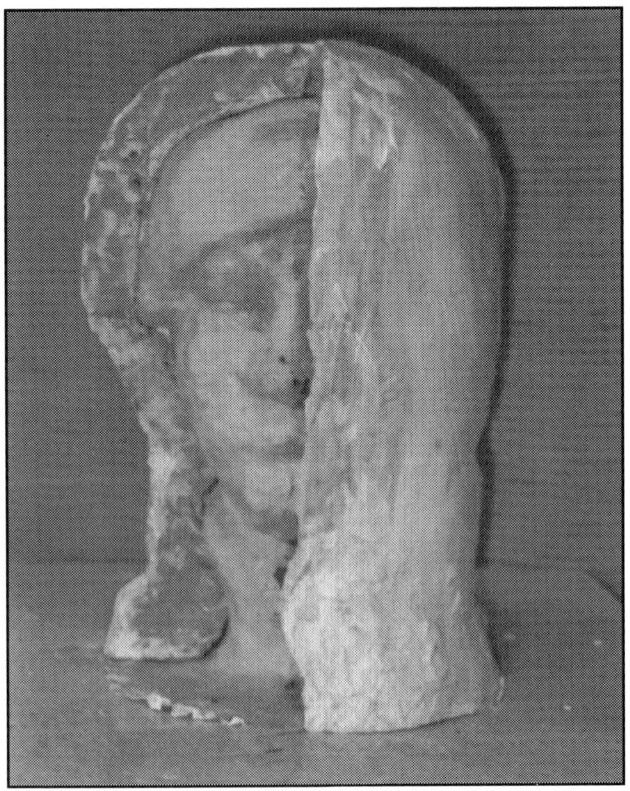

7. Front right of mother mold after construction of second section.

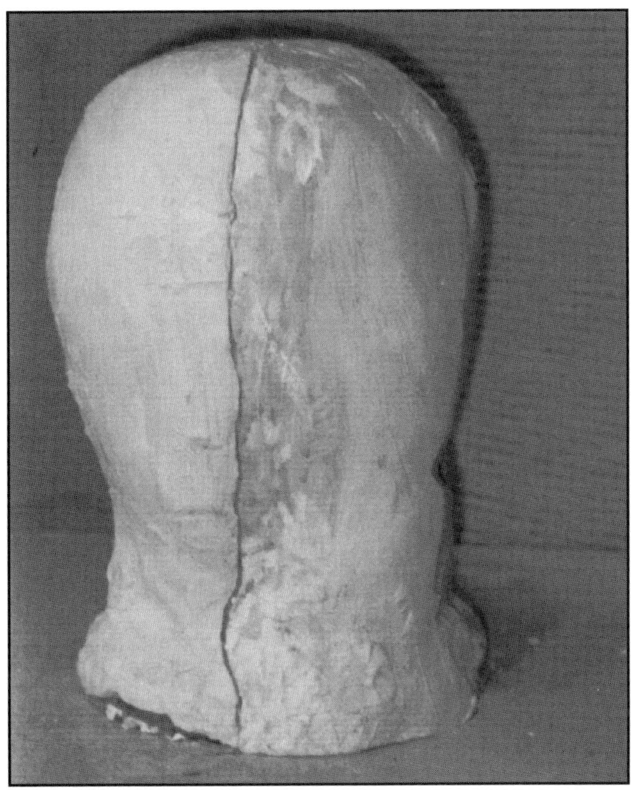

8. Front left of mother mold after construction of third section.

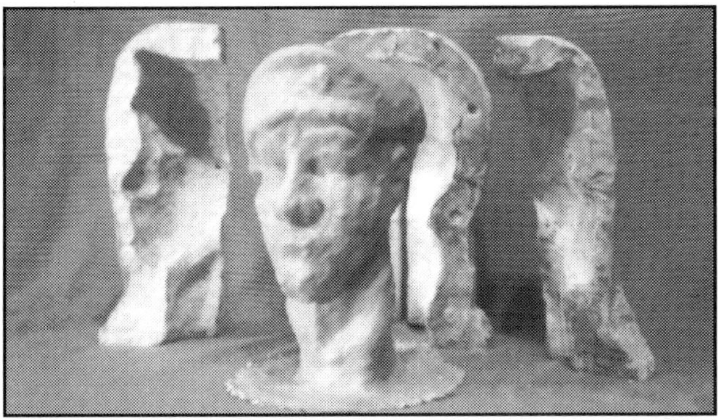

9. Three sections of mother mold and latex covered model.

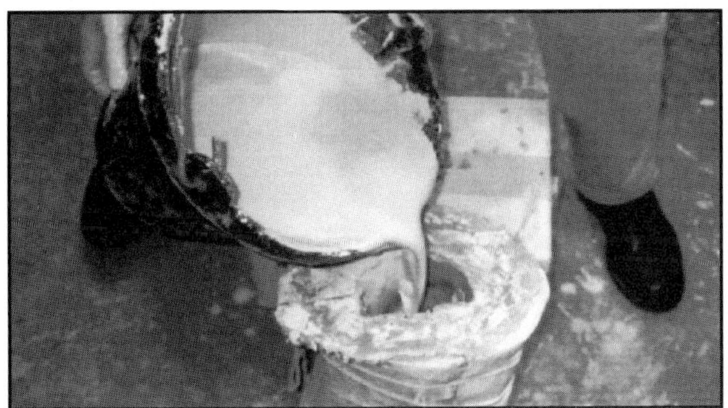

10. Casting into latex cavity after being secured in mother mold.

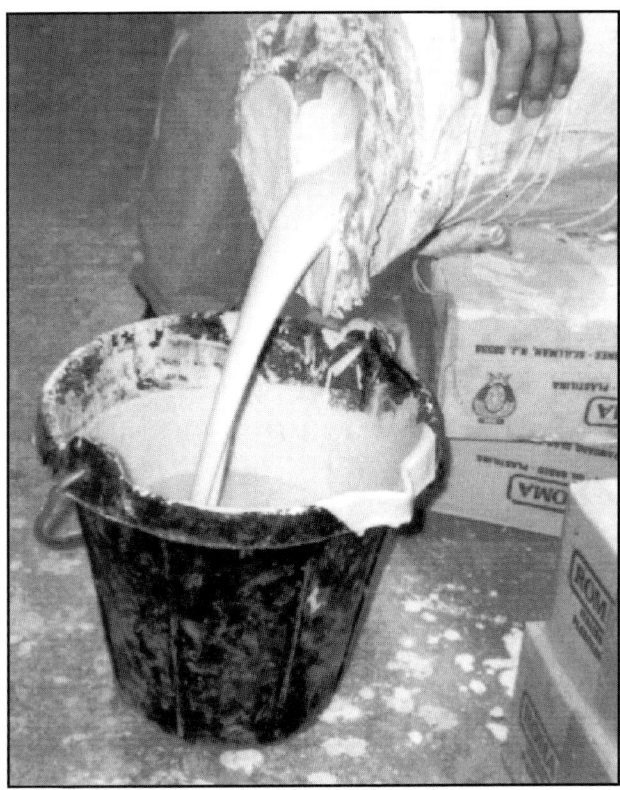

11. Removing casting plaster from mold after coating interior.

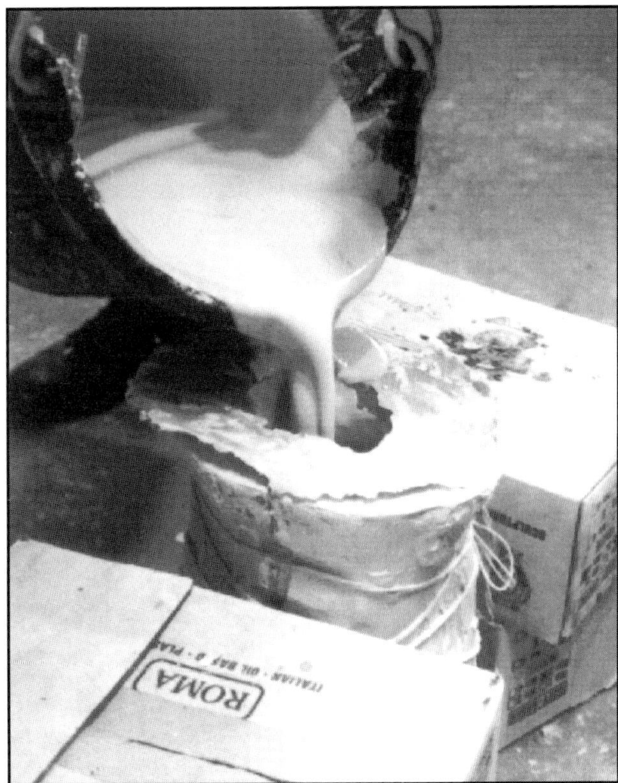

12. Filling mold second time for final cast.

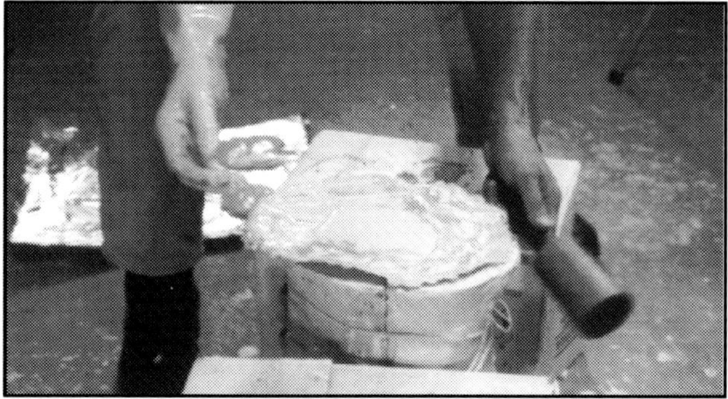

13. Tapping filled mold to release air bubbles.

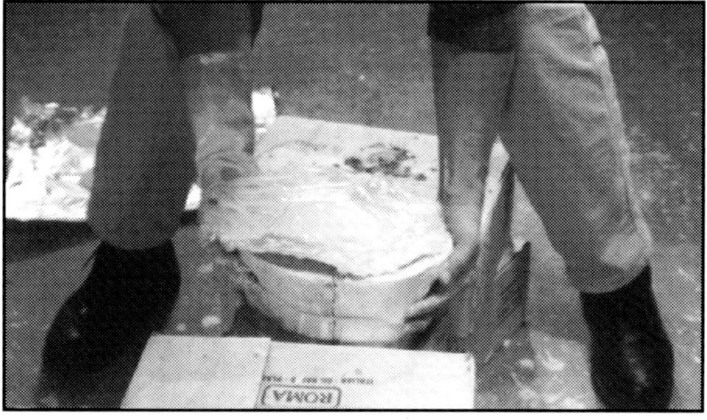

14. Bouncing mold after casting to release air bubbles.

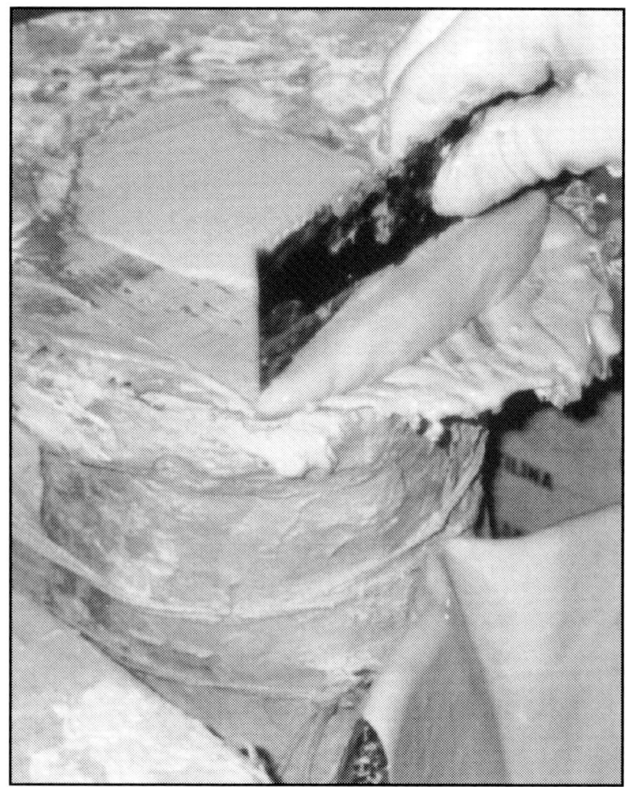

15. Scraping excess casting material from mold.

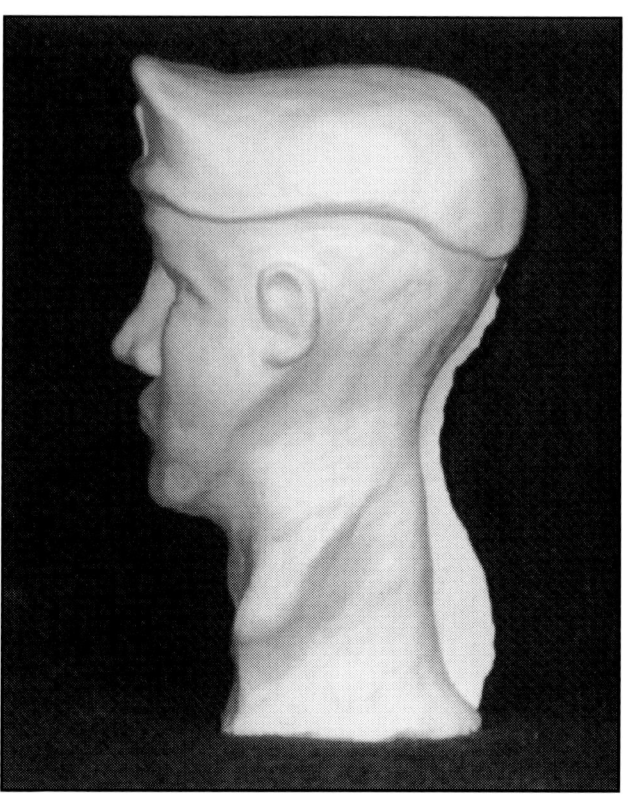

16. Cast with flange after removal of mother mold and latex mold.

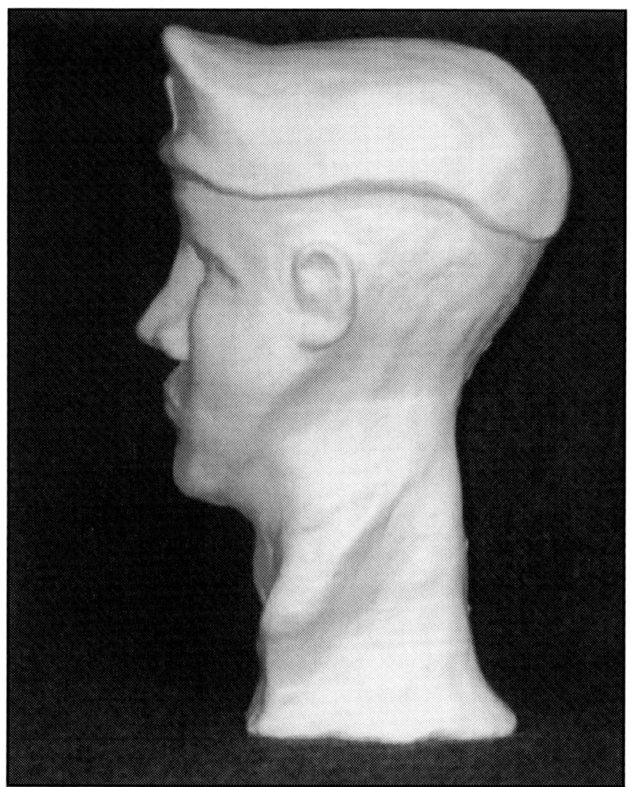

17. Flange removed from cast.

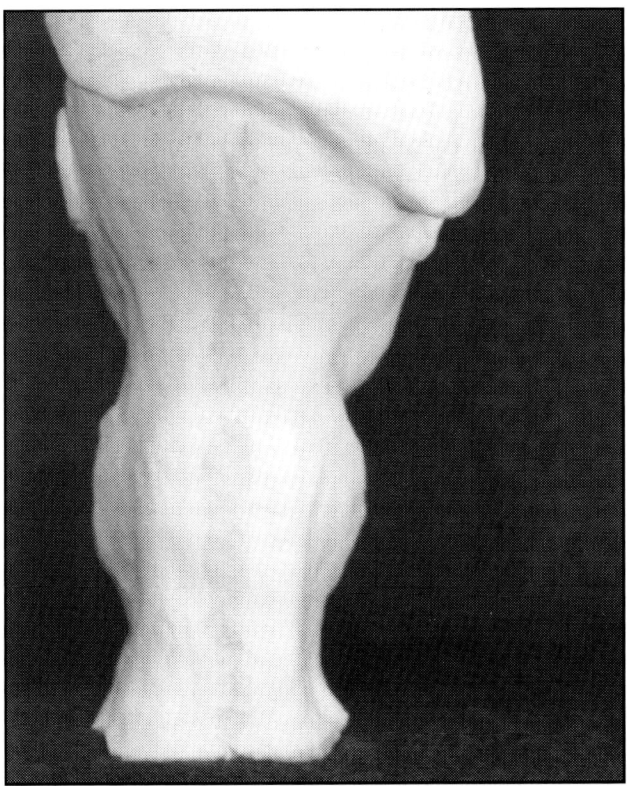

18. Seam line in back filled in, repaired and sanded smooth.

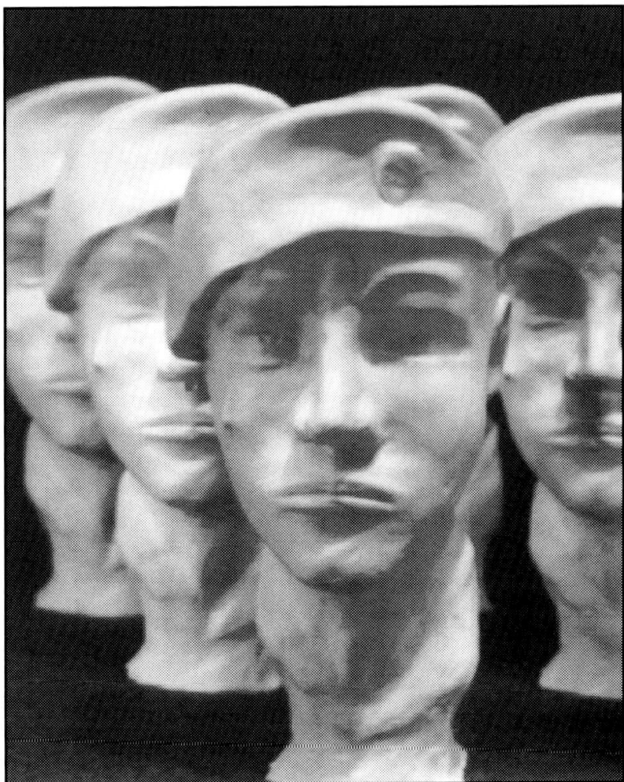

19. Multiple casts from a single latex mold.

CHAPTER 4

THREE PIECE WASTE MOLD

(Figure)

Type of Mold .... Plaster three piece
Type of Model .... 14 inch figure in the round, 14 inches high, 6 inches wide, 3 inches in diameter
Modeling Medium .... Claystone - air dry water base clay
Time Required .... Beginner, 6 hours
Casting Material .... Pristine white casting plaster

CONCEPT

The basic concept in making a waste mold of a 14 inch standing figure in the round, supported by an armature with an extended back iron, is to cover the entire model with a plaster shell or coating of plaster. This shell is made of several coats of plaster and can be removed from the armature and placed back together. The casting material is poured an allowed to set and the original plaster shell is removed by chipping with a ballet and chisel. It is understood that the original clay model and the plaster shell mold will both be destroyed in this process and the result will be a single plaster cast of the original model.

TOOLS AND MATERIALS

1. Clay model on armature supported by back iron, 14 inches high, in the round.
2. Shim, one roll, and household scissors.
3. 1 pt. of shellac.
4. 1 pt. alcohol.
5. 50 lbs. plaster for mold.
6. 2, 1-inch wide soft bristle brushes.
7. 1 qt. of mold lotion.
8. ¼ lb. of plaster bluing.
9. 1, 6-inch stiff with straight edge block scraper.
10. 1 flexible steel pallet tool.
11. 1 key tool or loop notch tool.
12. 1 mold makers chisel.
13. 1 ½ lb. wooden mallet.
14. 1, 3-inch rubber mixing bowl.
15. 1, 3-gal. large rubber pail.
16. 8 ¼-inch external support rods.
17. 12 ft. heavy twine rope or rubber bands.
18. 1 large roll of paper towels.
19. 1 sheet of 500 grit, wet dry sandpaper.
20. Base for mounting, optional.
21. Patina colors, optional.

BASIC STEPS

1) Seal the entire mold with the alcohol shellac mixture, mixed 1 to 1. Include an area of 3 inches from the base.
2) Place a dividing shim or fence separating the full front half and back half into three sections: front half, back upper half and back lower half. Place a clay plug at the point of insertion at the back.
3) Prepare the plaster and apply to the front of the model. Color or tint this initial coat. Attach support braces in the second coat and apply a third and final coat of white plaster.
4) Remove fence or shim and make key grooves and notches in the plaster wall. Seal the exposed plaster area.
5) Construct the lower back section of the mold, using colored plaster in the first coat and placing support braces in the second coat, before applying the third and final coat of white plaster.
6) Remove shim or fence and again make key grooves in the newly formed plaster wall, sealing the exposed area.

7) Place a clay plug at the top of the model and construct the top back half of the mold using colored plaster for the first coat and white plaster for the two additional coats. Place support braces in the second coat.

8) When it is set, remove plaster shell by prying and water. First remove the plug at the top of the mold, start with the top back, then do the lower back and the front.

9) Clean and repair mold sections.

10) Seal the interior surface of the mold and soak all sections prior to placing them back together and securing them with heavy twine or rubber bands.

11) Invert the secured mold and pout prepared casting material. Let set for at least 1 hour.

12) Remove plaster shell from the cast, chipping with mallet and chisel, starting with the upper back, then the lower back and front. Chip to the colored coat of plaster and leave delicate areas to last.

13) Repair the seam lined and any damaged areas.

14) Patina or color as desired.

PREPARING THE MODEL

The same basic procedures are followed in making a waste mold of the figure in the round as for the relief, head and bust molds. Since a figure with arms and legs is a more complicated piece, it follows that the mold will be more complicated. The preparation, application pouring, cleaning, and removal are all basically the same, however. The model that I am demonstrating on is a very simple figure with no outrageously extended appendages. Our mold can be made easily without complications of separation.

If the model has an arm, leg or torso position that hinders the separation of the mold such as an extended raised bent arm, the piece is likely to break when the mold and cast are made. The pieces must be rejoined in the final stages before the patina or coloring is applied. This is generally considered an advanced procedure not recommended for beginners. Take the model to a professional mold maker to have the mold and cast made or at least the molds.

Keep in mind, any type of figure is very difficult to cast. However, since this book is directed toward the beginner, I will try to guide you along with a minimal amount of frustration.

BUILDING THE FENCE - INSERTING THE SHIM

The first thing that must be done is to separate the model into sections. This is done so the mold can be made around, and removed from, the model and the section of back iron that is holding the model on the armature. Since we are using a model that is attached to the armature with a back iron located in the center lower back are, our mold will require three sections: (If you have a free standing figure, a two piece mold can be made.) a front half made in one solid section and two back halves, an upper and a lower, divided where the cross bar of the back iron is inserted in the lower back.

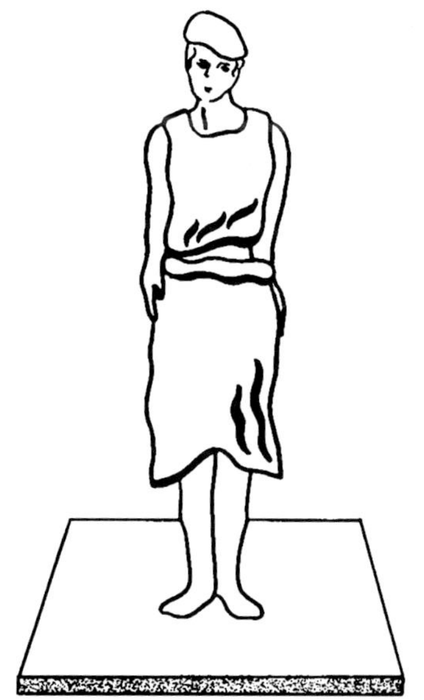

Figure 4.1. Model with back iron.

This will enable us to remove the mold sections from the model and armature. Reassemble the mold sections, making a full, solid, free standing cast in the round.

Cut the shim and place it in wedges, overlapping one another so there are no gaps between the shim pieces.

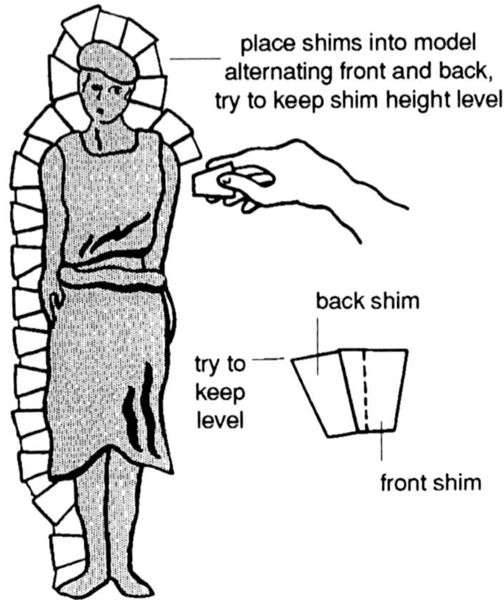

Figure 4.2. Inserting shim.

Place a clay plug made of a strip of moist clay of plastilina, 1½ inches in width and ¼ inch thick around the back iron. It should be long enough to wrap around the back iron support. Place the clay about the model and extend to the top of the shim line on a level plane.

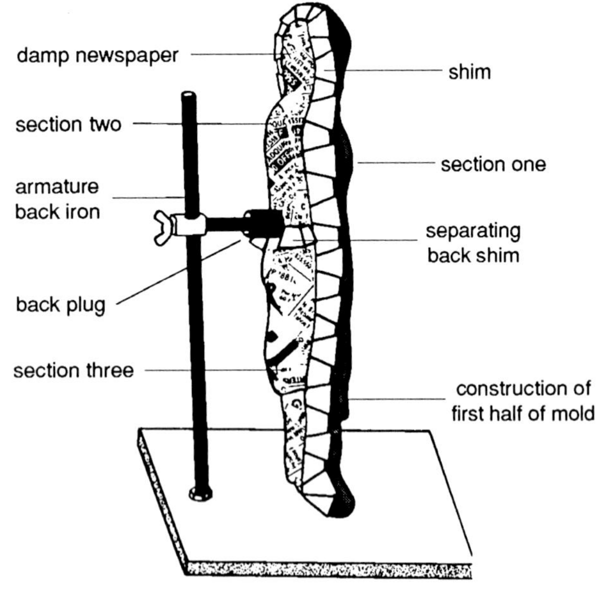

Figure 4.3. Back plug.

This shim or fence should extend from the clay plug down to the division of the upper and lower halves of the back and along the solid front half of the mold. It should form a solid divider between the legs, up to the groin area.

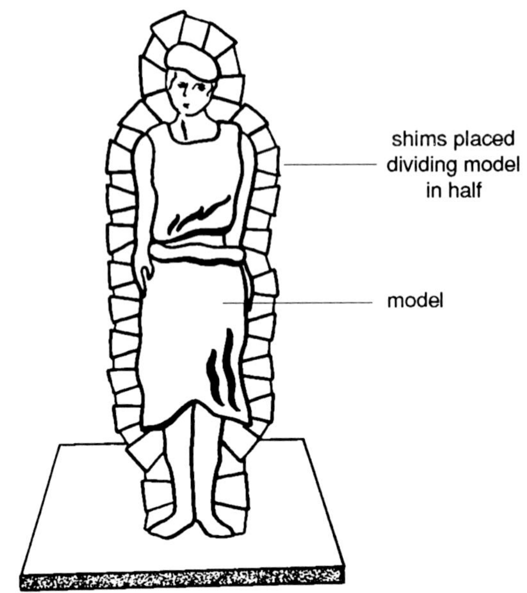

Figure 4.4. Total piece with shims.

SEALING THE MODEL

Once the model has been divided and the shim placed, so there are no gaps showing from on half to the other, apply a mixture of alcohol and shellac, cut 1 to 1 to the entire model. Include all three sections, both sides of the shim, and the clay plug around the back iron. Coat at least 3 inches from the base of the model around the work area.

When the first coat of shellac has dried, apply another thin coat. Remove any air bubbles or build up with a pointed tool. Make sure that all areas are coated. When mixing the alcohol with the shellac, **stir** the two together, **do not shake** the container, as this will cause air bubbles. The mixture should be applied with a soft bristle brush of high enough quality so the bristles do not come out and stick to the model. Soak the brush in paint thinner when not in use to keep it soft and pliable. Squeeze the excess lotion from the brush with a damp cloth before using.

FRONT OF MOLD

FIRST COAT (front half)

After the shellac coatings have dried, the first or front half of the mold will be made over the model. Place damp newspaper over the back areas of the model and base so thrown plaster will not damage these areas of the model. A coat of mold lotion should be applied to the front of the model before applying the plaster.

Mix a batch of colored plaster for the first coat. Refer to the weights and measures chart in Appendix F, to determine how much plaster will be required. Mix the plaster bluing with water **before** the plaster is added. The water should be a deep royal blue color since the plaster will dilute the strength of the coloring. Apply a ¼ inch thick coat over the entire front half of the model. Begin at the top and work downward to and including the base area extending out 2 to 3 inches. The colored coat of plaster will give you a warning that you are close to the cast when chipping the mold away. Leave the first coat rough and clean the base area with the block scraper. The next batch of plaster is white. Apply a coat of mold lotion over the dried blue plaster to assist with easier removal of the outer plaster coats.

SECOND COAT (front half)

Before applying the second coat, we will attach support irons of ¼ inch wire, cut and preformed to the basic length and contour of the mold. The support rods hold the mold together during the separation process. There is tremendous natural suction from the mold sections and we do not want the mold to break when separating them. Mix and apply a ¼ inch coat of white plaster to the front of the mold, beginning at the top and working downward. As the plaster is applied, we will place the support rods in a crisscross fashion and secure them with additional scoops of plaster (see Figure 4.5). The rods should be touching at the intersecting points and placed directly against the plaster of the mold.

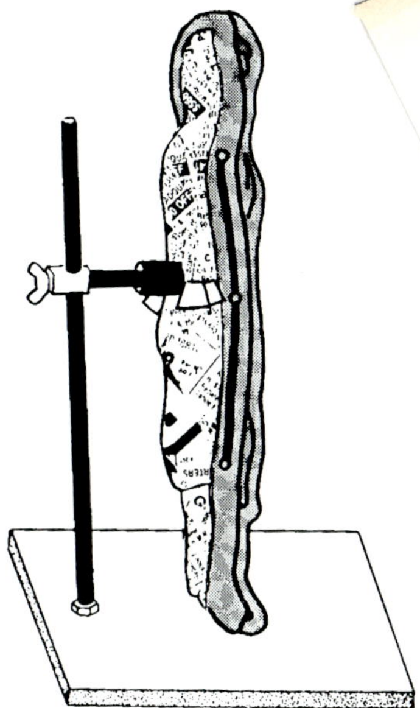

Figure 4.5. Attaching rods.

The second coat should also be left rough so the third coat will adhere easily. When the rods have been set in place and the area cleaned with a block scraper, we can begin mixing a third and final coat of plaster.

THIRD COAT (front half)

Apply the new batch of plaster for the third coat like the first two, starting at the top and working downward. Since this is the third and final coat of plaster, bring it to the top of the shim fence and level it evenly along the top of the shim with the block scraper. Cover the entire front surface of the mold including the support rods. Smooth this coat with the fingers while the plaster is still wet.

Clean the base area and let the plaster set. The front of the mold is now complete and we will begin the first section of the back half.

BACK OF MOLD
(Lower Half)

FIRST COAT (Lower Back)

When the front of the mold has dried thoroughly, remove the shim of fence exposing the flat, even plaster wall of the first half of the mold.

Remove the damp newspaper from the lower half of the model only. We must now make countersunk notches in the exposed plaster wall of the first half of the mold with the key groove or steel tool.

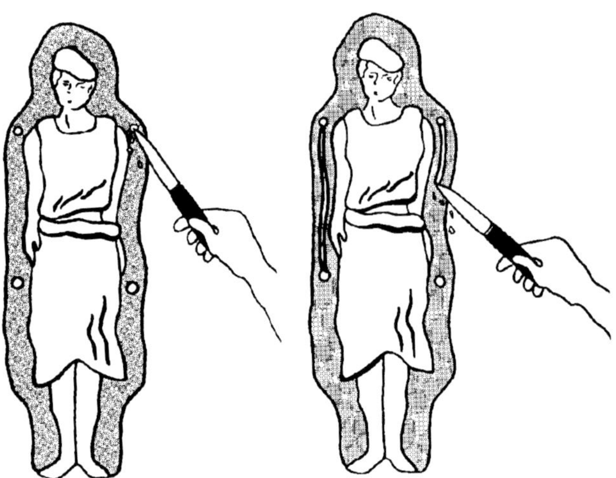

Figure 4.6. Cutting key grooves and notches.

Remove any plaster scrapings after the grooves and keys have been made, dusting with a dry brush and blowing gently, then wiping down with a damp cloth.

Seal the plaster wall with two thin coats of alcohol and shellac, 1 to 1. Let the first coat dry before applying the next. Also coat the top of the mold going in about 2 inches. This will enable you to remove any excess plaster that might get on the mold while making the back half. The shim separating the upper and lower halves of the back must be left in place. It divides the two halves at the back iron position facilitating removal of the sections of the mold from the model.

Mix the first batch of plaster, using bluing for color, and apply with the flicking motion. When applying the plaster to the under portion of the shim, it may be necessary to blow it in place. Cover the entire lower back half of the model and base area with the blue plaster, making the coat ¼ inch thick. Clean the base area of the work space and the parts of the first half that have plaster spattered on them. Leave this first coat rough so the next coat will adhere properly.

As an aside, I will mention that some mold makers place moist clay wedges at 4 inch intervals on the wall of the first coat, before applying the second. This ensures an easier separation. If you wish to do this, place the moist wedges like the plug in the top of the mold. They are removed in the same digging out manner.

SECOND COAT (Lower Back)

When the blue coat of plaster has been applied, we will begin to mix a new batch of white plaster for the second coat. We will again attach support irons of aluminum, ¼ inch thick rods, cut to the proper length, then shaped to the contour of the mold before applying the second coat. Make enough to guarantee adequate strength, depending on the size of the mold. In our example, we will be using four, two horizontal and two vertical.

Apply the second batch of plaster like the first. Use the "flicking" motion, being sure to get underneath the shim properly. When the coat is ¼ inch thick, insert the support rods into the wet plaster. At the crossing points, secure them with extra amounts of plaster lightly pressed into the wet plaster of the second coat. Leave this coat rough so the next coat will adhere better. With the scraper clean the work area and the areas of the mold that may have had plaster splattered on them. You are mow ready to prepare the third and final coat for the lower back half.

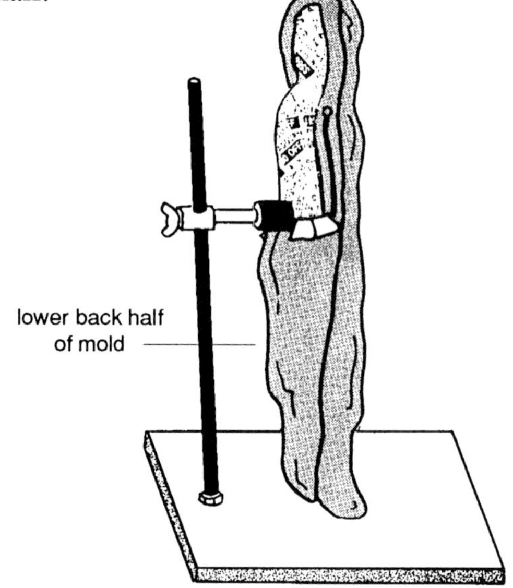

Figure 4.7. Rods and third coat.

THIRD COAT (Lower Back)

Apply the third batch of clean, white plaster with the flocking motion, even with the walls of the first coat and the shim, to a thickness of about 1¼ inches in all areas. With the block scraper, level all areas at the joining sections of the mold and shim, then clear the mold and the surrounding work space of plaster scraps. Let the plaster set-up for at least 1 hour before beginning the upper back half.

BACK OF MOLD

(Upper Half)

FIRST COAT (Upper Back Half)

When the plaster of the lower back half of the mold has set, remove the newspaper and shim from the upper section. The upper back half of the model will be exposed with the walls of the first half and the lower back half. Seal the wall of the lower back half with two thin coats of the alcohol and shellac mixture. Again, coat a few inches into the top of the lower mold surface so splattered plaster will not stick to it.

Some mold makers like to apply a coat of mold lotion between coats so each layer will come off separately. If you elect to do this, apply the lotion to the inner areas of the mold, not to the edges, so the coats of plaster will adhere better. Prior to sealing the exposed wall of the lower back half, make two countersunk notches to ensure a secure fit of the halves when they are placed back together. Remove any plaster scrapings before applying the shellac.

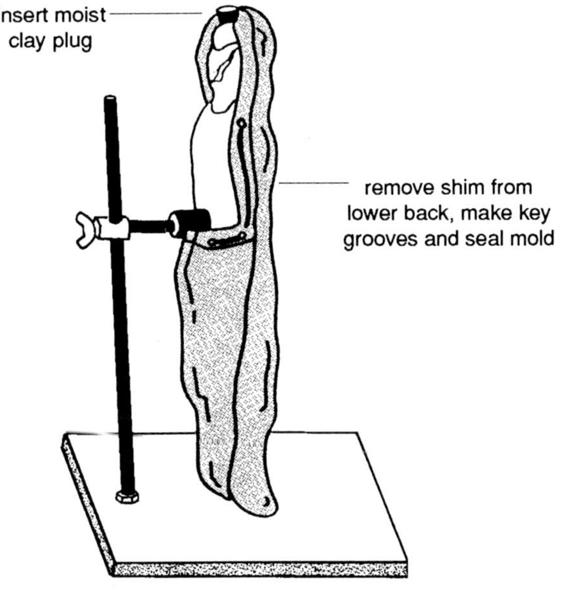

Figure 4.8. Notches.

When the grooves have been made and the shellac coats have dried, mix a batch of colored plaster for the first coat. Before making the upper second half of the mold place a moist clay wedge about 2 inches wide, 1/8 inch thick and 2 inches high at the top center of the first half of the mold. We will be using this to pour water into the mold for separating purposes.

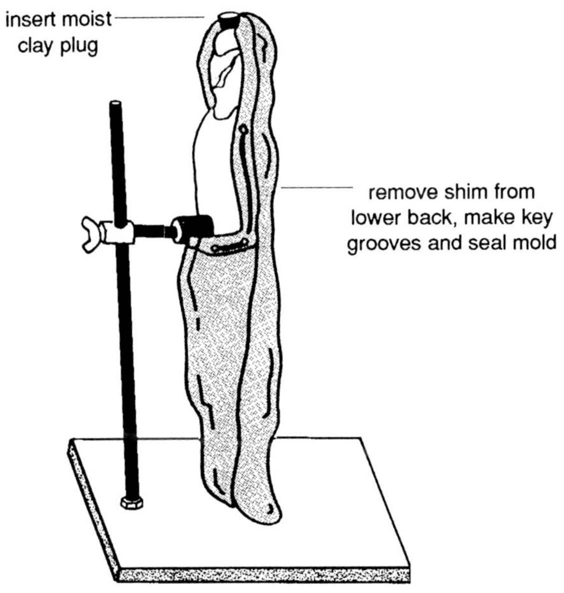

Figure 4.9. Plug.

Seal the plug and the mold with shellac and alcohol working from the top downward to the upper wall of the lower half of the mold.

Take extra time with the application of this mold section, so the plaster does not run off and onto the lower back half. Continuous cleaning and removal of spattered plaster is suggested. When the first coat has been applied, clean the work area and lower half of the mold of splattered plaster. Leave the surface rough and prepare a fresh clean batch of white plaster for the second coat.

SECOND COAT (Upper Back Half)

As with the other sections, we will be attaching rods with the second coat to strengthen the mold. Preform these rods to the contour of the mold after cutting to the proper length. Use ¼ inch aluminum wire. Now mix a batch of new white plaster in clean water and apply with a flicking motion to the upper section of the model starting at the top and working downward, cleaning splatters as you go.

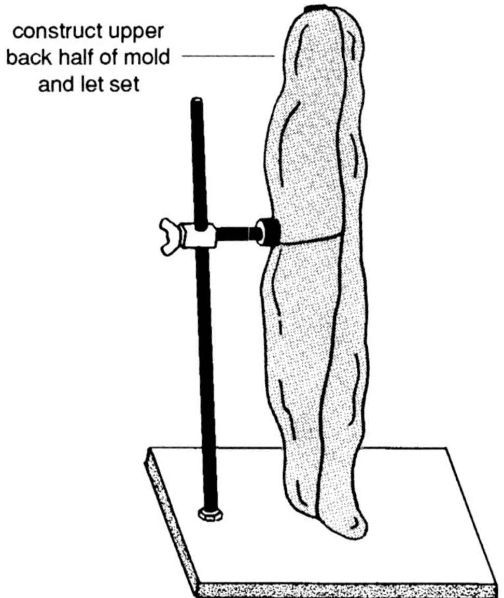

Figure 4.10. Upper second coat.

While the plaster is still wet, set the support rods in place and secure them with extra amounts of new plaster. Leave the surface of the second coat rough. Clean the base area and mold of unwanted plaster and prepare a new batch of white plaster for the third and final coat.

THIRD COAT (Upper Back Half)

Apply a new batch of white plaster over the entire upper back section of the mold covering the support rods even with the rest of the mold and the shim sides. Starting at the top, as before, work downward. The mold should now be the same thickness all over. With your fingers, smooth the entire area to an even surface.

Place an X or other distinctive mark to show where the key notches are, so the positive will not be mistakenly cut off when removing the mold from the model before casting. Let the plaster set-up for at least 1 hour. If you don't know where the notches are you can break the positive off when separating.

REMOVING THE MODEL

When the plaster has set, we will remove the mold from the model.

Remove the clay plug at the top of the mold and any wedges that have been inserted, digging the material out with a steel tool of chisel. Be sure not to damage the sides of the mold when doing this.

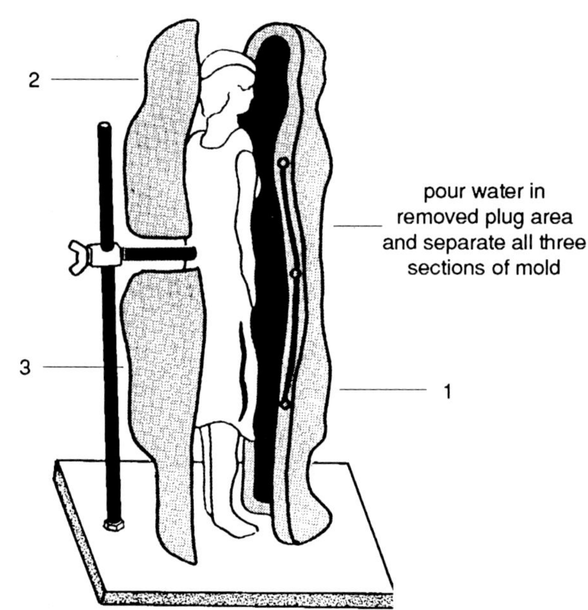

Figure 4.11. Removing mold sections.

We will begin with the top back section of the mold. Pour a cup of warm water into the open plug space and gently pry the upper back section from the model. Begin at the top center and work left to right down both sides to the top of the lower back half of the mold. Gradually the top back half will separate from the model and can be totally removed. Set aside well out of the way, so it will not be stepped on or knocked over.

In the same manner remove the bottom back section of the mold, starting from left to right, gently but firmly prying with the flat chisel. You will probably experience suction removing this section. You may need to dig into the model to gain leverage. Experienced mold makers may use wood wedges inserted at certain areas of the mold and lightly tapped to get this leverage, but it is not really necessary. Remember to go slowly from side to side and downward so as not to break the mold sections out in chunks.

As the lower back half comes off, do not be too quick to pull the last inch. It might hit the back iron support and be damaged. When the lower back half has loosened, slide it from underneath the back iron and set it aside with the upper back half. Give yourself plenty of room to place these sections out of the way so they will not be damaged.

We will now remove the large front half of the mold. This half is on the model alone and may seem a little awkward to get to. You can tilt the mold and base, and pout water into the seams of the mold to help with the release, but **this could be dangerous working alone.** Pry the plaster from the model with the straight chisel, starting at the top and working downward from left to right, going very slowly so as not to break the mold.

The tendency is to go fast and the suction will break a large section of the mold if you are not careful. You want to take the entire section in one piece. Take your time and have patience. Dig into the model and use it as leverage to remove the mold. If the model still does not want to release, you must dig it out from the mold with a heavy steel tool of the straight chisel.

CLEANING THE MOLD

All modeling material must be removed from the interior of each section of the mold before the casting. Use the steel loop tool or hook and steel tool. Be sure that all crevices and angles are checked carefully. You may also wash the mold with soap and warm water if desired.

After the mold has been cleaned, check all sections for any scrape marks, gouges, or air bubble holes that may have occurred during the construction or separating processes. Mix a small batch of plaster. Using the flexible steel pallet tool, fill in any holes and repair the marks. Smooth with a damp cloth or sand paper as necessary. Remove any dust or excess plaster with a damp cloth or by blowing.

PREPARING THE MOLD FOR CASTING

After the interior of the mold has been cleaned, repaired, and inspected to your satisfaction, each section must be sealed prior to casting.

Using a soft bristle brush, lather all areas of the mold interior and the walls of the mold sections with mold lotion or liquid green soap. Soap each section for at least 20 minutes. Soap liberally to ensure saturation of the lotion into the mold surface, to ease release of the cast from the mold.

When the soaping has been completed, remove any froth with a soft damp cloth and rub a small amount of olive oil over the entire surface area of each section. This should produce a dull sheen and drops of water should bead up on the mold surface, like water on a newly waxed car. If the water is absorbed by the mold, additional soaping or lotion may be required.

Next, soak each section of the mold in cold water. Submerge entirely for at least 15 to 20 minutes to ensure total saturation of the mold, thus enabling the mold to be chipped from the cast without adhering to it. Since the plaster has set and cured, the soaking will have no adverse effect. The plaster will remain strong and not decompose. Remove the sections from the soaking container and allow them to drip dry, but not dry out. Then reassemble them, forming the completed mold.

Start by placing the lower back section against the lower front section of the mold. Then snug the upper back section on the lower back and upper front sections, fitting them together securely with the grooves and keys locking.

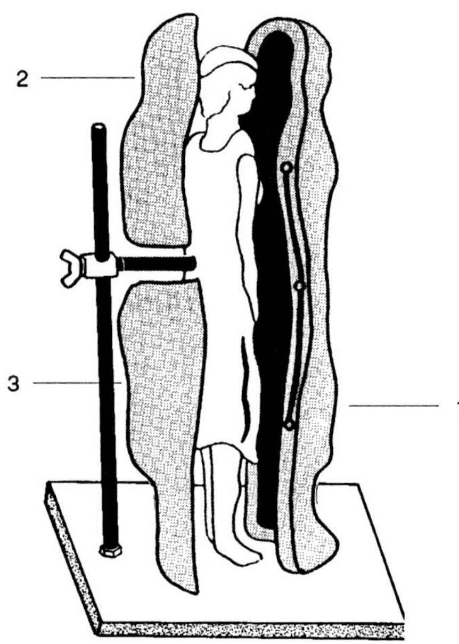

Figure 4.12. Placing mold back together.

They must be tight enough to withstand the pouring of the plaster into the mold. Secure them with heavy rubber bands or heavy twine. If you are using twine wedges can be inserted between the mold and tapped to form a tighter fit.

The mold should now appear free standing as it did when first completed over the model. With moist clay plug up or fill any holes made in the mold for separating purposes. These areas are the first to be plugged and are at the top of the mold where the plug was.

You can generally look at the mold and see any gaps that may have occurred, but you may want to double check by lowering the room lights and inverting the mold. Hold a flashlight to the access opening at the bottom of the mold; the light will shine through any openings you may have missed. Fill these areas with moist clay. Do not press too much clay into the openings since this will create an indentation in the cast or leave so much space that the casting material will cause a ridge that will have to be removed and cleaned later. If there is a decision to be made, opt for the cleaning rather than the filling.

Invert the mold so the head is at the bottom and the feet are up, with the feet opening exposed so the casting material can be poured easily. If two persons are doing the pouring it's simple, with one pouring and the other holding the mold. If you are pouring alone, give yourself plenty of room and support the mold well to avoid a mishap.

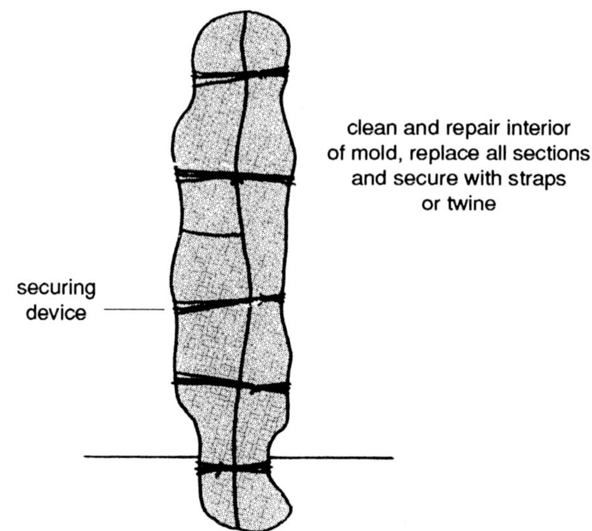

Figure 4.13. Inverted mold ready for pouring

POURING THE CAST

We will be using casting plaster for our cast. First determine how much plaster powder and water will be required to pour a solid cast into our mold, filling it completely. Refer to the weights and measures chart in Appendix F to determine the cubic area of the cavity and the amount of water and plaster you will need. If you are using some other material, determine the amount of that material you will need. Remember, you should have **more** than enough.

Refer to Appendix A for mixing instructions and procedures.

When the plaster is ready to pour, **tilt** the mold to a 45 degree angle and pour in enough casting material to fill the mold ¼ full. If you are pouring alone and cannot tilt the mold by yourself, pour directly into the upright mold trying not to cause air bubbles of allow air into the mold.

When the mold has been filled ¼ full, raise it and tap it gently to dislodge any air that may have entered while pouring.

Rotate the mold and at the same time pour the casting material back into the mixing container, coating the entire interior of the mold with casting material. Include both feet and leg openings. Repeat this process until you are sure that all the interior areas of the mold have a thin coating of plaster.

Now pour the casting material back into the mold filling it to the top. Lift the full mold and gently tap it on the work base area to dislodge any air bubbles. You may also tap the sides of the mold with a mallet, starting at the bottom and working around and upward to the top. Air bubbles will rise to the top of the mold and should be scraped away with the block scraper. You may also take a piece of thin gauge aluminum wire and insert it into the cavity of the mold. Place it down each leg and into the body of the cast in a plunging motion, so air is dislodged and plaster is forced into all the areas of the mold.

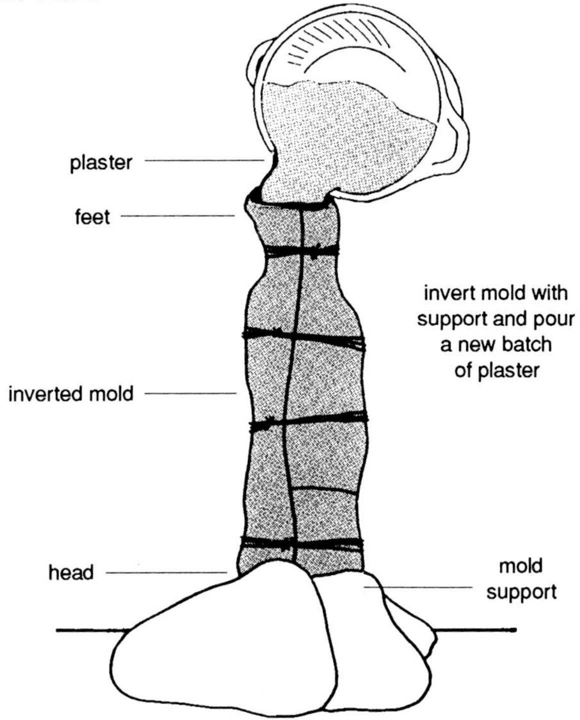

Figure 4.14. Pouring the cast.

Internal support is required within the cast and rods are set in place and left to give strength to the cast. These rods should be of a noncorrosive material since the water content in the plaster can rust the material and this will show through. Insert the rods when the plaster has set enough so they will not float to the outside edge of the mold but will stay in the center of the cast. Also place these thin wires in each leg opening, to depth of about 1 inch when the plaster is in an almost set state.

If the seam lines have not been properly placed together or the holes not properly plugged the casting material will escape through these cracks or holes. This is very common. To prevent it place a piece of moist clay over the area where plaster is coming through. Fill the mold to the top so that a level cast is made pouring all at once and in an even manner since the casting material will begin setting up after it is mixed. You will have about 15 to 20 minutes to accomplish all the pouring, insertions, and leveling. This is more than enough time, but not if you hesitate and waste time worrying. Begin and keep going until you are finished. Let the mold and cast set for at least 1 hour before removing. If you place your hand on the top of the cast about 10 minutes after pouring, you will notice the material is warm to the touch. This is the plaster setting up and is a natural reaction. The casting material will most likely recede somewhat from the mold as it sets.

REMOVING THE MOLD

The next step is to remove the outer shell or casing from the model. Do this by chipping the mold from the cast with a mallet and straight chisel. Return the mold to an upright position with the feet at the bottom and the head at the top. When the mold has been positioned properly, remove the twine of rubber bands that had been securing the mold while casting and begin chipping the white plaster from the mold. Begin at the top back and work downward and around the entire piece. If mold lotion was used between coats, there will be a layer that will seem to fall off.

Wear protective goggles as you are chipping. When you have chipped away to the blue coat, with all the white plaster removed, you must use caution

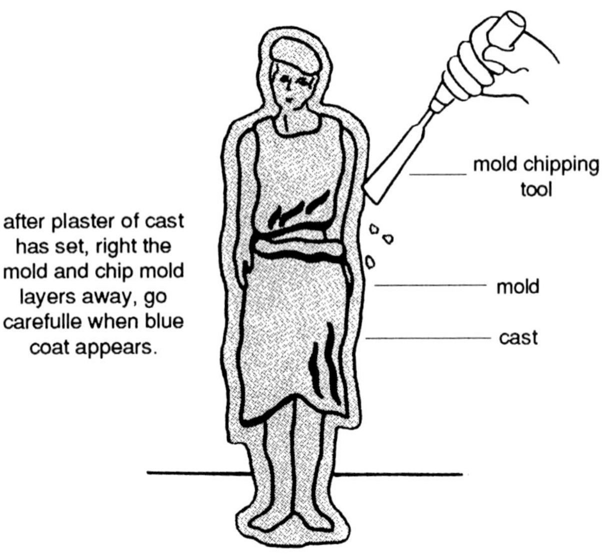

Figure 4.15. Chipping away the mold.

so the cast is not damaged. Leave the areas under the chin, the legs, arms and around the ears and eyes until last. Chip the blue plaster very **gently** and with great **caution**, until the whole cast has been revealed. Clean fallen pieces as necessary to facilitate the job.

REPAIRING THE CAST

Once all the mold pieces have been removed inspect the cast for damage and for air pockets where the casting material did not penetrate, leaving craters or holes. Repair these with plaster of the

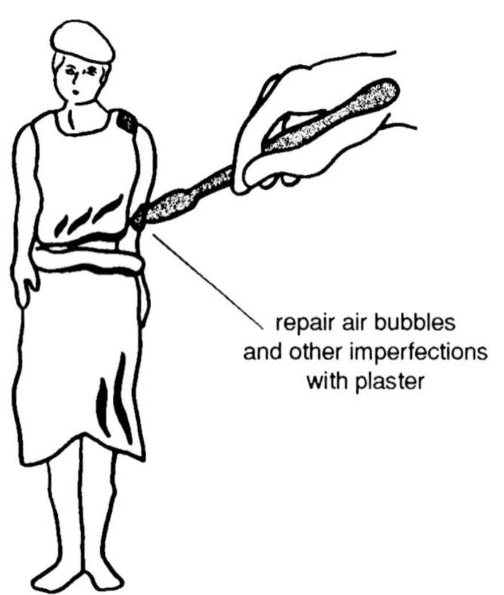

Figure 4.16. Repairing cast.

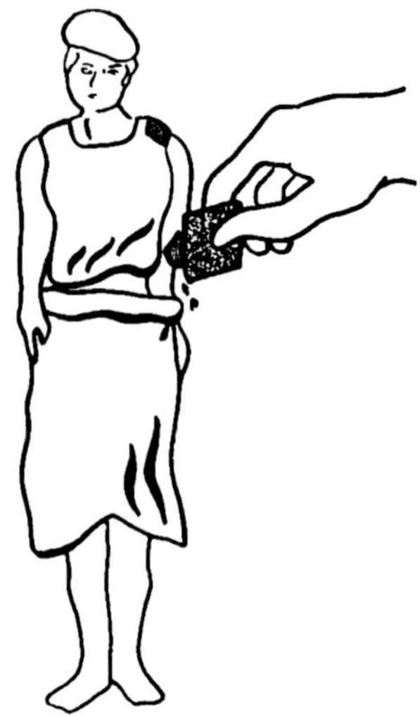

Figure 4.17. Sand off excess plaster and smooth over with a damp cloth.

same color as the cast. Once the holes have been filled in and other repairs have been made, remove the seam line and smooth down the areas where the plugs were inserted. Do this with the edge of a steel tool or block scraper. When the surface has been scraped to the original contour of the model, use sandpaper to complete the final smoothing.

Go over the cast one last time, inspecting for any defects that might need repair. Complete the final touch up. You are now ready to patina or color the cast and mount it to the desired base. For a comprehensive method of patina and mounting, refer to Chapters 8 and 9. If the cast is to remain white, you might want to apply two coats of white flat water based paint to the entire cast. This will cover any defects.

PICTORIAL OVERVIEW

Three Piece Waste Mold of the Figure

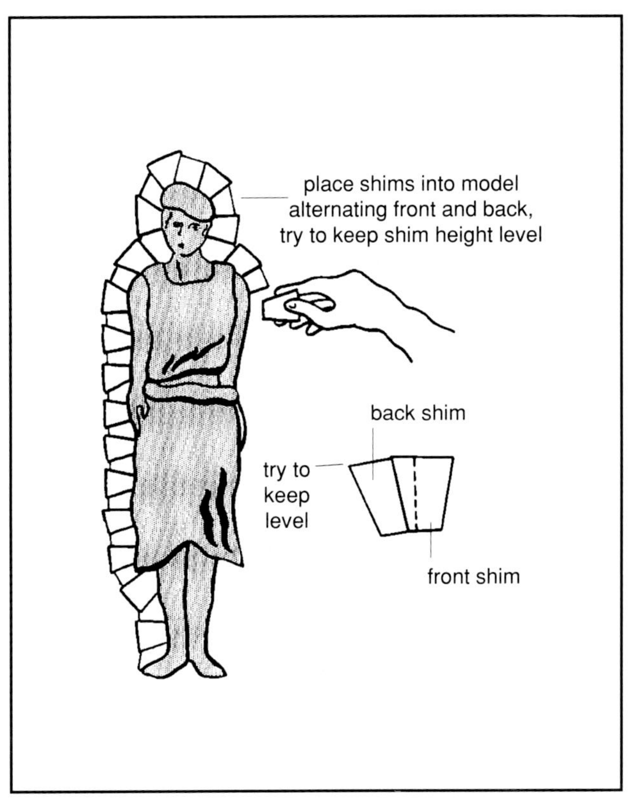

2. Inserting shim to separate the model into two halves.

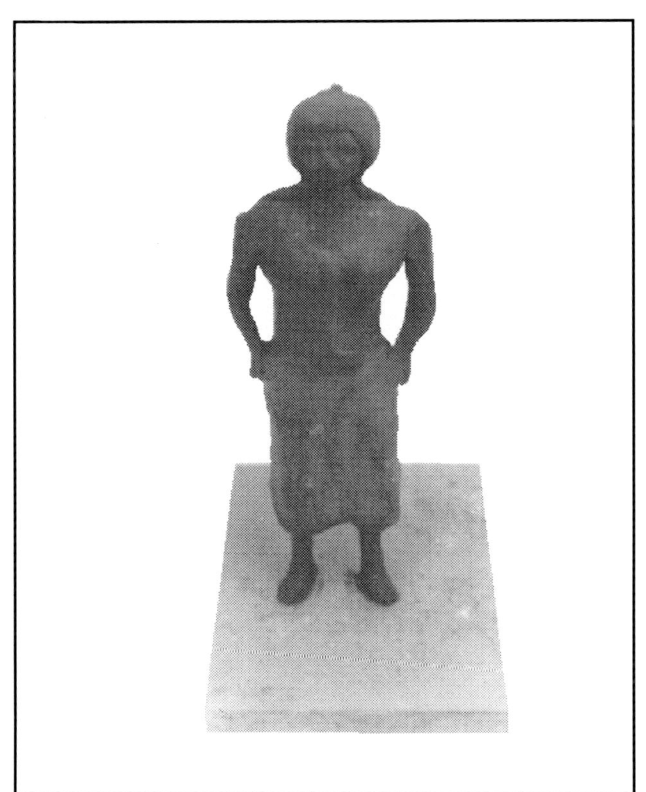

1. Model on armature ready for mold and cast to be made.

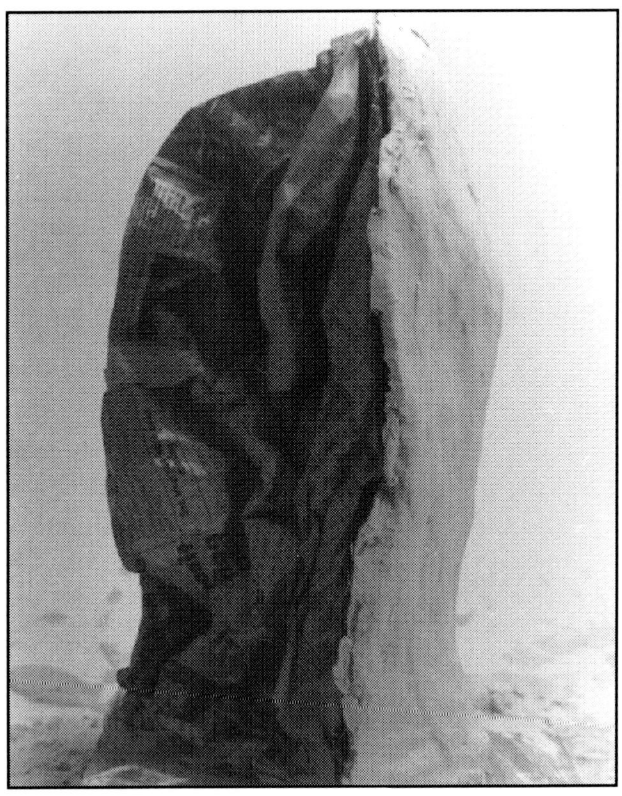

3. First half of the mold completed, with wet newspaper protecting back half of model from stray plaster.

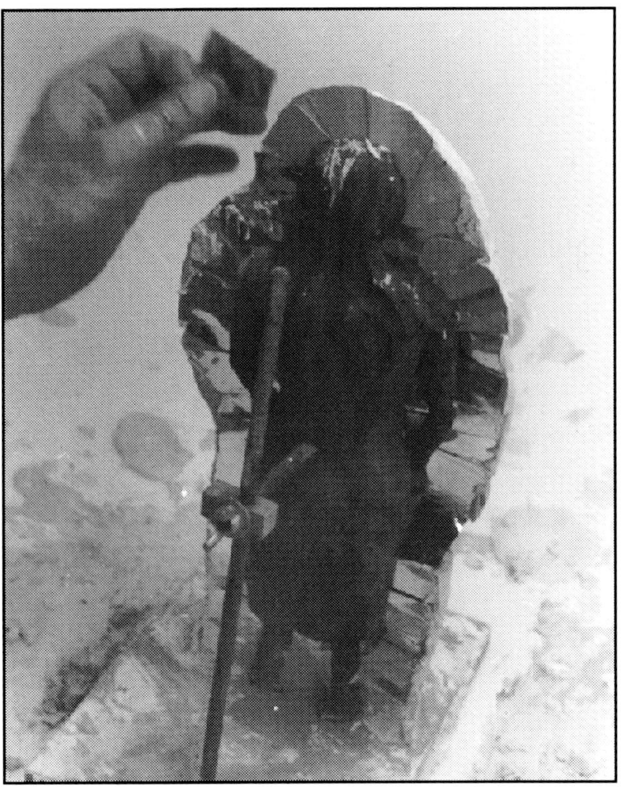

4. Shims being removed after front half of the mold is completed.

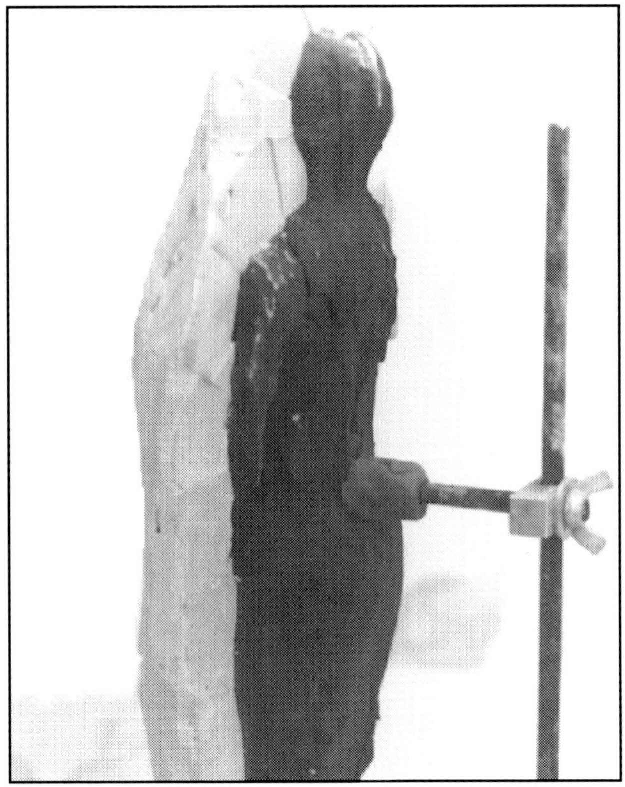

5. Front of the mold and the model on the armature.

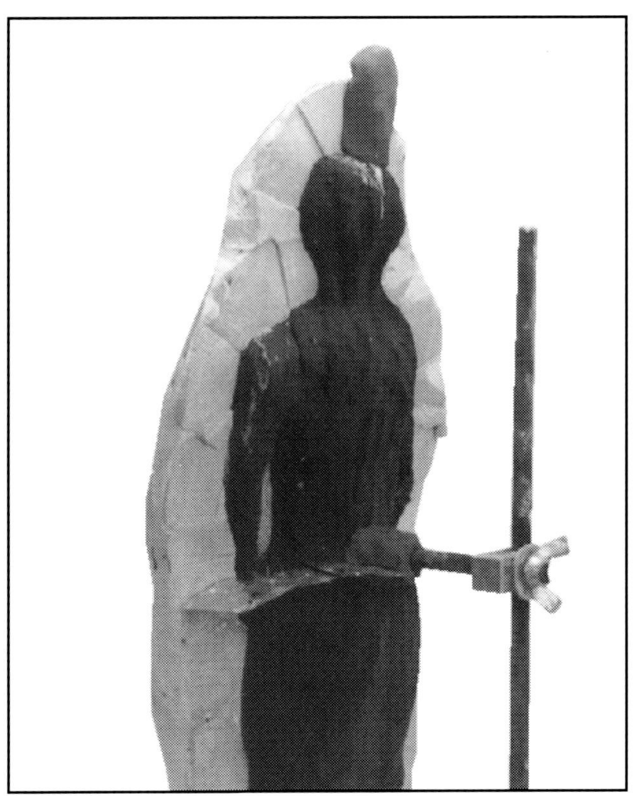

6. Shim sections on the back half of the model separating the upper and lower halves. Plug in top center.

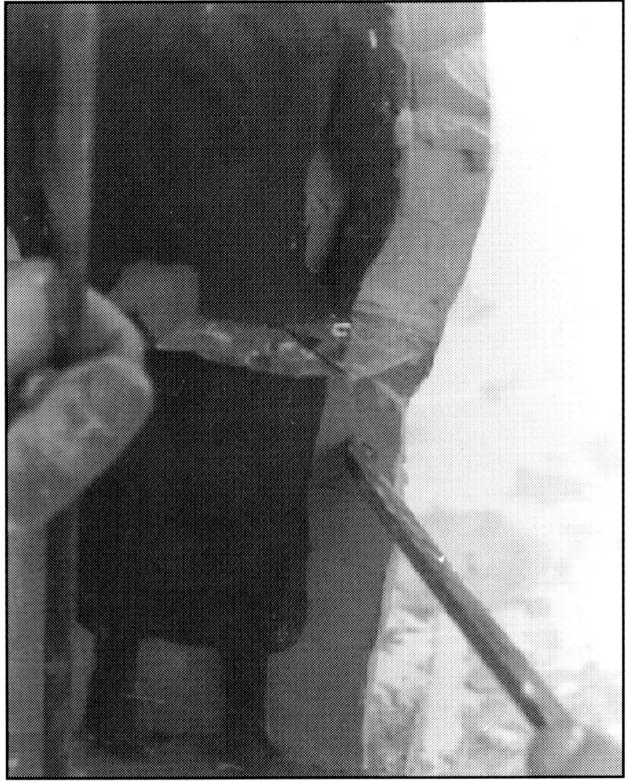

7. Cutting key grooves and notches in plaster mold.

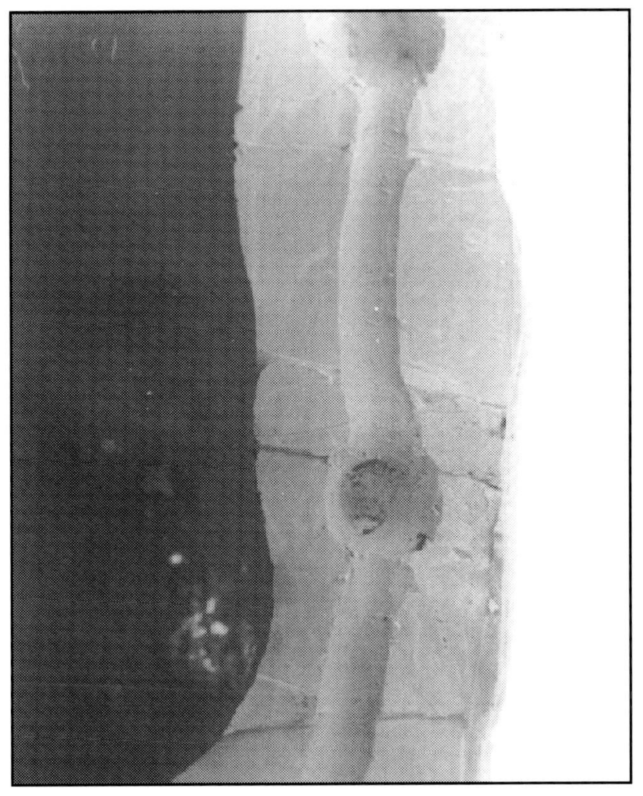

8. Close up of keys prior to being sealed and back of mold construction.

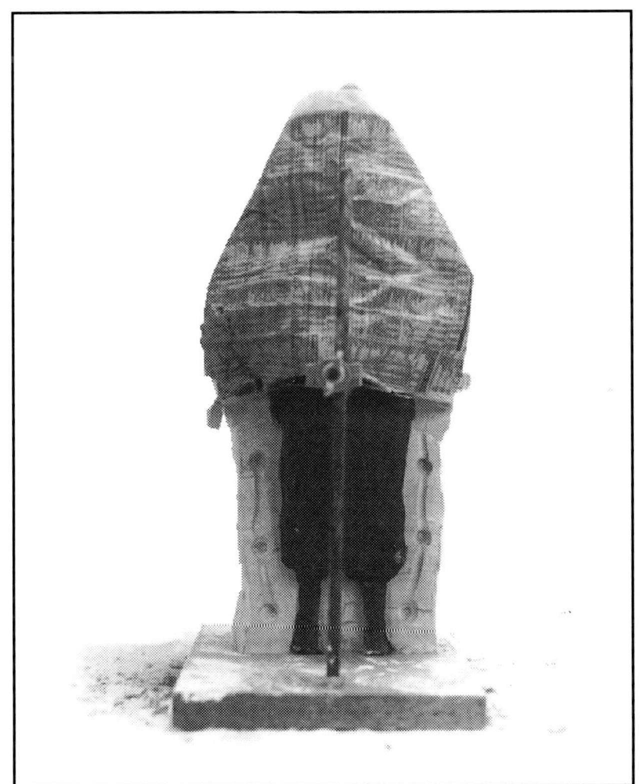

9. Damp newspaper covering top back half of model in preparation for making back lower half of mold.

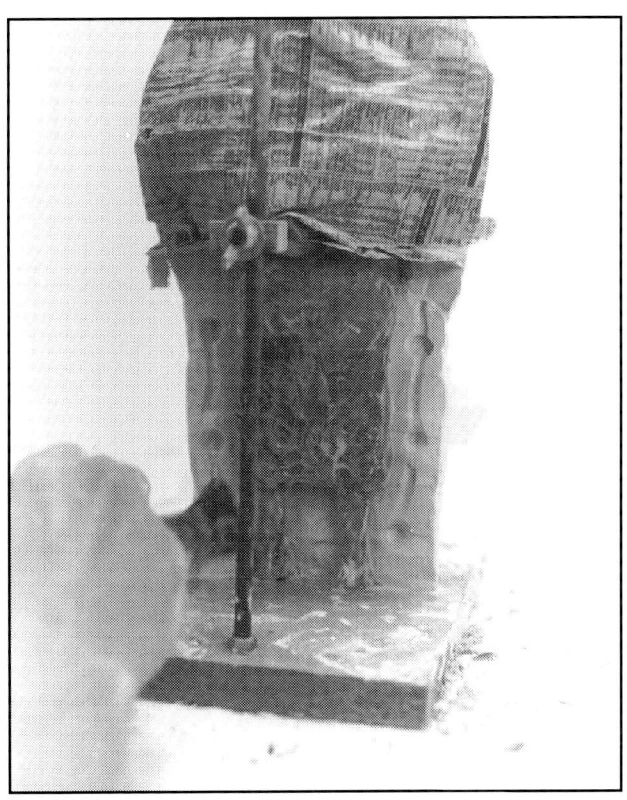

10. Sealing the back lower half of mold and model.

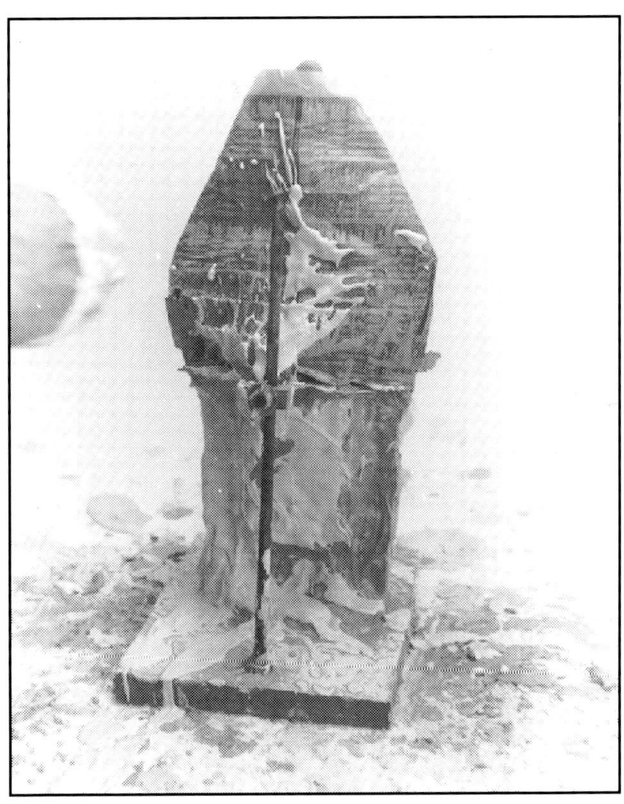

11. Applying back lower section of the mold using the back hand flip.

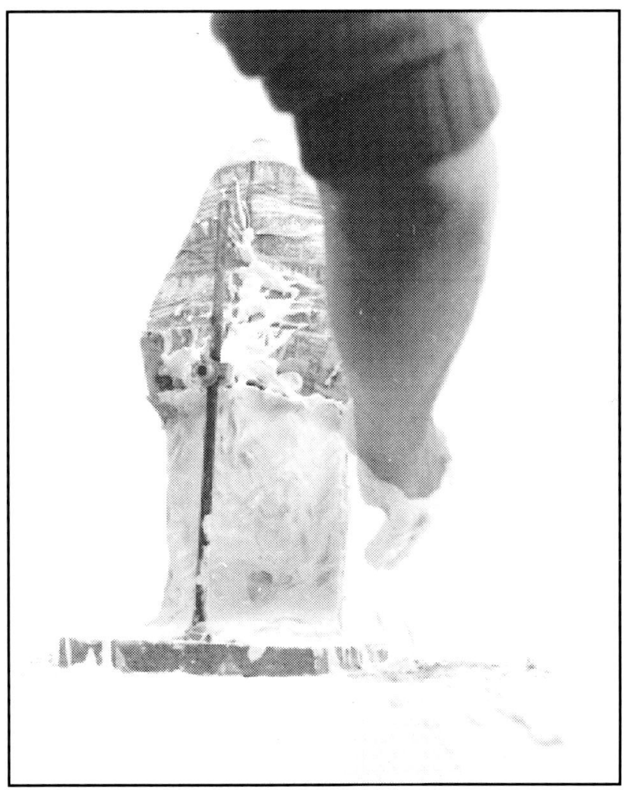

12. Building up mold section with plaster.

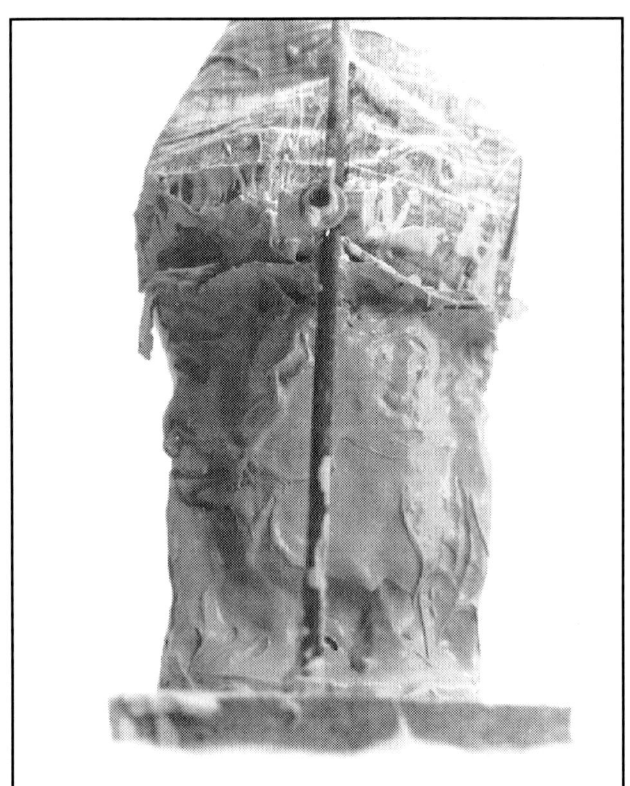

13. Additional building of the plaster lower back section.

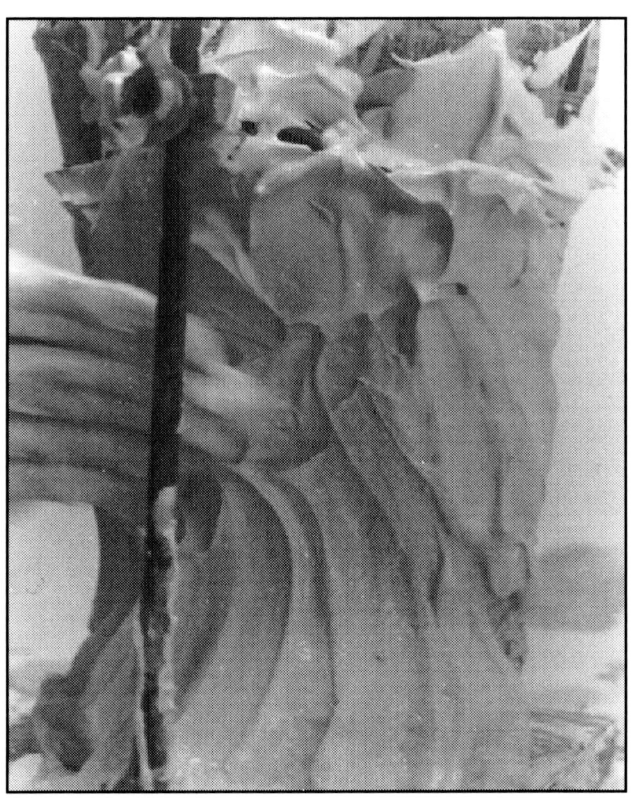

14. Smoothing the final areas of the lower back section of the mold.

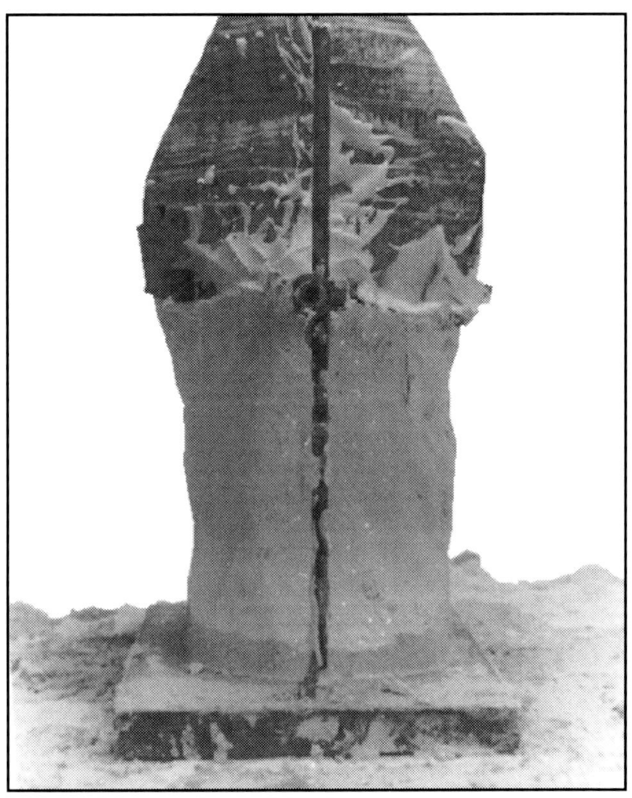

15. Completed lower back section of the mold, smoothed and trimmed.

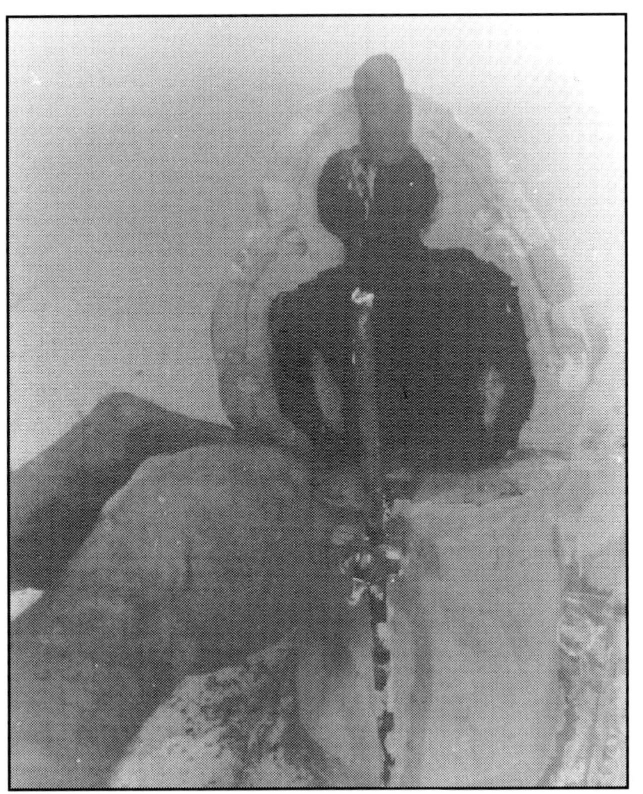

16. Removing shim from completed section of the mold after the plaster has set.

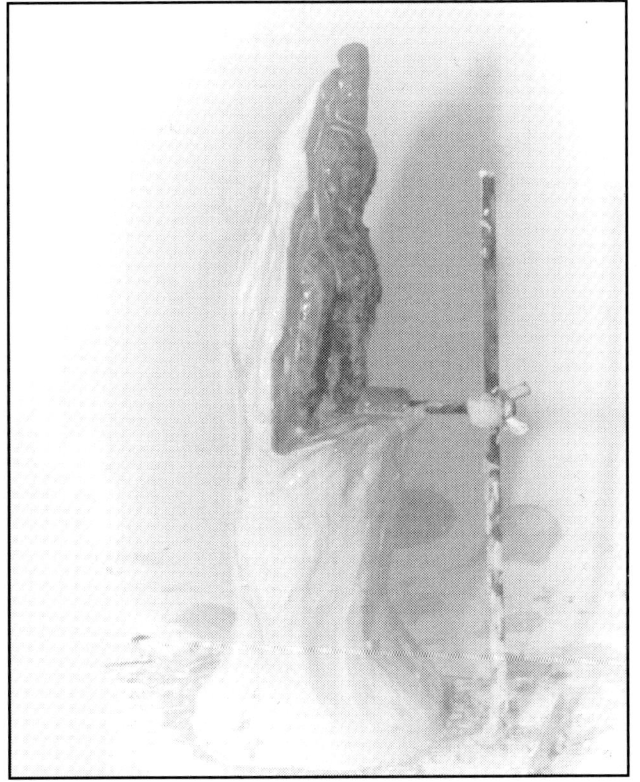

17. Side view of the lower back and front sections of the mold.

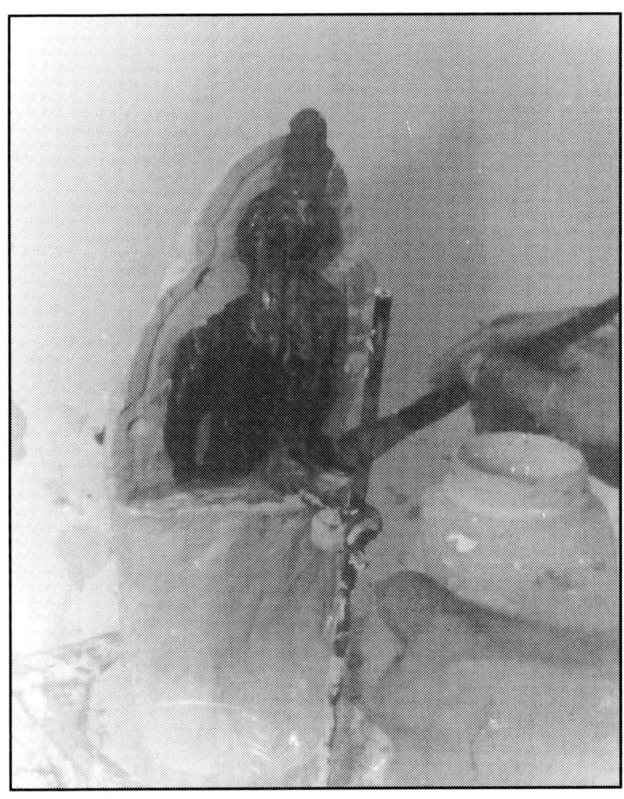

18. Sealing the exposed area of the lower back of the mold. Key grooves should be made in this area also.

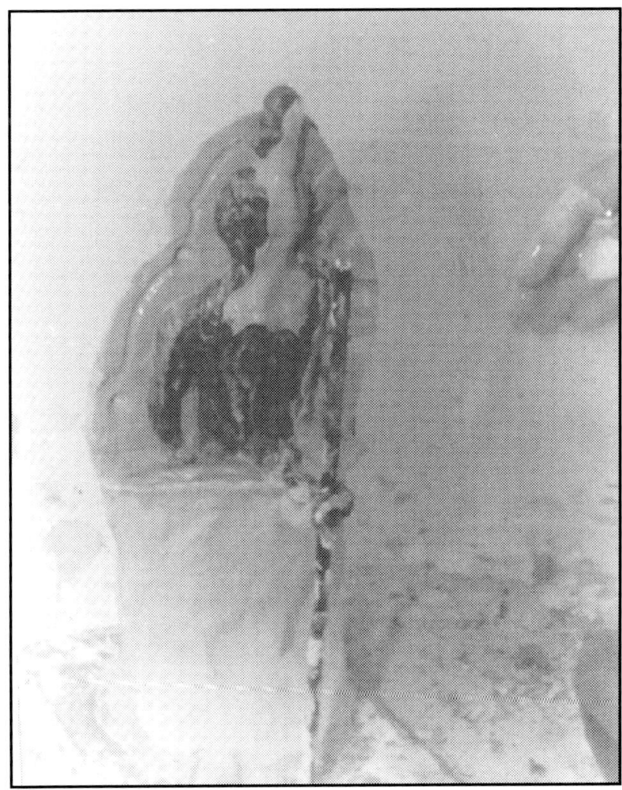

19. Applying initial plaster coat to the upper back section of the mold.

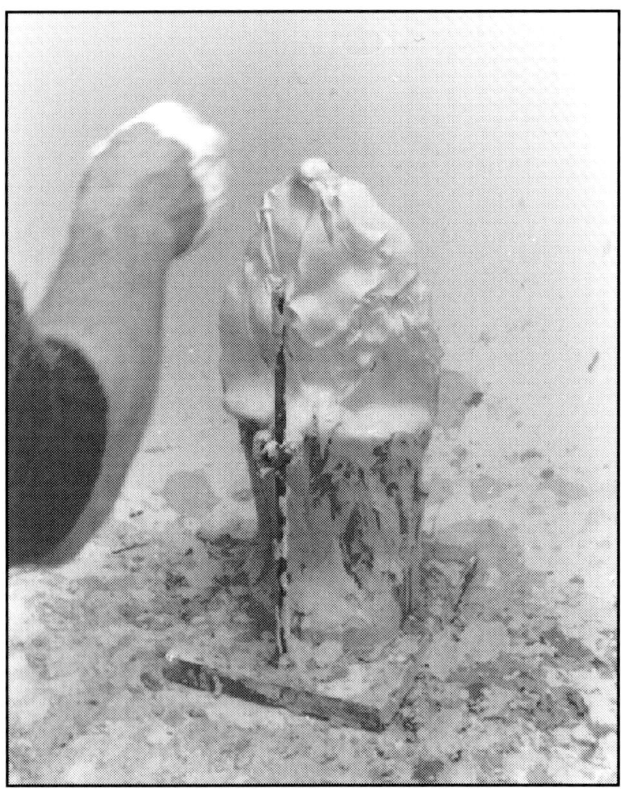

20. Building up plaster mold for the upper back.

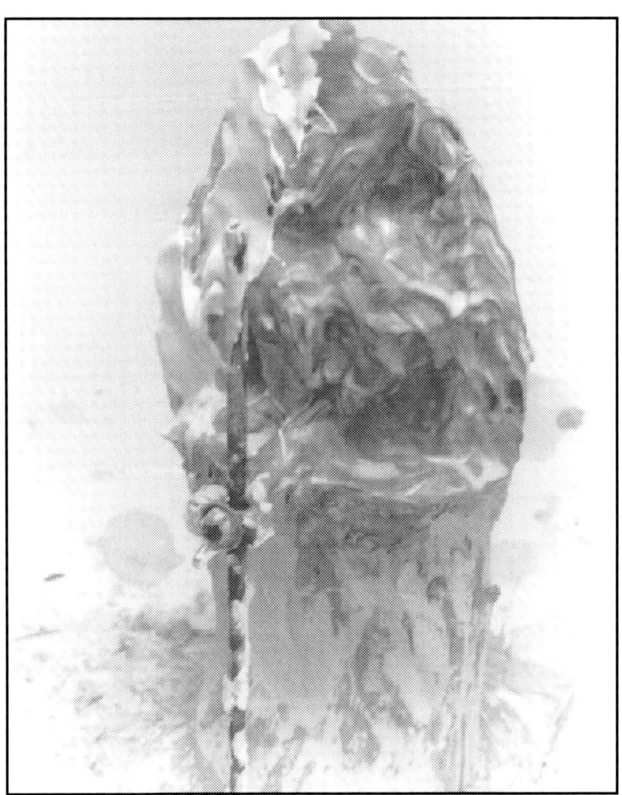

21. Building plaster mold on the upper back section of the mold.

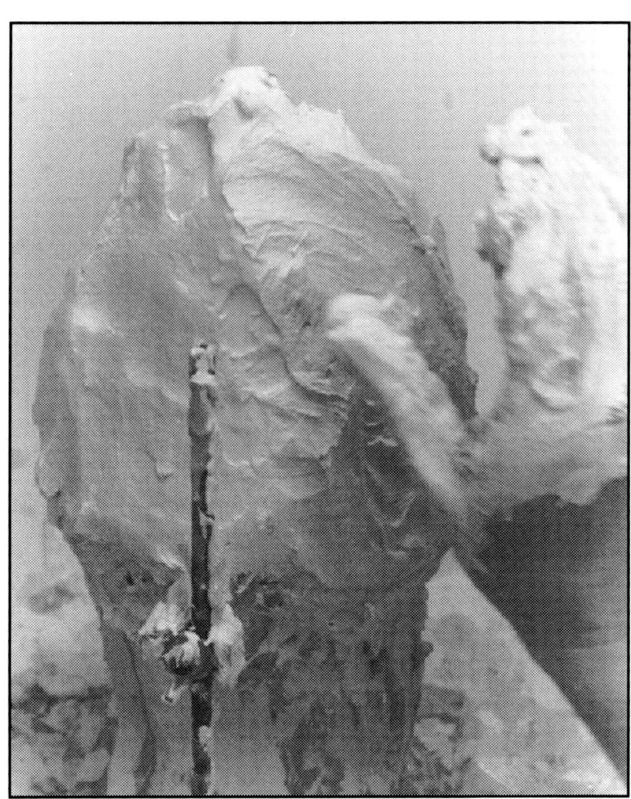

22. Smoothing the final coat of the upper back section of the mold.

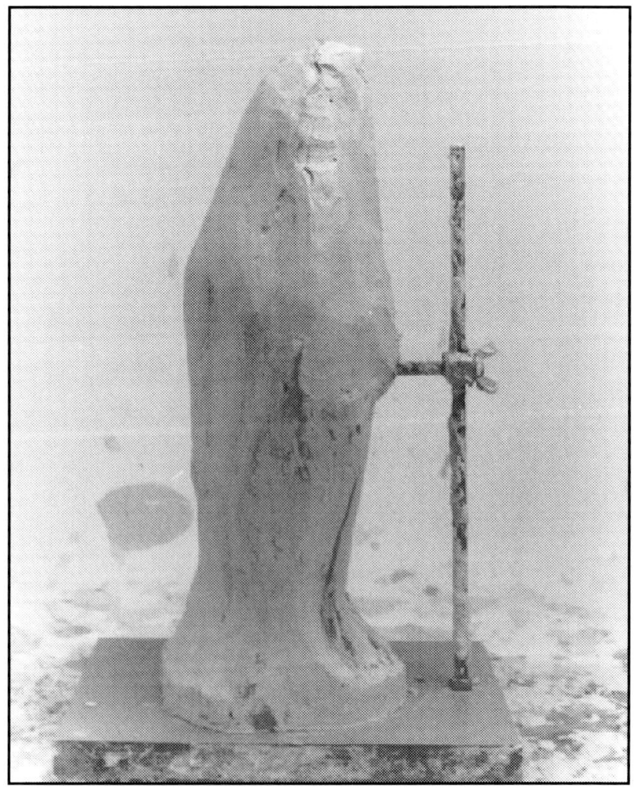

23. Completed side view of the mold made over the armature and model.

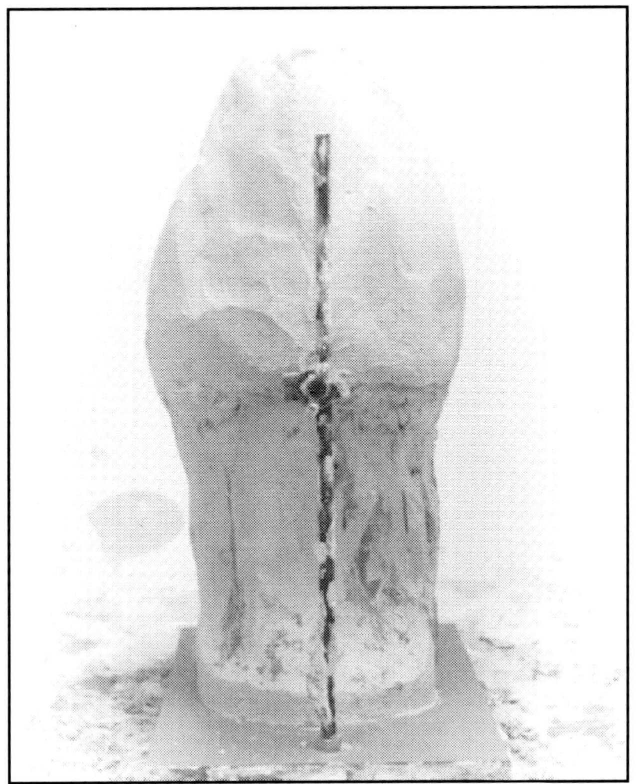

24. Completed back view of the mold over the model and armature.

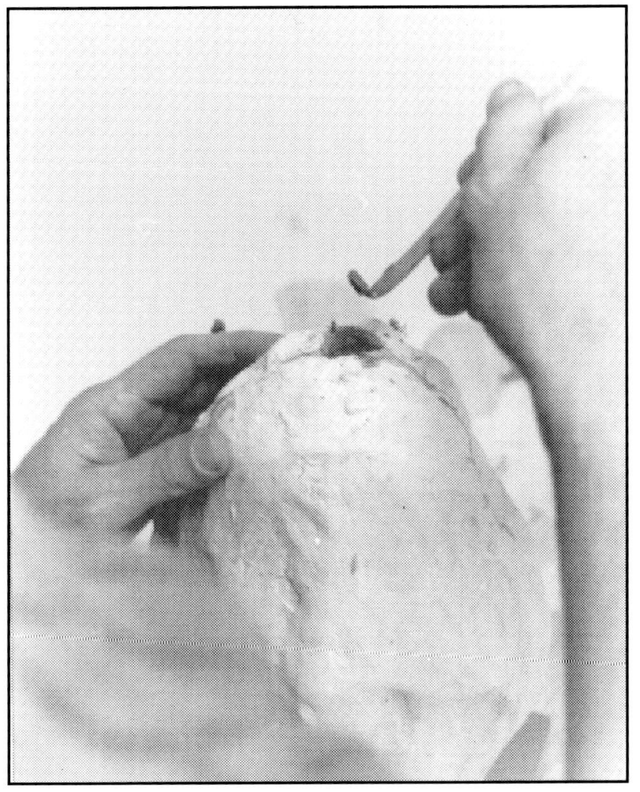

25. Removing the clay plug from top center of the completed mold.

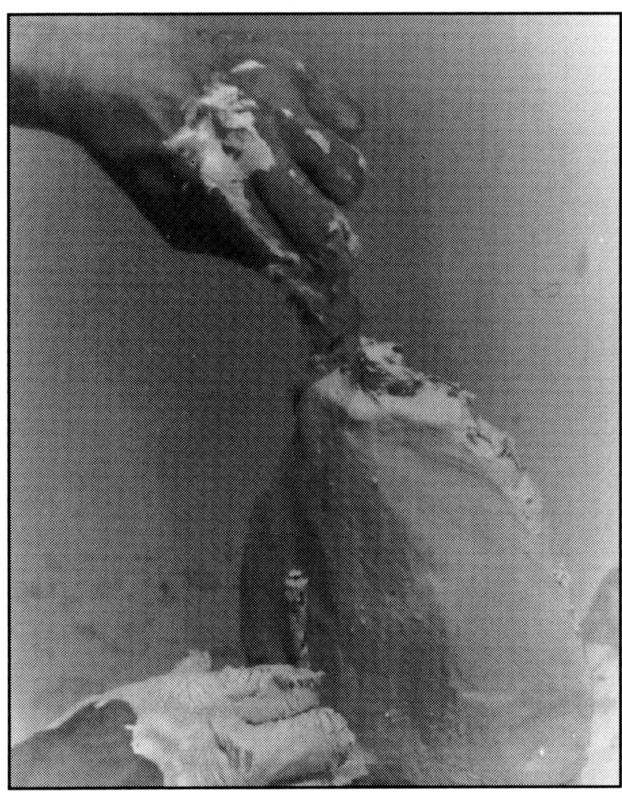

26. Leveling top section of mold with plug.

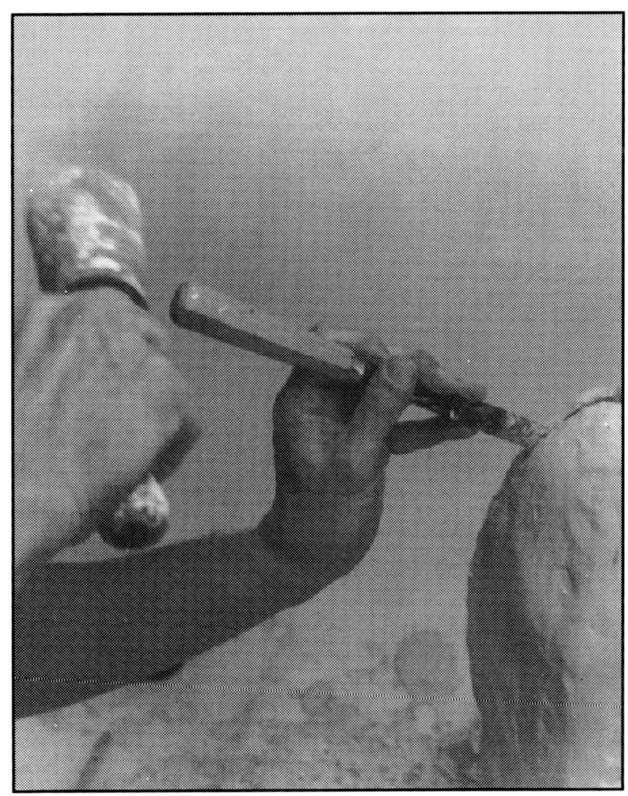

27. Separating halves of the front of the mold.

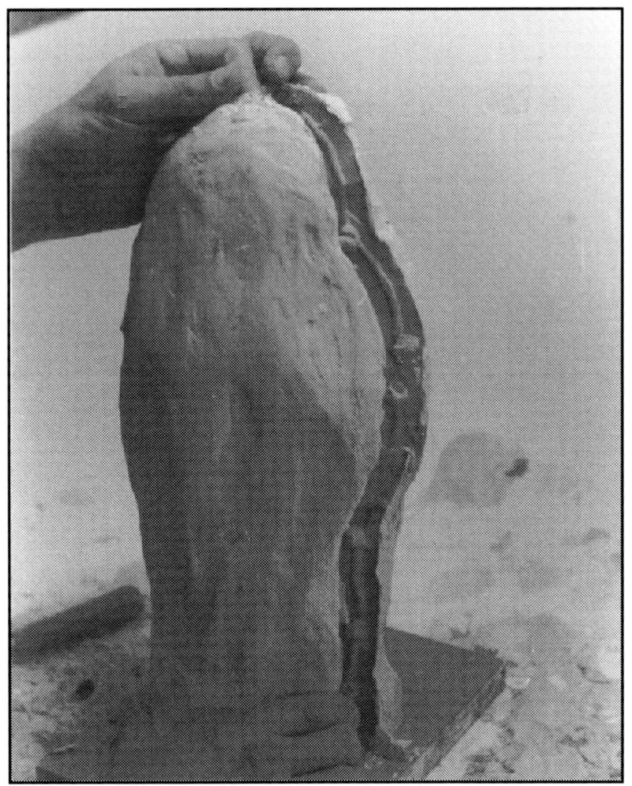

28. Removing the front half of the mold.

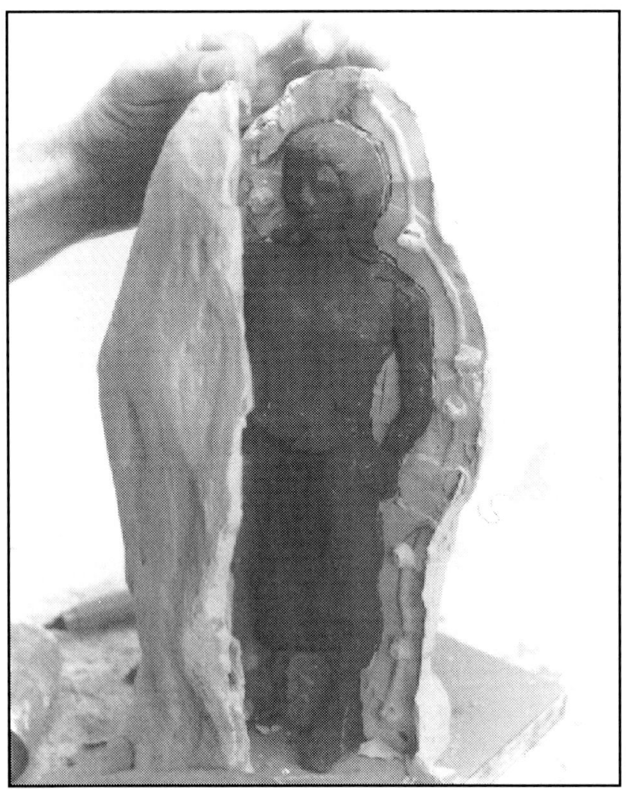

29. Final separation of the front half. Water has been poured in the plug area to help with removal.

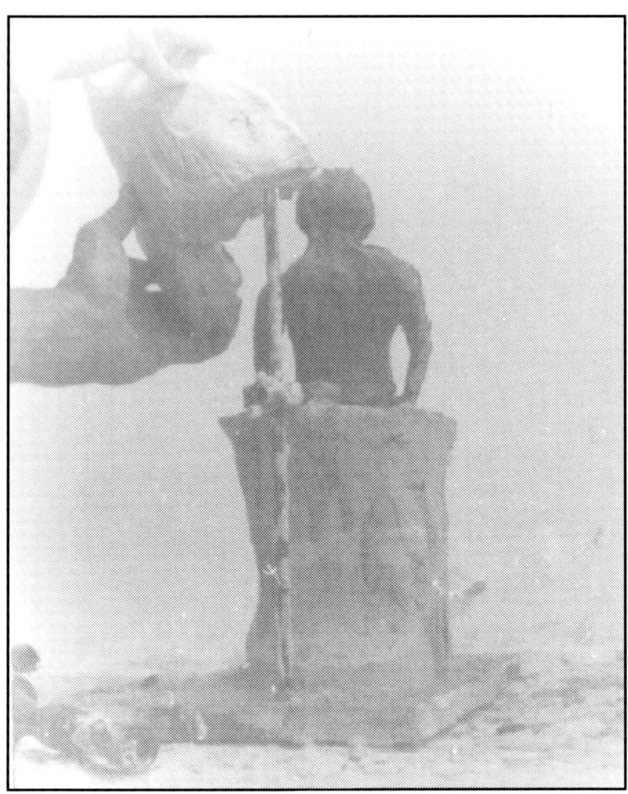

30. Removing the top back section of the mold.

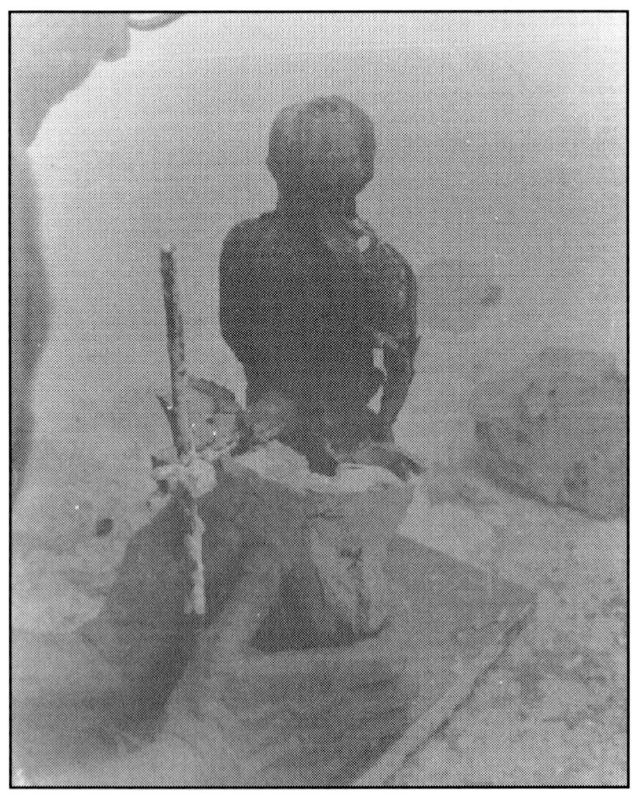

31. Removing the bottom back section of the mold.

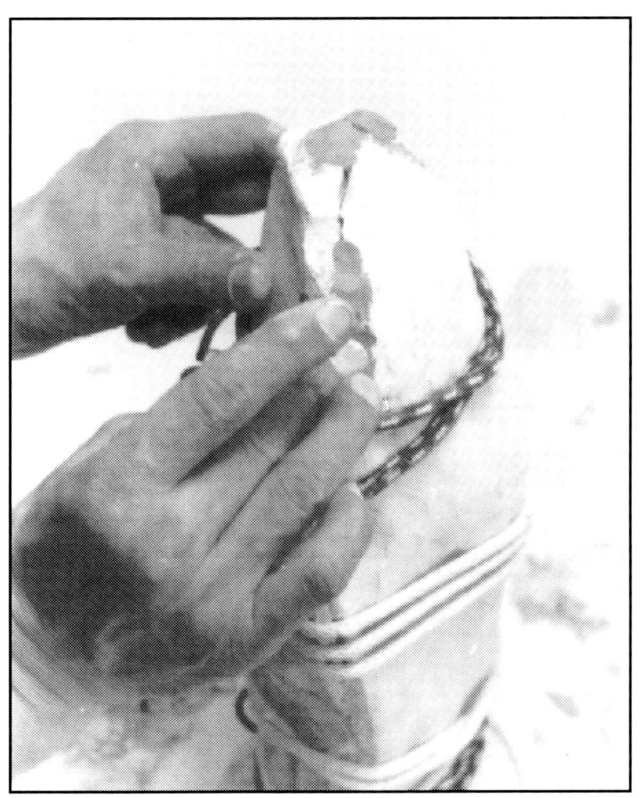

32. After repair and reassembling, the mold is sealed, secured, and any openings plugged with clay.

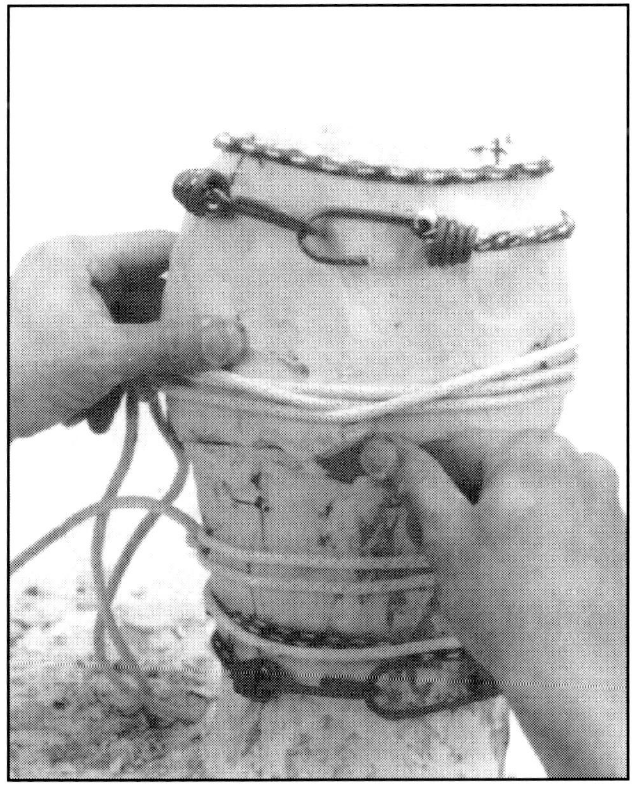

33. Straps are secured so the sections will not separate and the casting material is poured.

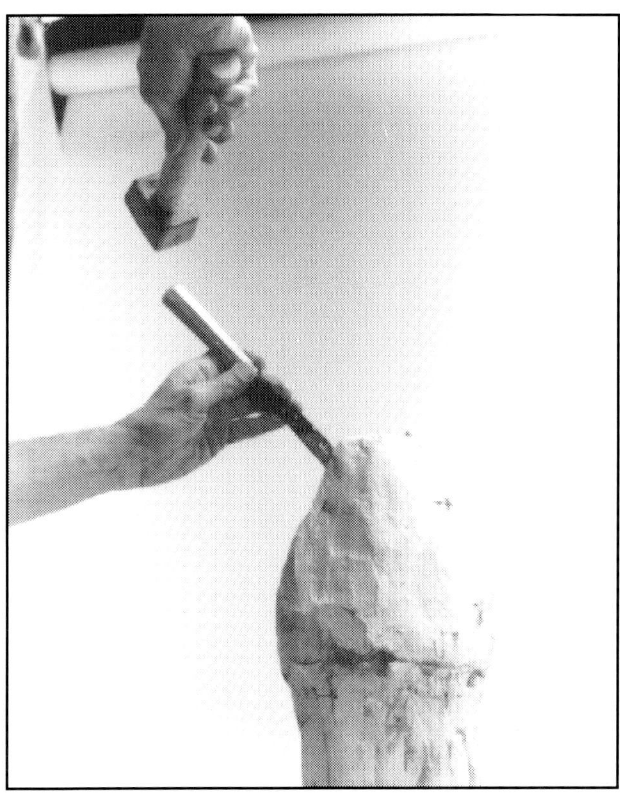

34. When the cast has set the bands are removed and the mold chipped away.

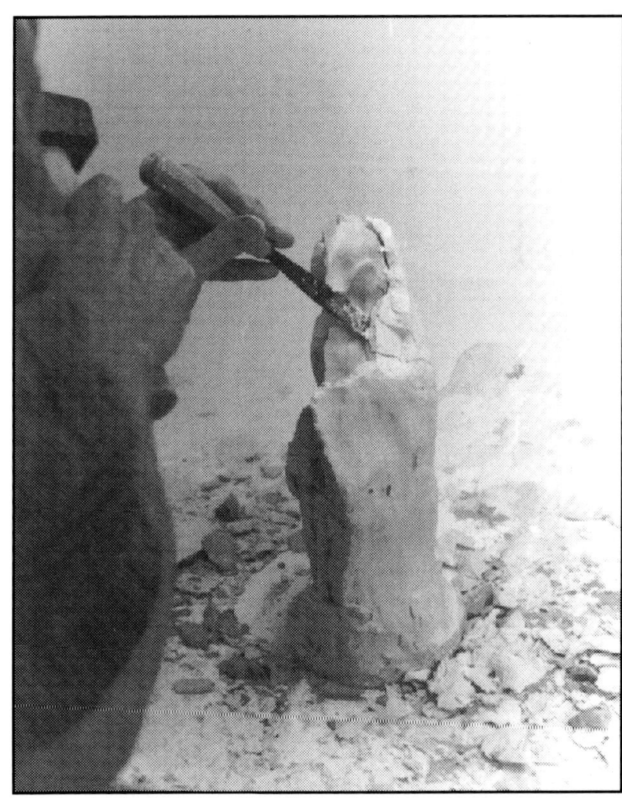

35. Mold almost completely chipped away from model casting.

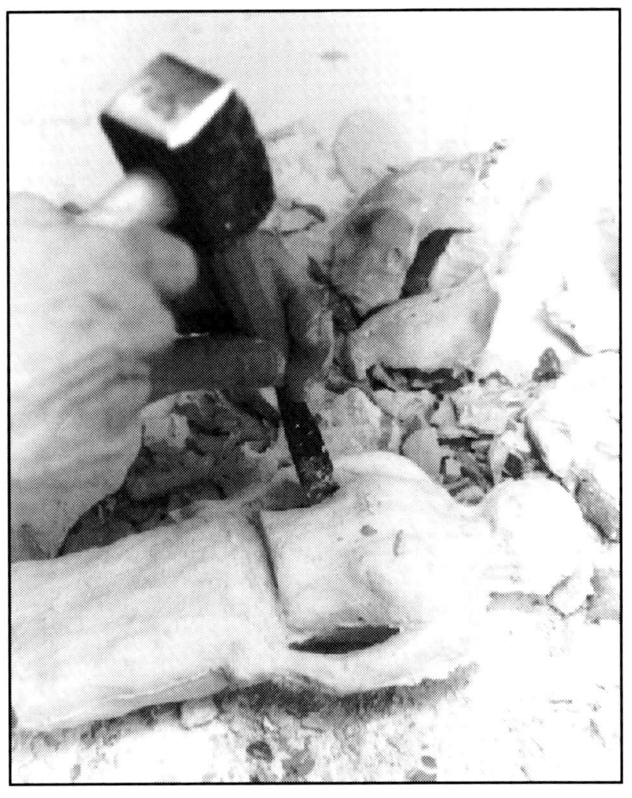

36. Final chipping of the webbing between the arm and hip area.

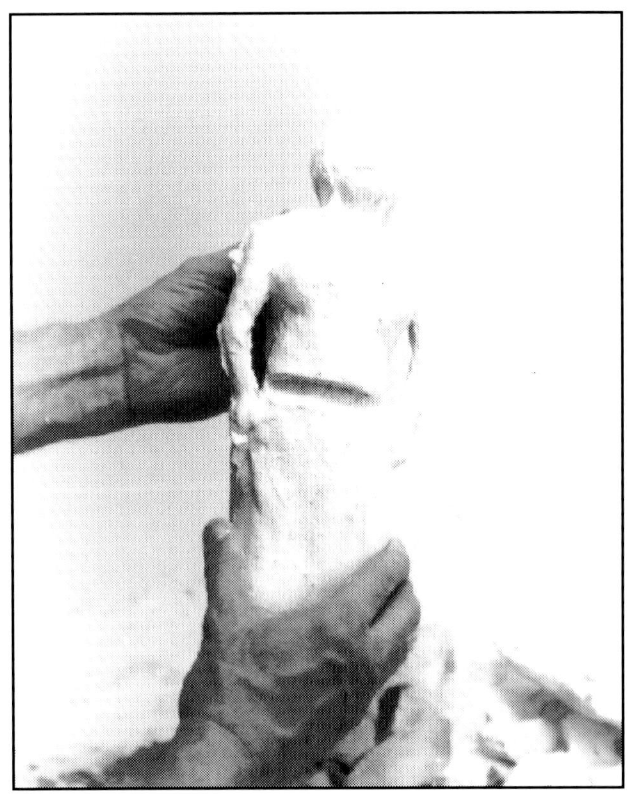

37. Final cast prior to cleaning and finishing for mounting.

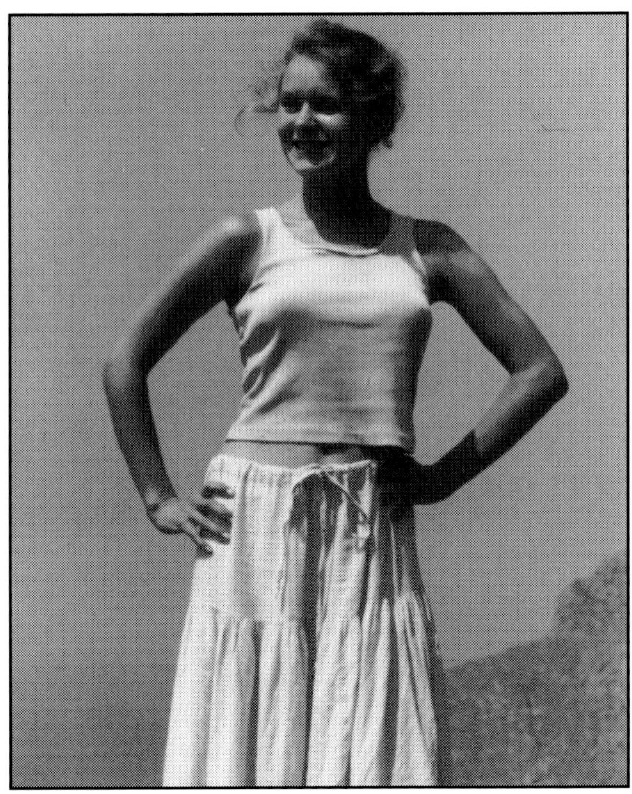

38. Original subject, Jennifer.

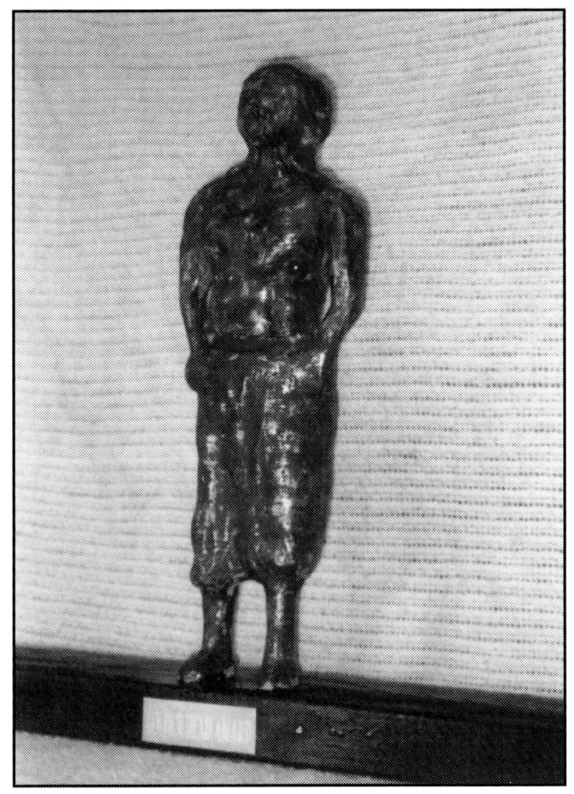

39. Finished cast with patina.

CHAPTER 5

MOULAGE MOLD

Type of Mold .... Moulage, Reusable
Size .... Life size
Type of Model .... Face from life
Time Required .... 3 hours

DESCRIPTION

Moulage is a rubber material that becomes a liquid when melted over indirect heat such as a double boiler. In this state it can be used as a base compound for molds, by itself or with the aid of wire of plaster backing. Moulage material before melting resembles large curd cottage cheese and has a moist and rubbery texture. It should be stored moist in an air tight container to keep its basic properties. Moulage is particularly useful in making molds of various parts of the body, as it is nontoxic, but it can be used to make molds of almost any object. Apply two thin coats of shellac (letting the first coat dry thoroughly before applying the second) to porous surfaces so the moulage material will not absorb into the surface.

Moulage is mainly used for casting various kinds of gypsum (plaster) products and wax (posmoulage) positives. Plastic resins and rubber materials are not compatible with the moulage material. Make a sample mold and casting before actual use to familiarize yourself with the proper techniques and procedures. Moulage is generally used in making plaques or relief molds since the material is air drying and is not suitable for hollow cavity case molds. With practice, piece molds backed with wire and plaster can be achieved. Moulage should not come into contact with any form of aluminum since they are not compatible.

After use, moulage can be cut into small pieces and stored in a plastic bag or other air tight container, with a small amount of water added to maintain its moisture content. It can be remelted and used over again, about 100 times before any deteriorating effects are noticeable. When using on a live subject, it's a good rule of thumb to place a small amount of cooled liquid moulage on a sensitive area, such as under the chin, to be sure there is no discomfort. When moulage is placed over a person's face, a sense of claustrophobia sometimes occurs. This is a totally unfounded feeling, since the material can be removed in seconds and does not harm the person in any way, but participants should be warned that it can occur. For breathing, place straws or rubber tubes in the nostrils as the last of the material is placed on the face. With experience you will be able to work around the nostrils without this aid. When inserting the tube, be careful not to damage the inner membrane causing a nose bleed. Having a nose bleed when your entire face is covered with moulage is not recommended.

Moulage should be applied in the liquid state and all at once, since gelled material will not adhere to itself and will cause layering of the mold. Working time for liquid moulage is approximately fifteen minutes. The amount of moulage material required for specific projects can be found in the weights and measures chart in Appendix E.

TOOLS AND MATERIALS

1. Moulage
2. Double boiler **(DO NOT USE ALUMINUM)**
3. 25 lbs. plaster
4. 3-gal. rubber mixing container.
5. Flexible mixing spatula, rubber cake mix type.
6. Cardboard, shower cap, and bath towel.

7. Vaseline, optional.
8. Casting material, pos-moulage, and plaster.

BASIC STEPS

1. Melt moulage in a double boiler of stainless steel, glass, or porcelain **(DO NOT USE ALUMINUM)**. Apply to object as a liquid. If the object is live, cool the material to 110 degrees Fahrenheit or until it is comfortable to the skin.
2. Build up material until approximately ½ inch thick. No release agent is necessary.
3. Let moulage set, about 20 minutes, then construct a plaster casing support mold or mother mold over the gel.
4. Remove plaster and moulage as one when plaster has set, about 15 minutes.
5. Cast positive into moulage negative, remove cast, and finish.

MAKING THE MOULAGE MOLD

When making a moulage mold of the face, first cut out a heavy section of cardboard or similar material to fit the contour of the face.

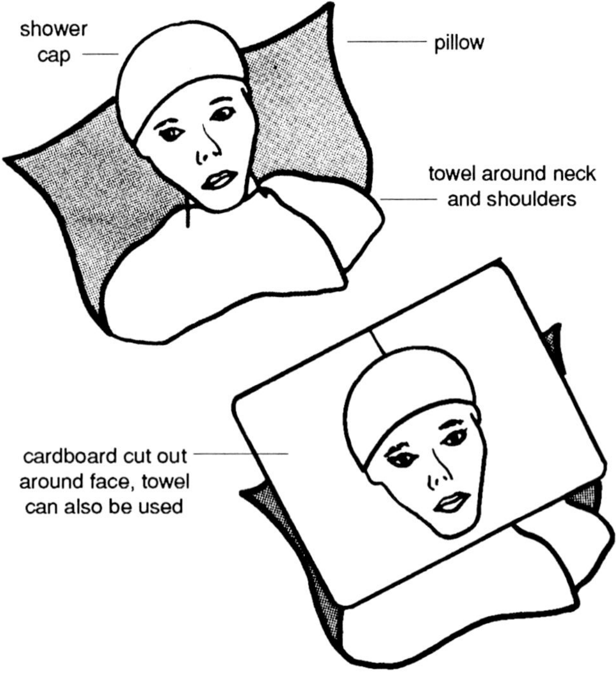

Figure 5.1. Cardboard surrounding face.

The cardboard should fit securely so the liquid moulage will not run down the neck and into the ear. Cotton may be placed in the ears as a safeguard and towels can be placed around the head and neck, under the cardboard, as support and to inhibit the flow of liquid in any area where there is a possible gap. It is not absolutely necessary to use cardboard and both may be used as the backstop.

Place the proper amount of moulage in the top of a double boiler, using only glass, stainless steel, or porcelain **(DO NOT USE ALUMINUM)**. Determine the proper amount by referring to the weights and measures chart in Appendix F. Heat the moulage over boiling water in the bottom section of the double boiler until it becomes a thick and creamy liquid.

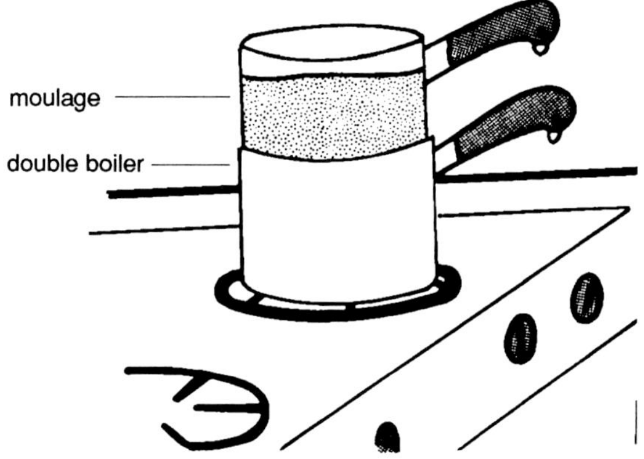

Figure 5.2. Moulage in container.

Let it cool to about 110 degrees Fahrenheit or until the material can be placed on a sensitive are such as under the chin without discomfort.

To cool the moulage more quickly replace the hot water in the bottom of the double boiler with cold and stir the mixture in the top half. When the moulage is cool, replace the cold water with warm water so the moulage will not get too cool.

If hair on the head or face will constitute part of the mold, mat the hair down with petroleum jelly or Vaseline so the moulage does not become embedded in the hair (how much vaseline will depend on the length of the hair). If moulage does become embedded into the hair, wait until it becomes firm and comb out with a fine tooth comb.

Once the moulage has melted and cooled, and the cardboard and/or bath towel has been set in place, you are now ready to apply the material. Use your hand, a spoon, brush, or flexible rubber spatula. The whole mold should be applied at the same time before the moulage material can cool. You will get separations in the mold if a layer has cooled and another placed over it. Have the subject lie down at a 20 degree angle at the most. Advise the subject to remain very still throughout the whole process and not to move the nose or lips while the moulage is setting. Build up a layer of about ½ inch over the entire area of the face. Begin with the top of the head and work downward. Leave the nostrils until last.

Before the nostrils are covered, insert soft rubber tubes or straws into the nostrils so the subject can breathe when moulage is placed around the nose and nostril area.

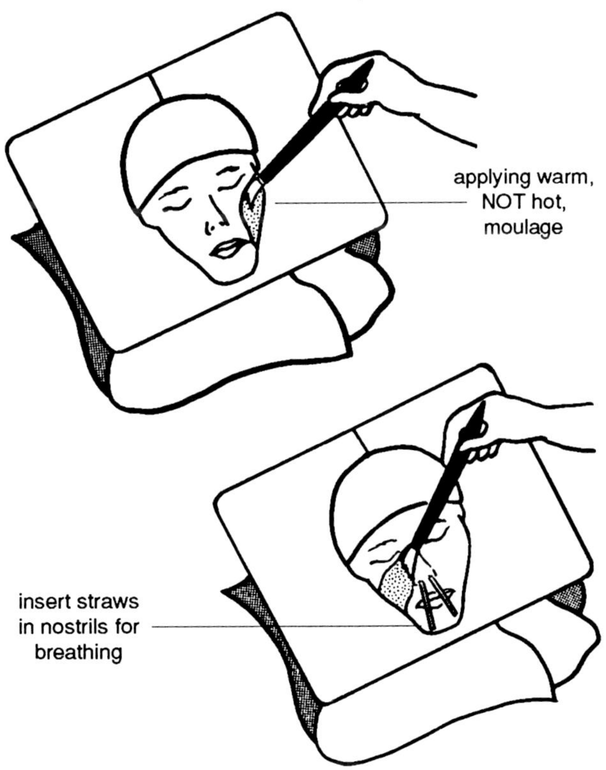

Figure 5.3. Applying moulage and Inserting straws.

Cut paper straws to about 3 inches in length for easy manipulation. Let the subject hold the tubes so he or she can assure the proper depth required. The subject must stay extremely still so as not to alter the mold. It is a good idea to keep up a continuous conversation with the subject to prevent apprehension. I also recommend playing the subject's favorite music.

While the moulage is gelling, mix a batch of plaster for another mold. This will support the moulage face mold, since the moulage material is not strong enough by itself to hold the weight of the casting material without distortion. Mix a batch of plaster following the guidelines in Appendix F to determine the correct amount required. Construct a plaster mother mold over the moulage to about ½ inch thickness. Apply only after the moulage has gelled.

Apply the plaster after it has set up enough so that the consistency is more like pudding then in a flowing state, somewhat like applying a mud pack. The plaster will give off a small amount of heat when setting. **ADVISE THE SUBJECT OF THIS!**

After applying the plaster, smooth it with your fingers or a damp cloth. Setting time will be about 15 minutes.

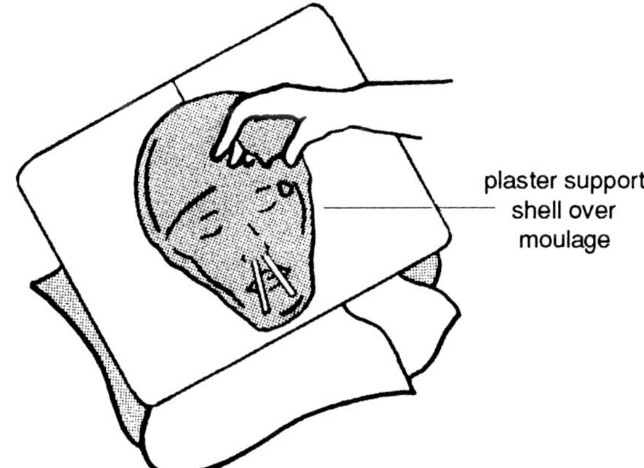

Figure 5.4. Apply plaster.

When the plaster has set, remove the moulage and plaster as a unit from the face lifting from the top. Or the subject can sit up and lean forward slightly, wriggling the face to allow the plaster and moulage to fall off by means of gravity.

One item found to be invaluable when making a moulage mold is a hand held blow dryer. Set on cool and directed toward your work, it cools the moulage as it is applied and your subject need not "be under" for quite so long.

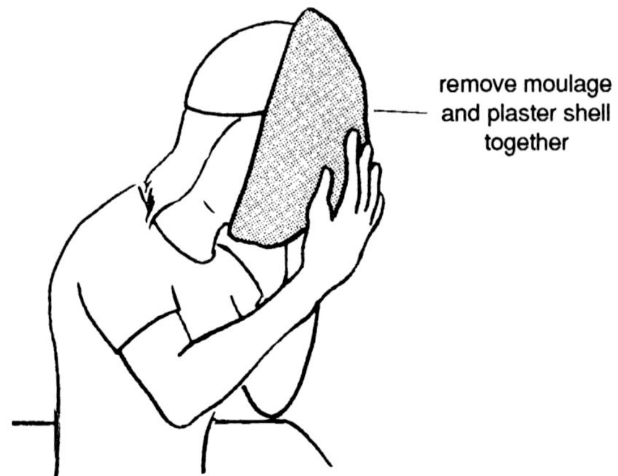

Figure 5.5. Removing both from face.

Once the moulage and plaster mother mold have been removed, you are ready to cast your positive. If using wax or pos-moulage, dry the interior of the moulage mold with a soft cloth or towel. Apply the wax by brushing it on to the desired thickness. Pos-moulage can be melted directly over a low flame in a metal, glass, or porcelain pot. **Do not** allow pos-moulage to get too hot, as it can "flash." Allow the pos-moulage to cool to about 130 or 140 degrees F. before pouring into the moulage mold. Use this same technique when casting cement or gypsum (plaster) based materials. Mix the casting material as per package instructions to a heavy cream consistency, them pour of brush into the mold to the desired thickness. No separating agent or release is required when casting these materials into a moulage mold.

Casting materials recommended for moulage molds are gypsum (plaster) based materials, cement, wax, and pos-moulage. The last named is a combination of wax materials that produces the finest details in a moulage mold. Like moulage, it can be remelted and used over and over again. Do not confuse pos-moulage with moulage, although the names are similar. Moulage is used for the "negative mold" and is placed directly on the object/subject. Pos-moulage is the "positive casting" material applied to the mold to achieve the positive cast. It should **NOT** be placed directly on the object or on exposed skin. (This would be the same as placing hot or melted wax on the subject.)

When the casting material placed in the mold has set-up properly, invert the plaster and moulage mold and tap to remove the casting.

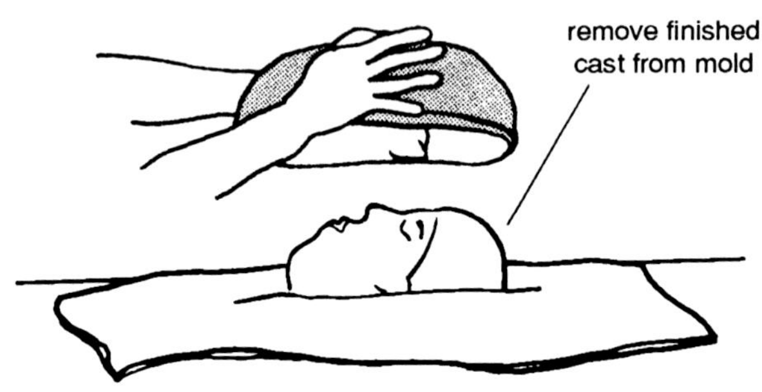

Figure 5.6. Removing the cast.

Inspect the cast for any damage or air bubbles and repair with plaster or wax as necessary. When you are satisfied with your cast, patina and mount as desired. Patina and mounting instructions are found in Chapters 8 and 9.

PICTORIAL OVERVIEW
Moulage Mold and Cast of the Face

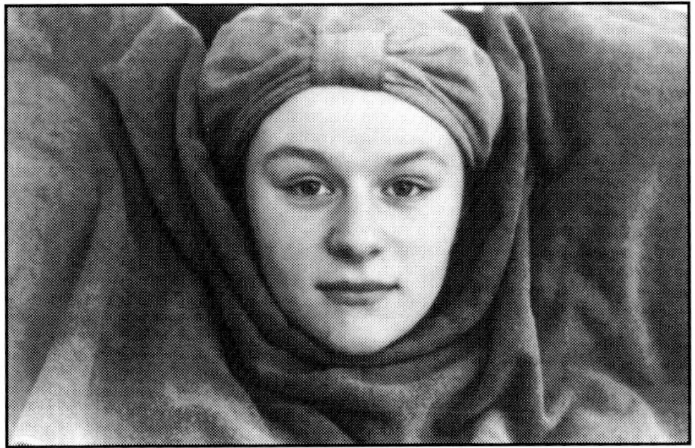

1. Reclining model with towels and shower cap covering head and neck.

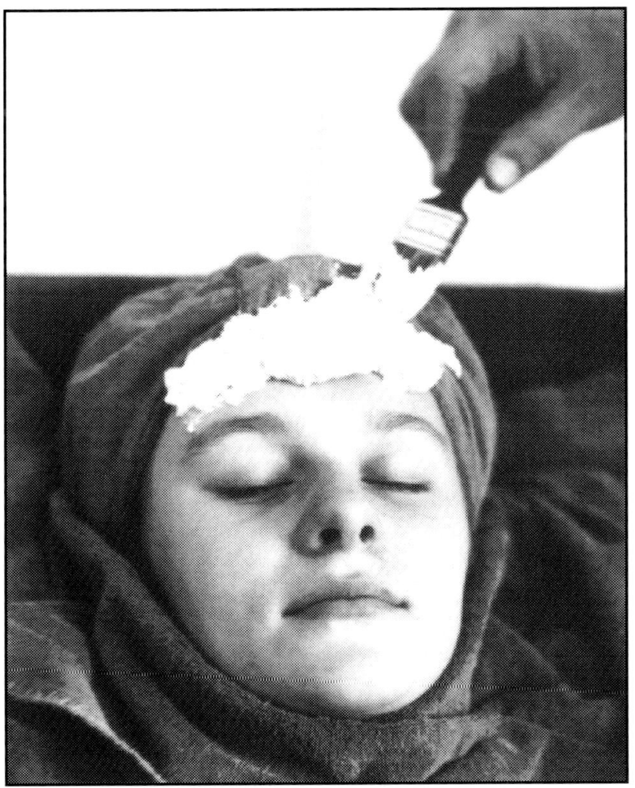

2. First application of melted moulage being applied to forehead.

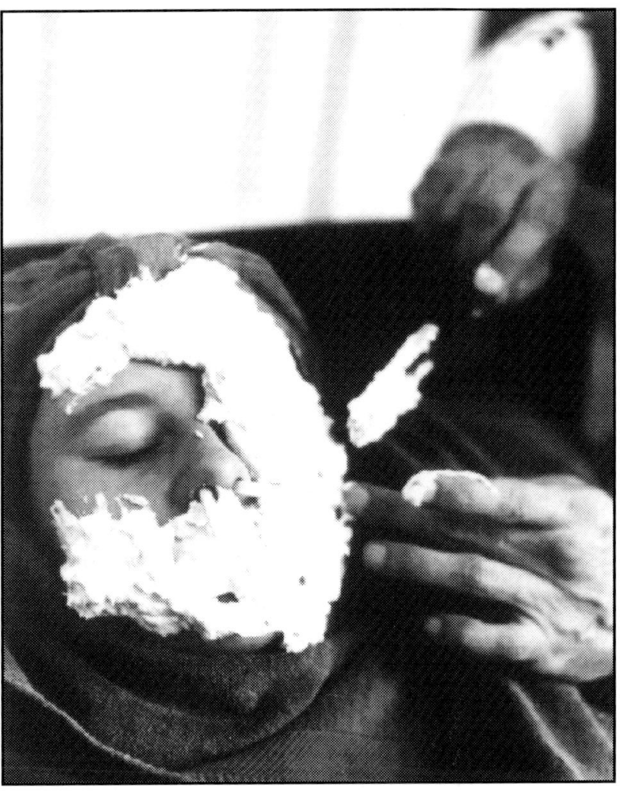

3. Final coats of moulage being applied with straw inserted in the nose for breathing.

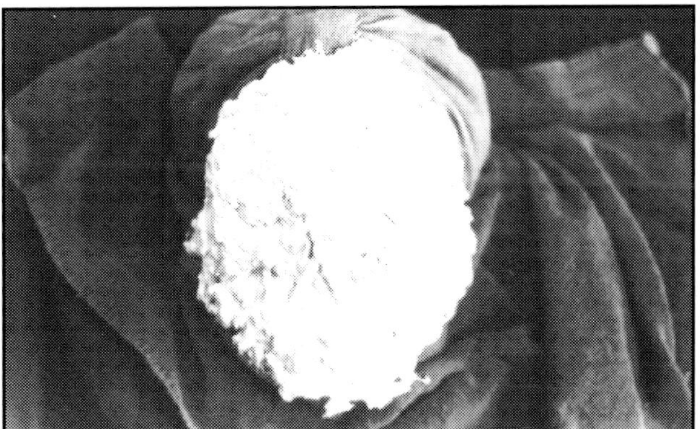

4. Completed moulage covering entire face of the model.

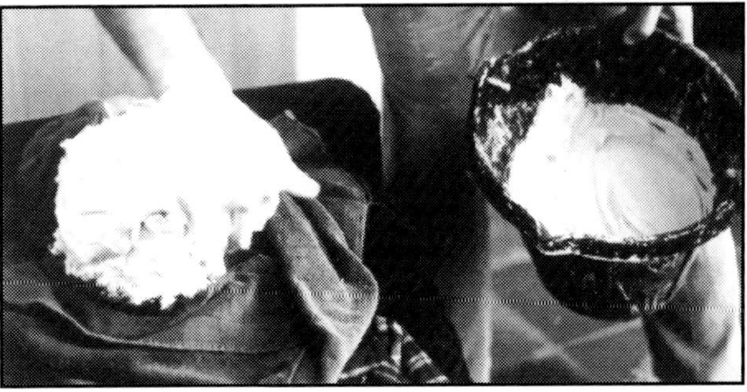

5. Application of plaster over the moulage to help retain shape of rubber when casting.

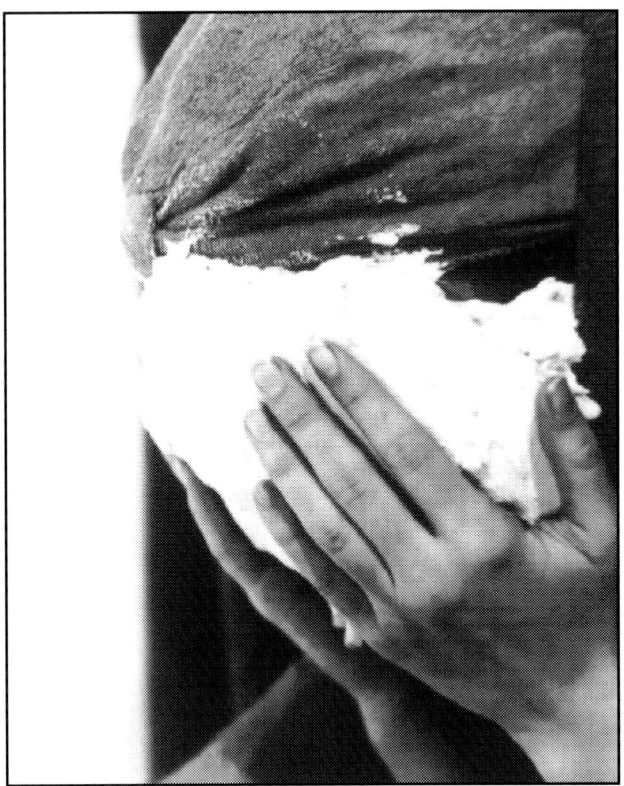

6. Removing the moulage and plaster mother mold by simple gravity.

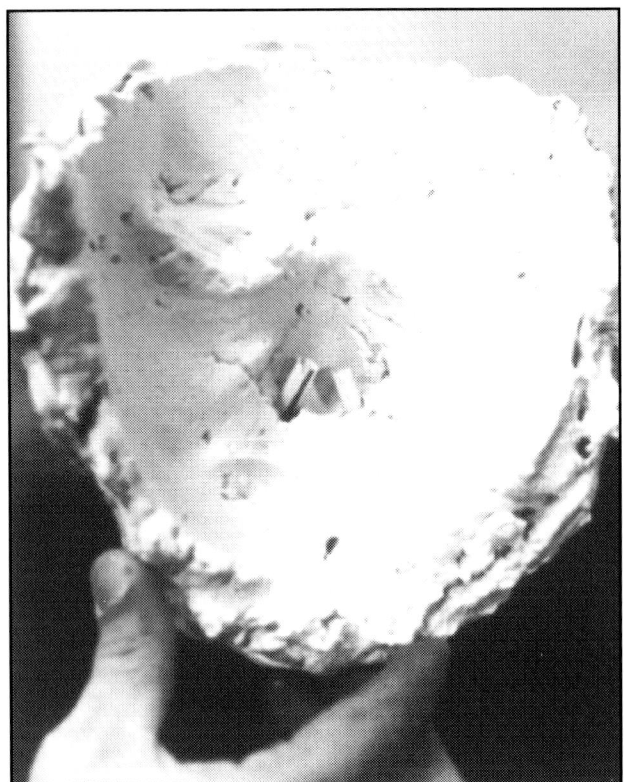

7. Interior section of the moulage and plaster mother mold.

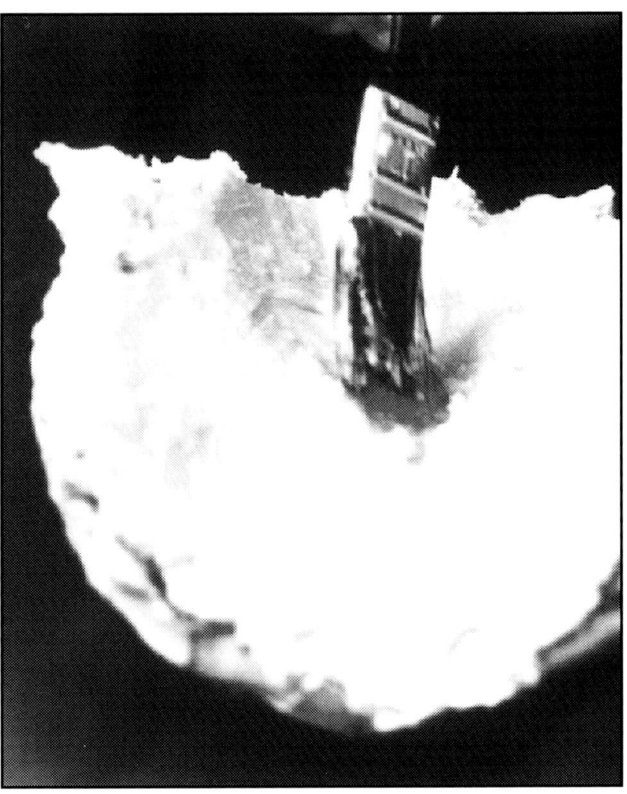

8. Applying melted pos-moulage to the interior of the mold. Pos-moulage is a neutral casting wax formula.

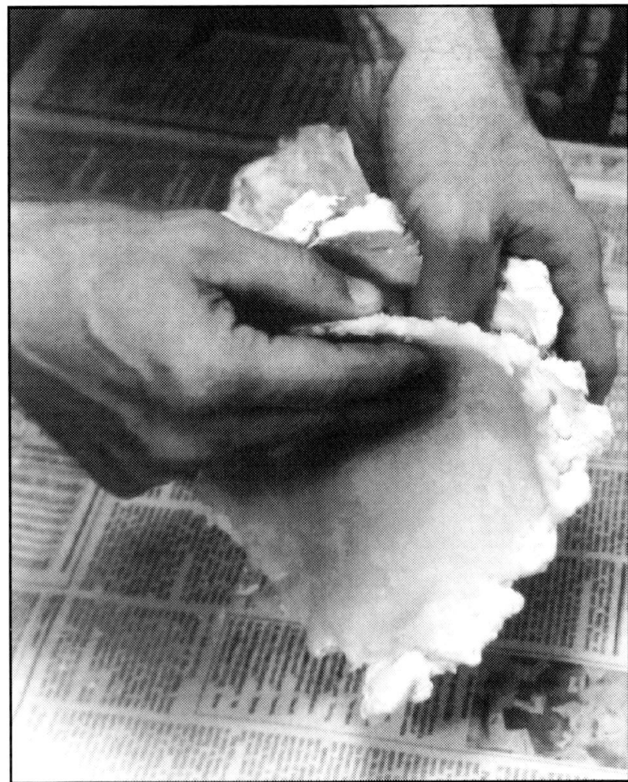

9. Removing the wax cast from the moulage mold.

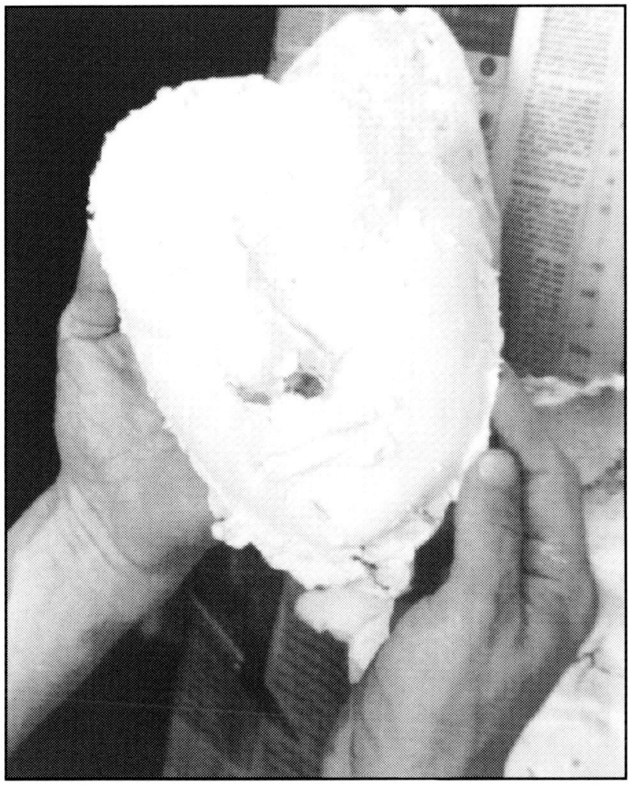

10. Completed wax (pos-moulage).

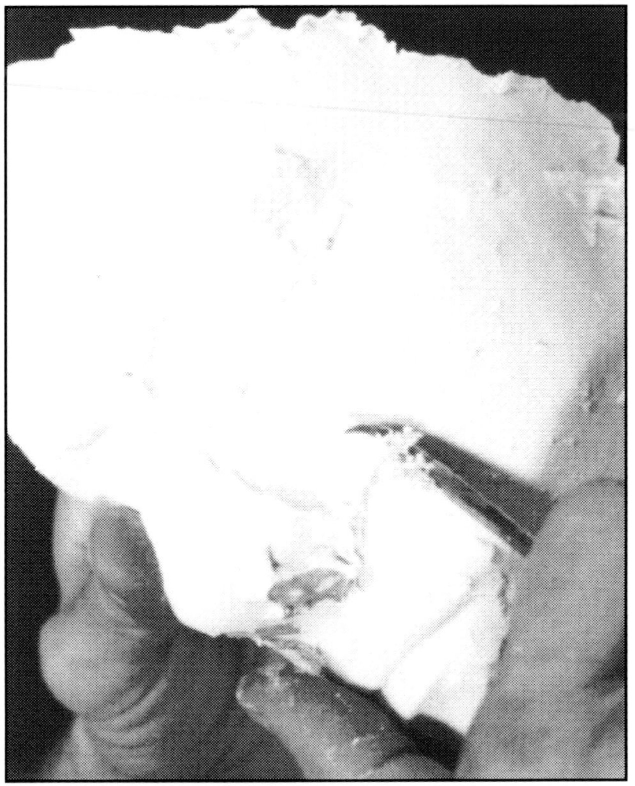

11. Removing and cleaning imperfections from the final cast.

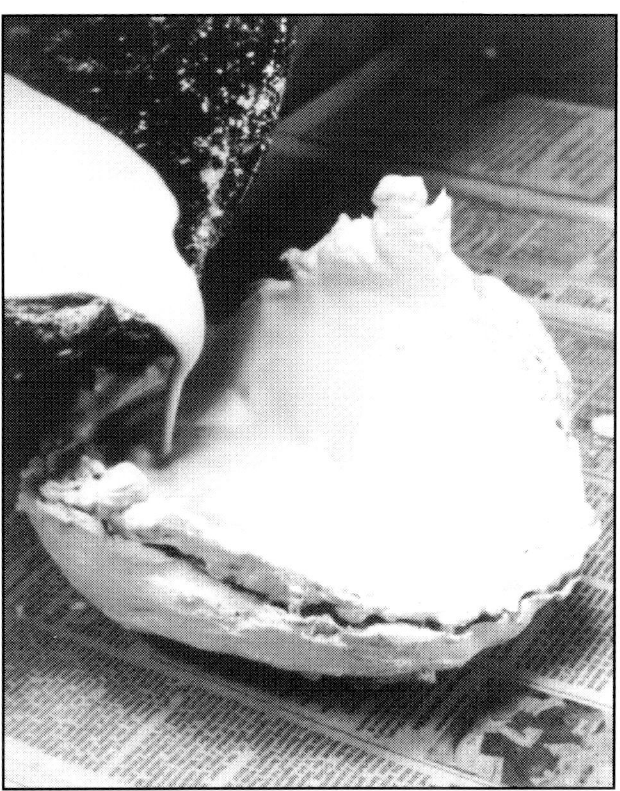

12. Pouring a plaster cast in the same mold from which the wax had been drawn.

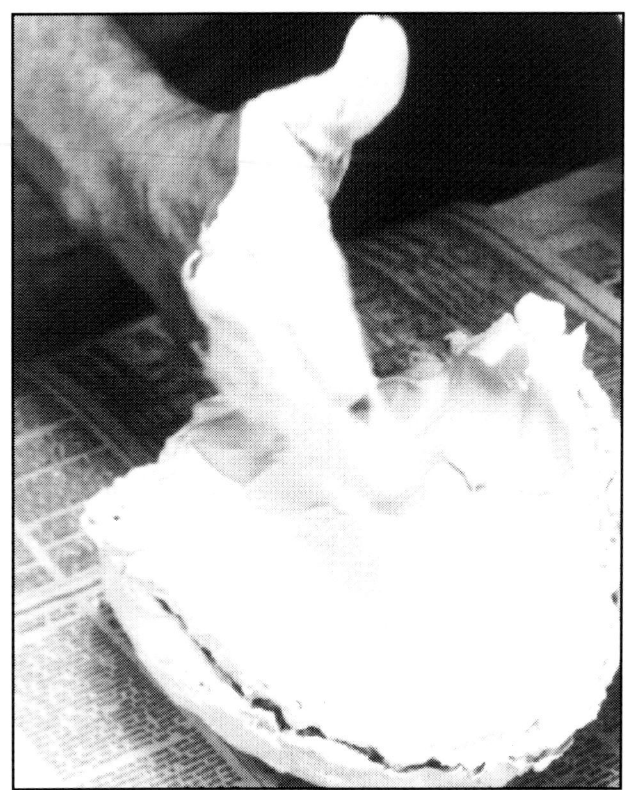

13. Smoothing the final casting of a plaster cast in the moulage mold.

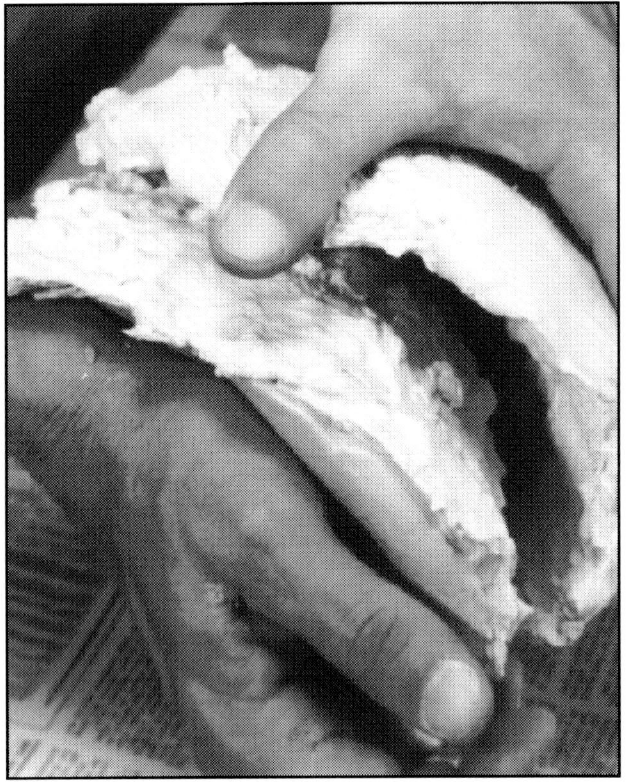

14. Removing the plaster cast from the moulage mold.

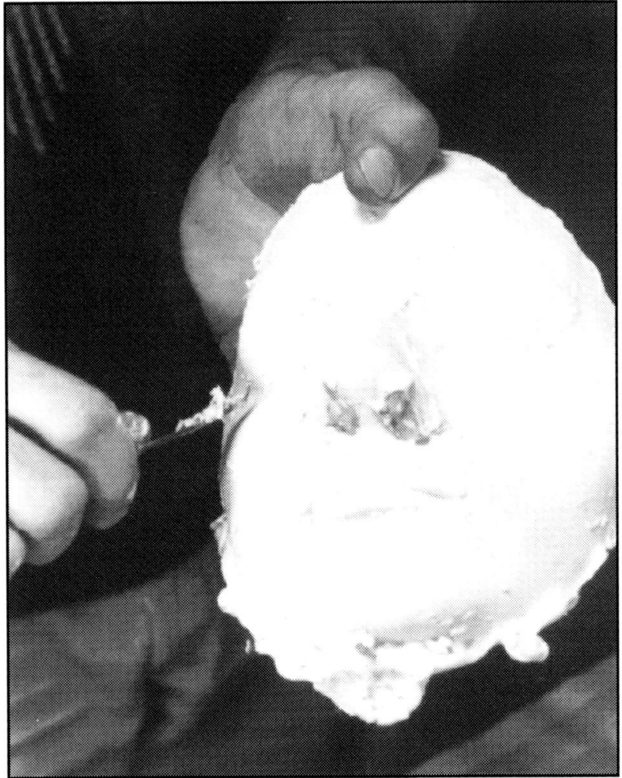

15. Cleaning and finishing the plaster cast.

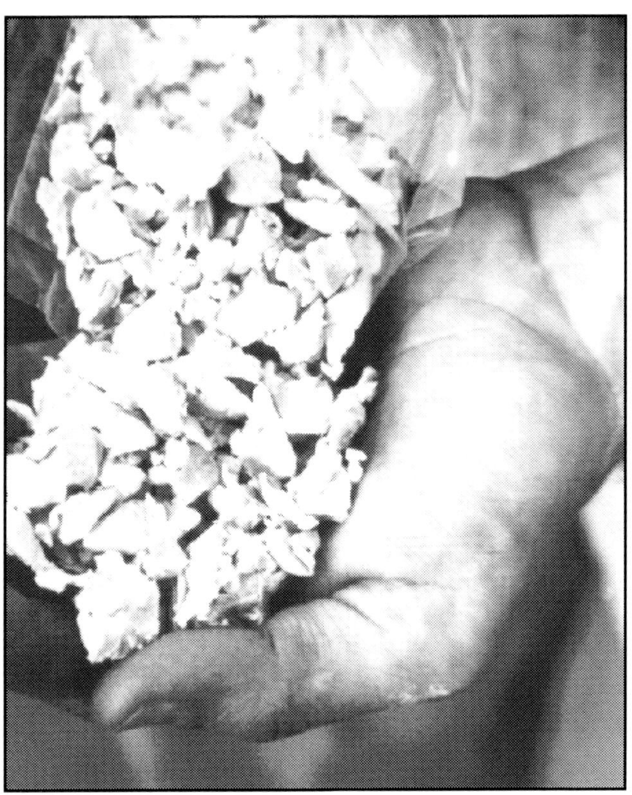

16. Before melting the moulage looks like moist large lump cottage cheese.

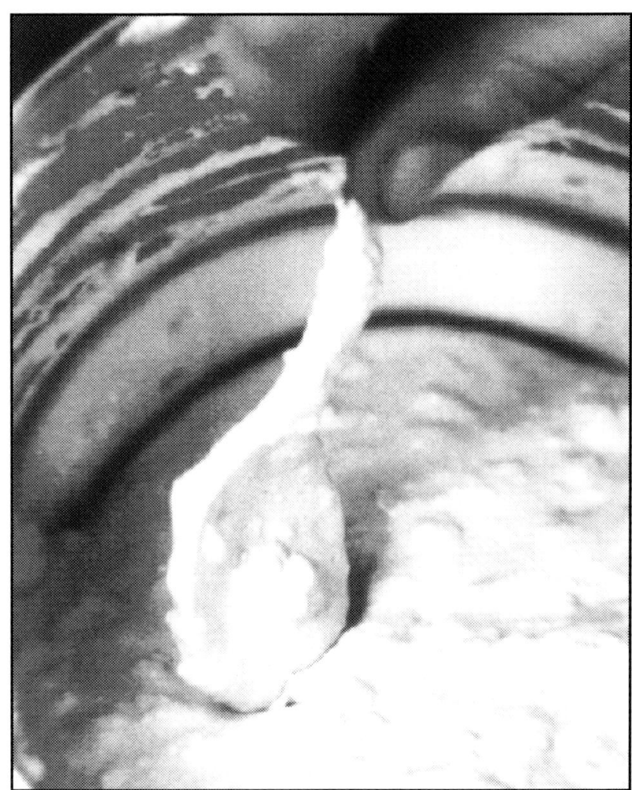

17. After heating moulage becomes smooth and creamy. Do not apply while too hot.

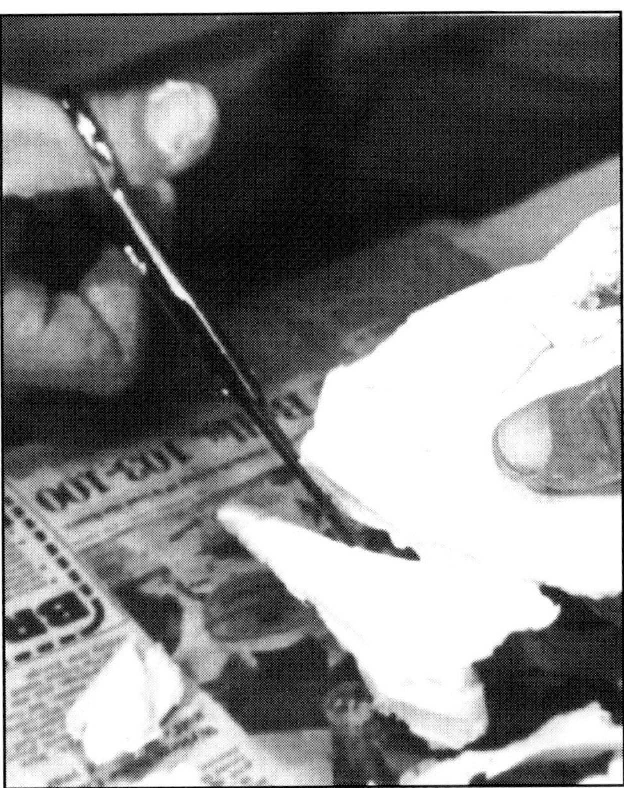

18. Cutting up finished moulage mold for melting and reuse.

CHAPTER 6

PLIATEX CASTING RUBBER

Pliatex Casting Rubber is a **positive** casting material, poured into a mold to obtain a positive cast. Do **not** confuse it with Pliatex Mold Rubber, a material used in making the negative or mold.

Casting rubber can only be used in plaster molds. No other type of mold will accommodate this material.

Pliatex Casting Rubber is a latex based rubber suspended in water and ammonia. When cast into a plaster, a positive rubber is achieved. This cast will be flexible unless a filler or hardener is used. The degree of flexibility or rigidity of the cast will be determined by the amount of filler mixed with the base rubber. The finished rubber cast can be painted with flexible rubber paint. If a more rigid cast is made, it can be patinaed in the conventional manner. I have found that the most common use of casting rubber is for masks of the human face or bas-reliefs. Casts in the round can be made but are extremely difficult and I would suggest leaving them to the professionals. I will go over all these points briefly but will discuss in detail only the use of casting rubber for a flexible cast or mask of the mold.

THE MOLD

The mold is probably the most critical element of the casting procedure. Casting rubber can only be cast into a dry plaster mold. Minimum thickness for even the smallest of jobs is at least 3 inches.

Casting rubber cannot be cast into any other but a dry plaster mold since the water in the rubber must be absorbed into the plaster, enabling the rubber to thicken and set. The larger the piece to be cast, the greater must be the thickness of the mold walls to absorb the greater amount of water from the larger amount of rubber.

With a cast made in the round, special locking keys must be incorporated into the mold, so it will be extremely secure and will not shift or leak when the cast rubber is poured.

THE MASK OR FACE MOLD

This will be a relief type of mold, with only the face are indented (negative). I do not recommend making a plaster mold directly on the face. The first step, therefore, is to create a positive plaster mold of the object to be cast. This mold must be at least 2 inches thick, no matter how small the object may be.

If the object is larger than 8 inches, increase the thickness of the mold so the moisture from the rubber will be able to absorb properly into the plaster, thus creating the cast.

Since we will be creating a face mask, we must first make a positive of the face to be cast. Using a moulage mold or negative of the face we will cast a pos-moulage positive into the mold, creating a positive wax or pos-moulage cast.

For the procedure for making the moulage mold, please see Chapter 5.

In making the positive be sure the build-up of the wax material is flush and that an even base supports the entire mask. Fill in positive mask so it will lie flat with no gaps or spaces underneath.

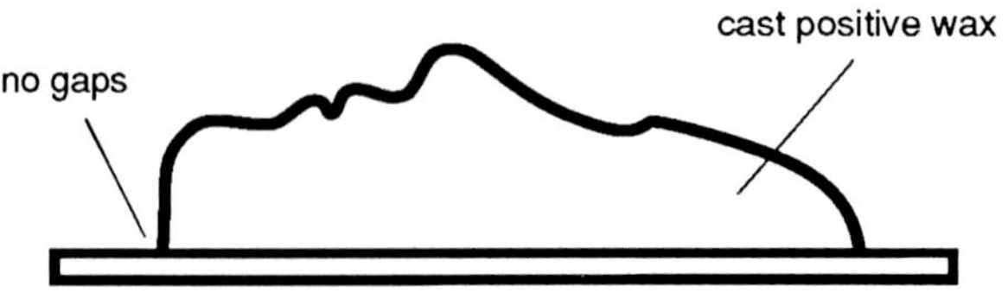

Figure 6.1. The mask.

A retaining box will now be built around the mask. You can use an old shipping carton, cut down. You must have at least 2 inches space around the entire perimeter of the mask and 2 inches above the highest point, usually the nose.

The next step is to line the entire interior of the box with heavy duty aluminum foil. Tape any cracks or crevices, since you do not want the liquid plaster to seep through to the box.

Once your box has been lined with foil, place the positive cast, flat side down, on the bottom of the box, centering it and leaving at least 2 inches on all sides and 2 inches above the nose. The top of the box will be open. If the positive cast is made of wax or pos-moulage, no release is required; the material should come out of the mold easily. If plaster has been used for the positive cast, soak it for at least 20 minutes after shellacking it twice and soaping with mold release or green soap. (This last should be done for about half an hour.) Mix a batch of fresh plaster to pour into the box, covering the mask.

The plaster should fill the entire box. Refer to the chart in Appendix F to determine the amount of plaster required. Remember it is always better to have a little too much rather than not enough.

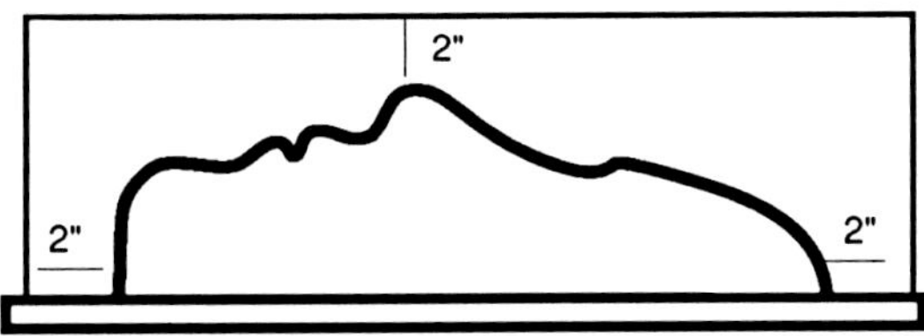

Figure 6.2. Cast in foil lined box.

Pour the plaster into the box, filling it to the top. Tap the sides to release any air bubbles, then scrape the top level flat. Remember we will be inverting this mold to make the cast, so it must be flat on the bottom.

Let the mold cure for at least 1 hour or until it has dried sufficiently to be removed from the box.

Remove the sides of the retaining box and remove the positive cast, leaving your negative plaster mold. You may have to dig out pieces of the cast but this is to be expected. The next step is very important. Let the mold dry, absolutely bone dry, before preparing to pour the casting rubber.

It is essential that the mold be completely dry, since the water in the rubber must be absorbed into the plaster mold for the rubber to set. You will discover that a large amount of rubber is required to fill the mold for even a thin face mask. No release agent is applied to the mold. Simply fill the entire cavity with rubber and let set. A normal mold will absorb enough water into the mold from the rubber to create a 1/16 inch thick solid layer within a two hour period.

As the water is absorbed and the rubber thickens the time for absorbing will increase; to achieve a 1/8 inch thickness, it will require an additional hour. These times are approximate and may vary according to the mold and type of plaster used.

I am using Pristine White Casting Plaster for this project, but if pottery plaster is used, absorption might be a little faster. When the mold has been filled and leveled, let set for the period of time required, usually 2 or 3 hours. Then pour the excess rubber back into its airtight container and reseal. This rubber can thus be kept for later use. The residue that remained in the cavity of the plaster mold will be left overnight to dry and set.

As setting occurs, the rubber will release itself from the mold and can be easily removed from the plaster.

If the cast is made of straight rubber it will be extremely flexible. To increase the stiffness of the rubber, a filler, Pliatex Casting Filler, is required. The degree of flexibility will vary depending on the amount of filler used.

A ratio of two parts filler to one part rubber (2:1) by volume, will result in a firm or medium hardness. A mix ratio of one to one (1:1) will create a firm to very firm medium and a mix ratio of three parts filler to one part rubber (3:1) will make a hard, almost unbendable cast. I suggest you make several small molds in dixie cups to test samples and select the hardness you prefer.

Fill a small dixie cup with fresh plaster and as it hardens, take a spoon and dig out a small scoop from the center leaving an indentation of about ¼ of an inch. In another disposable cup mix the filler and rubber in the ratio desired and pour into the dry plaster mold made in the cup.

When it has set for two hours, remove the excess liquid rubber and let the remainder set over night or until dry. The cast rubber section can be removed easily and its rigidity will give you an idea of the ratio of filler to rubber you will need. Be sure to keep a record of the ratio mix and the time set. **Do not pour** the mixed rubber **back into** the same container the rubber came from. Fill the hollow cavity of the dried plaster mold level with casting rubber and let sit for two to three hours.

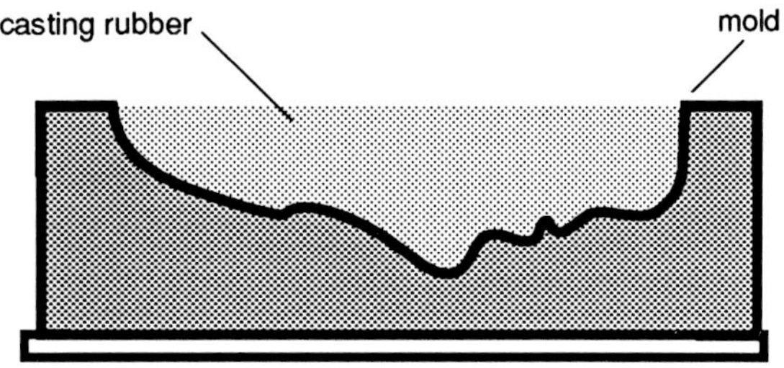

Figure 6.3. Fill the hollow cavity of the dried plaster mold level with casting rubber and let sit for two to three hours..

PAINTING THE CAST RUBBER

When you are finished with it, you might like to color or patina the cast. This is easily done. The patina procedure can be found in Chapter 8. You can paint the cast with conventional latex or water color paints, but the piece should them be of a firmer cast. If the rubber is flexible, the paint will tend to crack when the piece is bent. Flexible rubber paints are available, but they should be sprayed on with an air gun if possible. Thin coats will work, but the tendency is to apply too much paint, causing cracking.

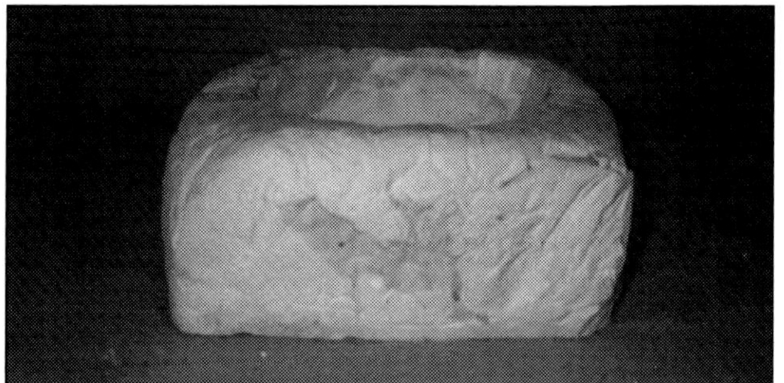

1. Plaster mold for casting rubber, side view.

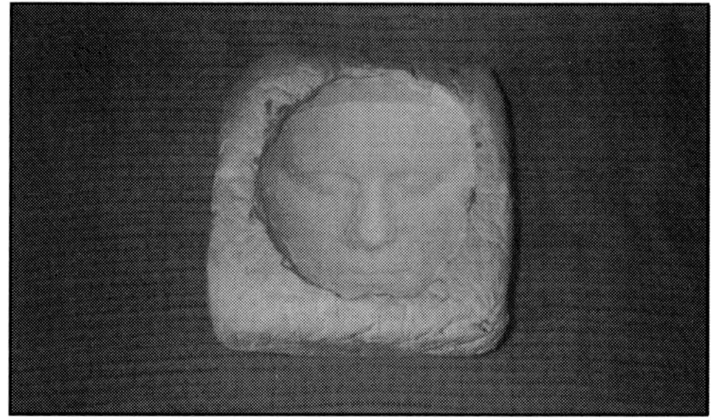

2. Interior of plaster negative for casting rubber.

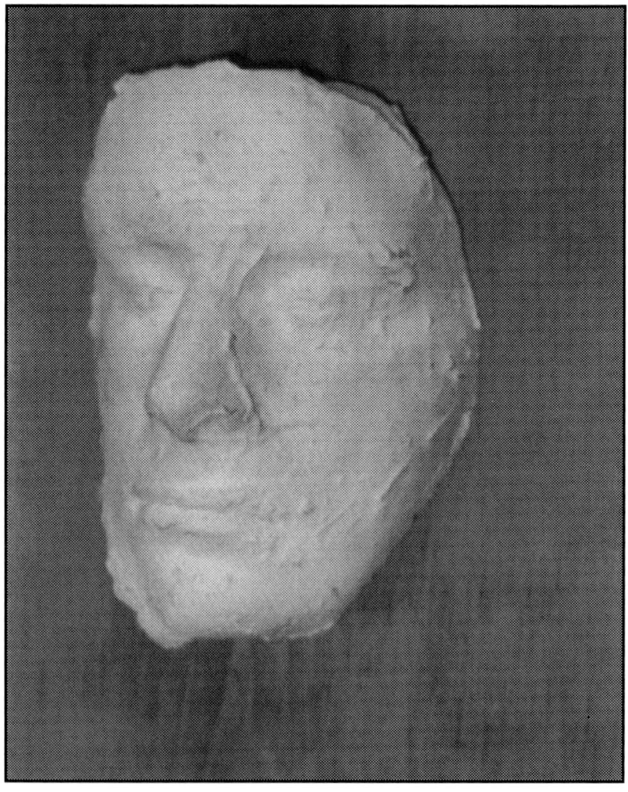

3. Cast rubber mask of Jennifer from moulage life mask.

CHAPTER 7

REPAIRING CASTS & MOLDS

A cast may be in need of repair for any number of reasons. Most commonly the cast breaks when being demolded or is knocked over or dropped.

When a piece breaks while being removed from the mold, it is generally a figure and the arms and/or legs tend to be the major problem. This most often occurs when the arms and legs do not have internal support; thin delicate areas like these tend to break off easily. Fortunately, the pieces usually break clean and can be rejoined or fused back on satisfactorily.

First, drill a small hole in each piece at the break. Insert into each a rod of noncorrosive metal or wire (aluminum). Apply glue or epoxy to the pieces of wire and the two broken sections of the piece. Fit the pieces back together and secure until the bonding material has set. If the break or crack line is extremely noticeable, mix a small amount of fresh plaster and fill in the area. When this new plaster has dried, it can be sanded to the original shape and contour of the piece.

If the cast has been dropped, the process is somewhat different and a little more complex. If the pieces are well defined, follow the directions above. If there are no whole pieces that can be reattached, the damaged area must be built back up with a new batch of fresh plaster.

Mix a small batch of fresh plaster and apply to the damaged areas of the cast. If there are large areas to be mended, the process may have to be repeated several times until the plaster has been built up enough to rasp or sand to the original definition of the piece. I like to take a few pictures of the piece before casting, so if anything goes wrong, I will have a guide as to the original design.

After the repaired areas are finished to your satisfaction, you can patina them. The broken areas will be hardly noticeable. It will take close examination to determine the area of breakage.

When a mold is broken, it is usually while demolding a cast because of the natural suction. This usually happens because the mold has been moved sooner than it should have been or the sections of the molds were not built up enough. These sections will naturally break clean and can be glued back together, drilling each section and inserting an epoxy coated pin into each half. Apply glue or epoxy to the broken sections of the mold, rejoin them, and secure until the material has dried. Mix up a fresh batch of plaster and build up the areas that have been damaged. Dipping cheese cloth or strips of burlap into the liquid plaster and laying them over the damaged area will ensure a strong and, it is hoped, salvaged mold. Cover the pieces with fresh plaster and smooth to complete the process. I have broken many molds and this manner of repair has always worked fine.

AIR BUBBLES FORM IN THE CAST

Fill in air bubbles with fresh plaster and let dry. Then smooth or sand as necessary. This will bring the piece back to its original contour. Many times there will be so many air holes that you will need several small batches of plaster. This is not uncommon and should be expected. Don't think one small batch will do the entire job, but if you mix a large amount of plaster and there are a lot of air bubbles, the plaster will set hard before you complete the job properly.

When you feel you are finished with all the repairs, go over the entire piece once again, from top to bottom. You will be surprised at how many defects you have missed. Repeat the process of repairing. When all air holes have been repaired and the plaster has set, sand those areas to the finished state and patina.

CHAPTER 8

PATINAS

For Gypsum (plaster) Based Materials

A patina is a multitude of different colors combining with a basic hue in natural form to give and object a distinct color. A patina usually forms on objects exposed to the elements and has different effects depending on the objects' composition and geographic location. The natural patina of wood on a house located on the Florida coast will form the same as that on a barn siding in upstate Maine, but the look and effect will be somewhat different. Bronze, copper, aluminum, granite, marble, and the temple bells of Japan over time will all acquire a unique and distinct patina. None will be exactly the same, but each will be beautiful in its own right.

When examined closely with a magnifying glass, patinas will display a great many different colors, combining to form what the surface of the object reflects as its own coloring or patina.

When dealing with gypsum based products that cannot be exposed to the elements to from their own patina, it must be applied with pigment by hand. The options can range from ebony, bronze brown, grey-green, and terra cotta to almost any other effect the imagination can think of. I will go over the basic and most commonly used effects of patina and a few that are unusual that I personally prefer. You can create other patinas by experimentation and testing. This chapter will give you a guide or stepping stone of basic techniques to build on.

Since all the products we are dealing with are gypsum based materials, I will stick with these as examples with Pristine White Casting Plaster as the base material. Other harder materials will accept these patinas in the same fashion.

It is imperative to do tests before working on the piece. Keep records of the materials used, in what order, and how they were applied, plus any other information that might help you to recreate the process . Too many times you will create a wonderful patina and not be able to duplicate it because you didn't keep notes. I have cast 50 separate tiles of plaster with holes drilled in the top for display. I have created a patina for each, numbered the backs, and recorded the techniques used in a book. Thus I need only consult my notes to duplicate an effect. These have become my private record.

If you don't want to go to the trouble of casting tiles, place a few blobs of plaster on a sheet of waxed paper or tin foil, smooth the surfaces, and let them set up. This will give you something to practice on before you patina your piece. Remember that creating a patina is a learned art form and every patina is different. Many casting studios take pride in their ability to produce great patinas and are very secretive about how they are accomplished. In all likelihood, you will feel the same once you have perfected your technique.

BASE COLORING

When working with gypsum products, the base color for patina can be achieved in several different ways. It is extremely important to get the base color correct, since the balance of the patina will be created from it.

An easy way to get a good solid deep base color is to add a water soluble pigment to the water of the casting mix. Thus, if the cast is chipped, a white area will not be exposed. Dilute the pigment in water and add to the water that will be used for the casting material. The coloring should be rather strong since its strength will be diluted when the plaster is added to the water. With practice, you will learn exactly how much to mix in order to get the desired effect. The only drawback is that the color may stain the mold and you may want casts of a different color from the same mold.

Another way is to apply a base coat directly on a white cast plaster piece with whatever medium is to be used. This can include pastels, oil paints, water colors, latex house paints, wood furniture stains, or other easily absorbed materials that will create unusual patinas.

STAINS

Furniture stains provide a very common method of obtaining a unique base color or natural base. These stains are usually alcohol or water based and absorb well into the plaster. In addition, the range of colors is great. You can use ebony, walnut, cherry, fruit wood, pine, birch and any other that may interest you.

When the stain has been selected, make sure to mix it well in the container so you will have a good strong even color. Brush onto the plaster cast as desired and let the stain soak in and dry. Several coats may be necessary to get the correct effect since the plaster will draw the material in. The strength of the color is your personal preference. When the stain has been applied, it may look a little drab but as the other applications are added, it will take shape.

PAINTS

Paints are probably the most common and best base material that can be used as a patina medium. All the household paints can be used as a base color. They can be mixed to create special colors and come in flat, semi-gloss and gloss. The plaster will absorb the patina so if a high gloss is desired, seal the plaster with several coats of shellac before applying the paint. You may also use art supply store paints such as water colors, acrylics, tempera, or oil paints. I have even used gesso (canvas primer), for a different effect. Remember that the plaster will draw the pigment color away leaving a very washed out pale coat. To offset this, apply a coat or two of shellac or a coat of wax to the plaster before applying the color. Experiment until you get the effect you want. A very common use of paint is a solid white finish. The paint is applied to cover any marks of repairs and seam lines. When finished, you should not even be able to tell where the seam line was. I enjoy looking closely at commercial casts or ceramic pieces to see if I can't do better. At any rate, a coat or two of water based flat white paint will do wonders for a plaster cast.

AEROSOL SPRAYS

Aerosol sprays are quite often used to get an even, solid base coat especially when metallic gold, bronze and silver effects are desired. A sealing coat of clear matte or gloss acrylic spray is generally applied as the last coat once your patina has acquired the desired effect. All these can usually be purchased in a hardware or art material store.

SPECIAL EFFECTS

There are different ways to create special effects when applying a patina. I will list a few of these; let your imagination do the rest.

Milk Wash

Something as simple as applying a few coats of skim, whole, or buttermilk to a white plaster cast will give a unique and deep luster to the cast. A piece is often left as is after the milk wash has been applied.

Egg Yolk

A few sculptors beat an egg with milk or water and apply this mixture to the plaster before sealing. You can also separate the yolk and white and apply one or the other.

Marble Look

Many people ask how to get a marble look to a piece of plaster. This is rather easy. Use a sharpened grease pencil purchased at the hardware store and draw the veins as you would like them to appear directly on the cast before sealing. If you want a specific color marble, make the markings and then apply a thin wash of the desired color before sealing. A good example is Portuguese pink or Belgium Black marble with the base color applied and veins highlighted with the black grease pencil before sealing.

Shoe Polish

Liquid or wax based shoe polish is another favorite of a great many sculptors for a patina base color. The colors vary widely and the solid polishes have the wax and pigment combined when they are manufactured. You may want to experiment with both types.

PATINA ON BRONZE OR METAL

This is a very complicated and skilled technique requiring a great deal of experience and safety equipment. I **do not** suggest that this be attempted by the novice or even the more advanced caster, but rather have a professional do the work with proper ventilation, tools and materials. I will list just a few of the basic items needed for putting a patina on bronze and will go no further.

After reviewing this list, I suggest that you do the same: **go no further**!

Chemicals Hot and Cold:
- ferric nitrate
- liver of sulphur
- ferric chloride
- copper sulfate
- ammonium chloride
- sodium thiosulfate
- nitric acid
- sulfuric acid

Tools and Equipment:
- propane torch
- gas-air or mapp
- elephant trunk ventilation
- air brush compressor
- copper-brass wire brush
- labeled glass containers for corrosive chemicals
- running water
- oxyacetylene torch
- face mask with chemical filters
- safety goggles
- shoes, safety
- cap
- gloves

just to begin with for your own safety.

If you would still like to pursue this I have listed in the sources section on page __, an excellent book that you can purchase, Patination. I strongly recommend leaving the patina of bronze and other metals to the professionals or to nature.

APPLICATION, PLASTER MATERIALS

Once you have decided on the base color for your patina, you will want to highlight certain areas, deepening some and thinning others. Then seal the patina so that it will not be disturbed. For gypsum based materials (plaster) you will require only the following items:

1. Base Color
2. Shellac
3. Pigments powdered, a small amount of each color: red, green, blue, bronze brown, gold, silver and some actual bronze powder.
4. Brushes: 2 1-inch soft bristle.
5. Neutral paste wax.
6. Aerosol transparent acrylic spray.
7. Pallet for mixing pigments, non-porous.
8. Talc, baby powder

FIRST STEP

Apply the base coat over the entire model, heavy in some areas, light in others, as your fancy dictates. It is sometime a good idea to apply a coat of shellac or neutral wax to the plaster surface before applying the base coat. This will allow the pigments to adhere better.

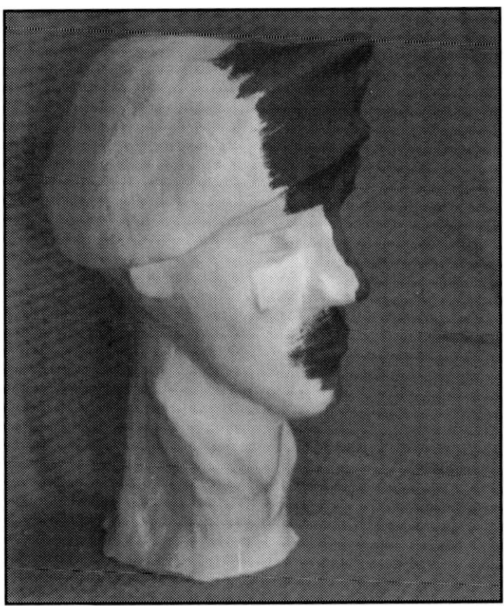

Figure 8.1. Base coat.

Again this is a matter of personal preference and should be done after experimentation. Untreated plaster will absorb the color of the base material and you must judge how you wish to proceed.

SECOND STEP

Once the base coat has been applied to the entire cast, coat the piece with a thin layer of neutral paste wax. It may also be shellacked. The piece should have at least one coat of either wax or shellac.

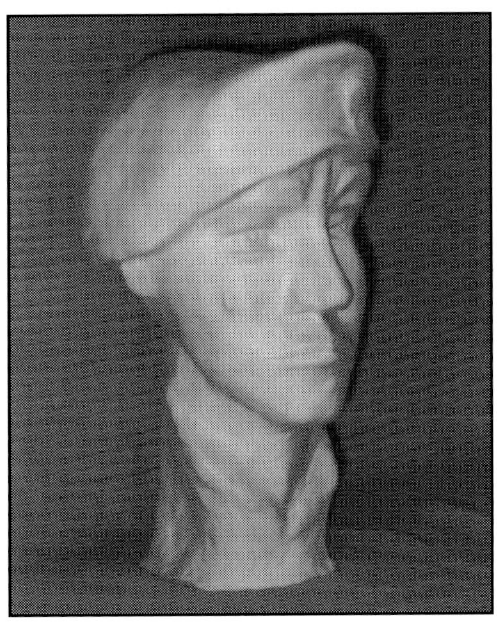

Figure 8.2. Coating cast.

THIRD STEP

Place a small amount of pigment on the nonporous pallet surface near your piece (Figure 8.3). Add a small amount of shellac, since this will serve as a bonding agent. You should have a small amount of all the colors listed previously to create a complete patina.

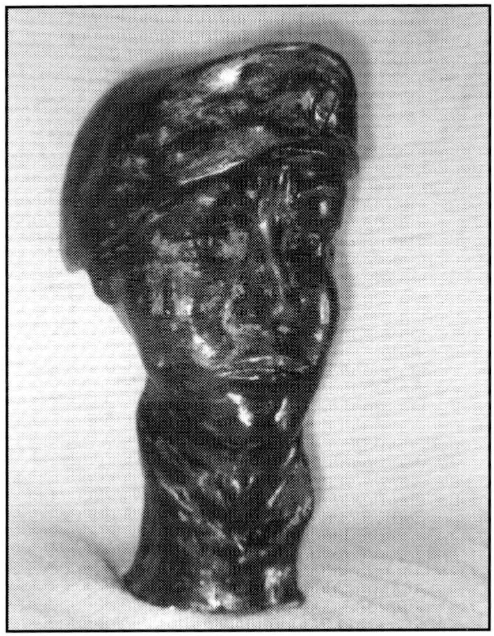

Figure 8.3. Pigmentation.

FOURTH STEP

Take the brush and dip in the shellac first so there is enough on the brush to make the pigment soluble. Pick up a small amount of the desired pigment, taking it from the edge of the mound, not the top or middle. Similar to an artist mixing oil paints on the palette to create a certain color.

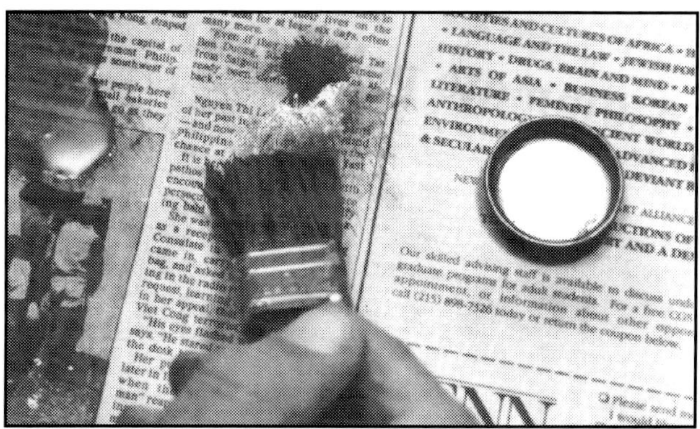

Figure 8.4. Application.

Apply the pigment in the strength you feel appropriate. Continue with the colors as desired. As stated earlier, sample tests are recommended.

When applying the pigments, take great care not to get too much on the brush at one time. The material will go a long way. Always pick up the shellac first before you pick up the pigment. Mix the colors in whatever way you want. It's a little like a chef creating a recipe, a dab of this, a pinch of that, testing and adding. Do not apply the pigments like a coat of paint, in a solid manner, but sparingly in different areas. If for some reason you feel the need to remove any part of the patina it can easily be done with alcohol. This will lighten the color and enable you to make changes.

FIFTH STEP

Now that the base colors and the primary colors have been applied, you may want to highlight the prominent areas with gold, silver, or bronze powder to get a metallic effect. These colors can be used individually, combined, or mixing with shellac.

Lightly brush the prominent areas of the piece with the desired colors. Remember they are concentrated and a small amount will be sufficient.

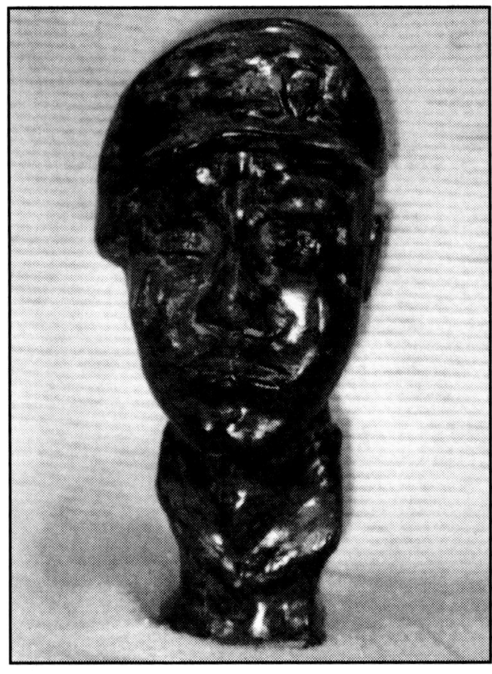

Figure 8.5. Highlight.

They are meant only for highlighting the base or primary colors and should be used sparingly. When the highlights have been dusted on lightly, you may wish to use talc to soften or lighten certain areas. This is the final step before sealing.

SIXTH STEP

When the colors and highlights have been applied to your satisfaction, you are ready to seal the patina to make it permanent. Apply several coats of transparent acrylic spray or a thin coat of neutral paste wax. Let the sealant dry and leave as is or buff it to a semi-gloss.

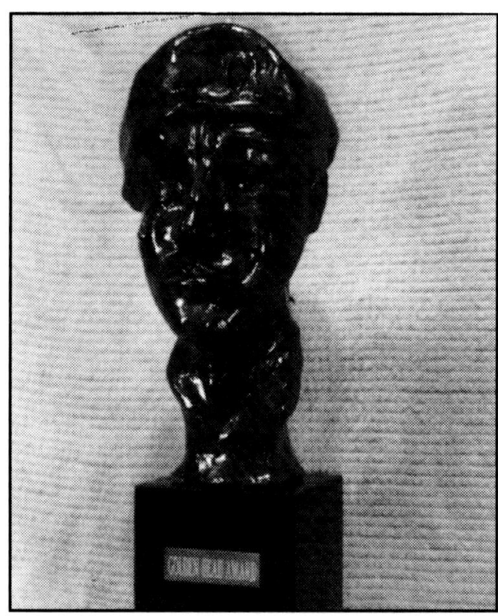

Figure 8.6. Sealing and mounting.

Your piece is now ready to be mounted for display. Remember the whole patina process is done individually, you can go in any direction you desire. Relax, be creative, and have a good time!

CHAPTER 9

MOUNTING

MARBLE, WOOD, AND MICARTA BASES

When your piece has been finished to your satisfaction, the last thing to be done is to display it appropriately. If the piece has a natural cast base, your choice is simple. A plain pedestal of either white or black in a solid gloss or matte, built to the dimensions of you sculpture, can be made to order. These pedestals come in a number of varied surfaces including clear lucite.

The most important requirement is the correct measurements. The base area should accommodate the resting area of your piece. The height should fit the size of the sculpture in the proper proportion. If possible, take your piece to a professional base or pedestal producer, usually found in the yellow pages under Sculpture or foundry. Go over the designs and measurements with him or her. If you intend to make your own base, purchase a do-it-yourself book on furniture or cabinetmaking. There should be quite a few designs for boxes or enclosed containers.

Most of the conventional and small to medium size pieces require some type of base for mounting. Figures, animals, or modern and abstract pieces tend to be enhanced by the temperament of the proper marble, micarta, or other such base. Some sculptures may not need a base, for example, a reclining nude placed by itself on a mantle or bookshelf. A base of polished gloss black marble might detract from its beauty instead of enhancing it. This is a personal choice. You are the sculptor and it's your finished product. I am only offering suggestions.

The most common base in the sculpture field is the gloss black micarta base. Plexiglass, lucite, stone, and wood bases are generally used for certain types of effects. Another favorite is the dark green or black marble base. These are generally precut at the quarries and are available only in standard dimensions. Most shops do not have the facilities to cut marble, which requires a diamond saw, running water, and proper drainage.

The micarta bases are made of either solid or hollow wood boxes covered with micarta, which is a thin form of plastic. The micarta is glued to the bases which can be made to a custom size, large or small. The cost of the micarta is usually figured on the square, dimension of the top, multiplied by a dollar amount, and an additional dollar amount for each inch in height. Marble, custom plexiglass, and lucite bases are priced according to their specific dimensions and difficulty of production.

Custom made bases can be round, oval, tapered, or kidney shaped. As long as the manufacturer has the ability to produce your design, the selections are endless. Bases can be predrilled to accommodate any type of sculpture. If you decide to go the custom made route remember that the proper dimensions are of the utmost importance. Another idea is to attach your piece to an object such as fieldstone, slate, or other interesting forms of stone.

Natural wood shapes are quite often used as bases for sculptures. Sanded, finished, and stained or left in the natural state, they can produce unique effects.

Whatever base you choose for your sculpture, remember to **mount your sculpture securely to the base** so it will not easily come free.

The most common way to attach a piece is with glue or epoxy, with pins or screws the next most popular. I will go over the basic methods of each. They can be used separately or in conjunction with one another, depending on the size and weight of the piece.

GLUE-EPOXY

Once the base has been selected, one of the fastest and easiest ways to secure the sculpture to it is with a glue or epoxy that is compatible with both the base material and the sculpture. Some glues and epoxies may have a reaction to plastic materials. Review the instructions for use on the epoxy container first.

Let's start by roughing-up each area that is to have contact with the glue. This will provide for a more solid adhesion. Before attaching the sculpture, seal the base with two coats of shellac and let dry. This will prevent the glue or epoxy from being absorbed into the plaster. Then as per the instructions, apply a small amount of glue or epoxy to each of the pieces.

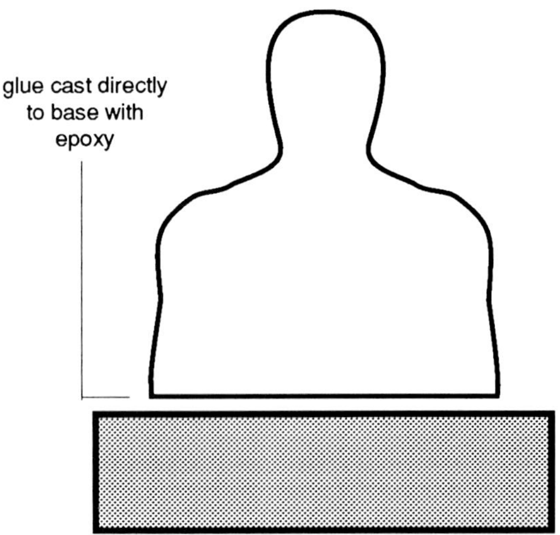

Figure 9.1. Applying epoxy.

Place the sculpture and base together, then separate them from each other. Let the material set-up for a few minutes, or as suggested on the package, then put the base and sculpture back together again. This will make for a tighter and stronger bond. If required, a clamp, twine or heavy rubber bands may be used to hold the two pieces together until the glue has sufficiently bonded. In most cases, the weight of the standing object will be enough.

PINS, SCREWS AND RODS

When inserting pins, screws, or rods, drilling is usually required to prevent damage to the base or the sculpture. Be extremely careful not to damage the sculpture by drilling too deeply or in thin area that will not accommodate the drill. When the correct diameter of the pin, screw, or rod has been determined, align the base to the sculpture. Mark the position where the hole will be drilled for pin insertion.

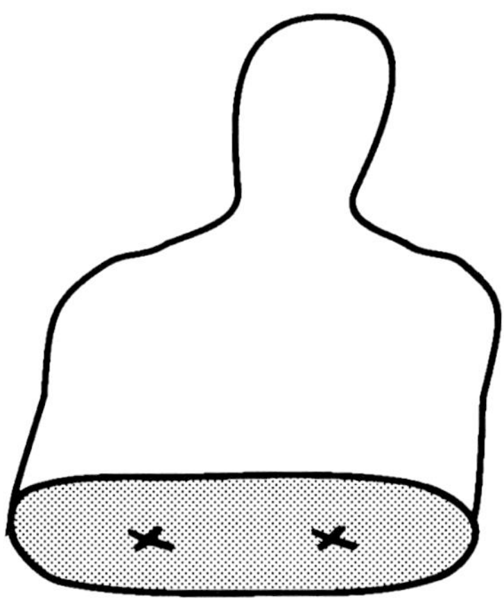

Figure 9.2. Marking and drilling cast.

Use drill of the same size as the pin, rod, or screw to drill both the base and the sculpture.

Drill into the sculpture to a depth that will hold half the length of the rod, screw, or pin. The other half will go into the base. If the rod, screw, or pin is 1 inch long, the holes in both the base and the sculpture must be 1/2 inch deep.

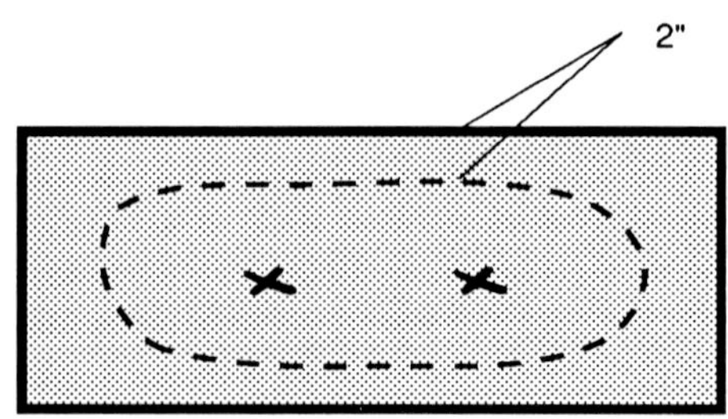

Figure 9.3. Marking and drilling cast base.

Mark the drill with the correct depth so your hole will not be too short or too deep. I place a piece of white adhesive tape around the drill to indicate the depth I want to go into the base.

When the holes have been properly drilled in both the base and the sculpture, place a small amount of glue or epoxy on half of each rod or screw and insert those halves into the drilled holes in the sculpture (figure 9.4). When the rods are properly bonded, place a small amount of glue onto the other end of each one, fix the sculpture to the base, and let it set. Some sculptors also smear additional glue or epoxy onto the surfaces of the base and piece that will be touching.

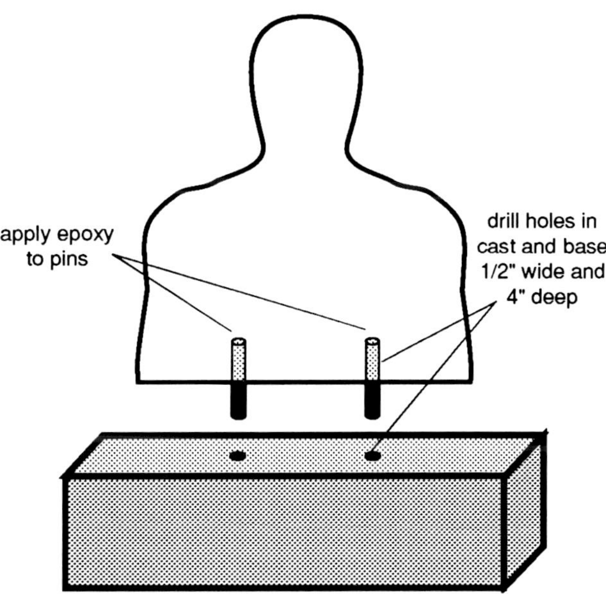

Figure 9.4. Epoxy on rod.

A small amount of seepage may occur around the edges of the base and sculpture. Wipe this away immediately before it sets-up.

FELT, CUSHION BOTTOMS

It is a nice touch to add a felt bottom or rubber bumpers to the bottom of the base (or the sculpture if you are not using a base). This will protect table tops, bookshelves, or counters from scratching. Cut the piece of felt to fit the contours of the base. It can be trimmed after installation if necessary. The most common type of felt bottom is black but felt comes in a variety of colors and can be purchased at any fabric store.

When the material has been cut, apply a thin coat of adhesive, usually Elmer's white glue, to the entire base area. Start at one end and roll the material onto the base. Do not use excessive amounts of adhesive as it binds and causes ripples in the fabric. Secure the material and allow it to dry evenly and adhere properly to the base. Be sure to follow the instructions on the adhesive container so the materials will join properly.

Rubber bumpers or pads can be attached in this same fashion. These come in different shapes, sizes, and thicknesses and can be found in most hardware stores and picture framing stores.

Before attaching these items, read the instructions. When used directly on plaster, the bottom part of the cast may have to be sealed with shellac, so the glue will adhere properly.

APPENDIX A

MIXING PROCEDURES FOR PLASTER

MIXING PROCEDURE FOR MOLD

Place the proper amount of water in a container large enough to hold both the plaster and the water after they are mixed together. The container should be flexible yet strong enough to maintain its original shape. A 3 or 3 1/2 gallon bucket reinforced with fiberglass is most commonly used.

When mixing plaster, the powder is **ALWAYS** added to the water. Sprinkle the powder over the surface of the water and let it settle to the bottom of the container; build up until a small mound or iceberg effect is achieved, extending about 1 inch above the water's surface.

Sprinkle the plaster powder into the water in a circular motion, sifting the plaster through the fingers.

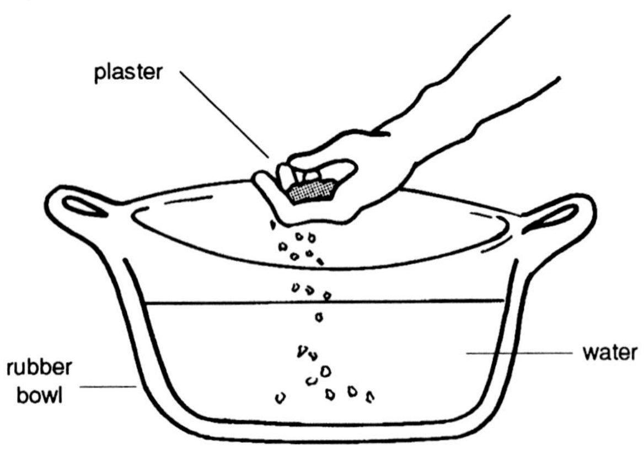

Figure 10.1. Sprinkled powder.

This will break up any lumps formed while the plaster was sitting in the package. There should be no solid pieces in the powder; if any are found, they should be removed since they will affect the surface of the mold and possibly the cast.

When the plaster has been added to the water and a peak has formed above the water line, let it stand between 4 or 5 minutes. This will allow the plaster to absorb the water.

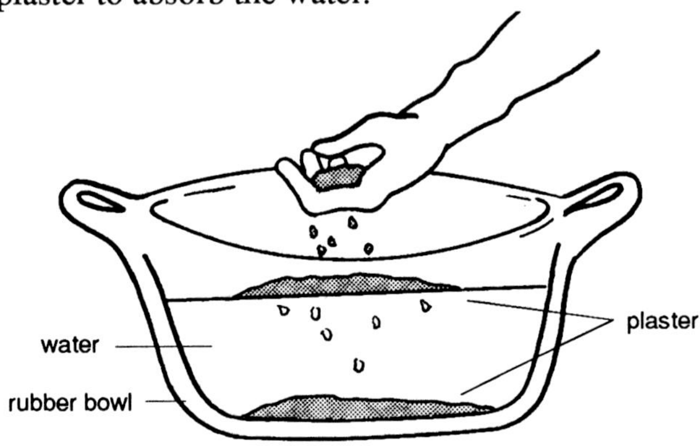

Figure 10.2. Let plaster powder float to the bottom of bowl forming a mound.

Then, with a slight agitation of the spread fingers, gently mix the plaster from the bottom of the container. Do not allow excess air into the plaster mix since it will cause air bubbles in the mold walls.

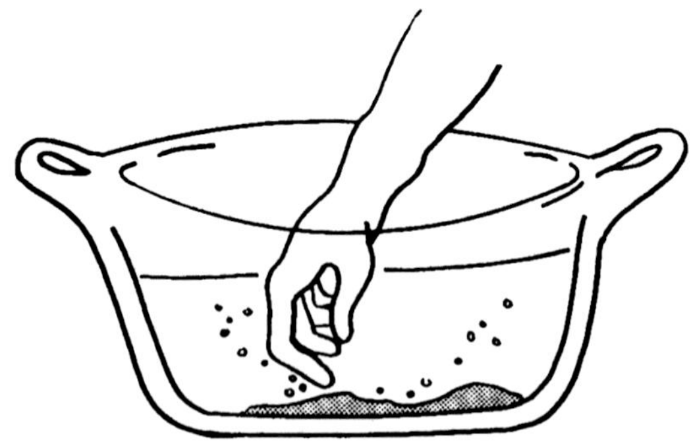

Figure 10.3. Hand mixing and dissolvling plaster.

As the plaster thickens, scrape down the sides of the container to make even, smooth, heavy cream mixture. When the plaster is just short of the consistency of thick pudding and somewhat heavier than heavy cream, it is ready to apply to the model.

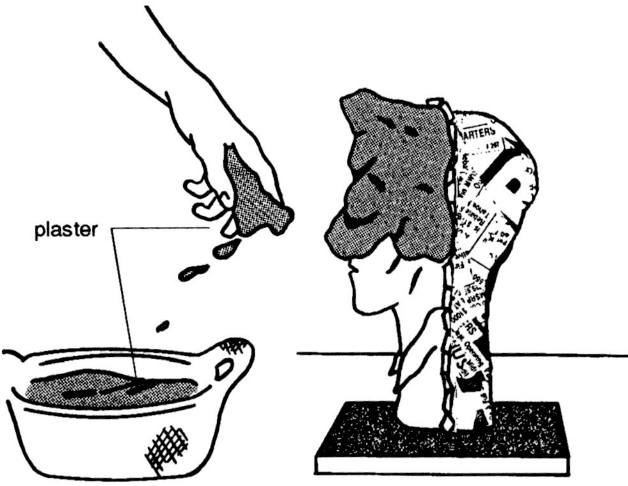

Figure 10.4. Backhand flip.

Always begin at the top of the model when applying the plaster since the force of gravity will cause the plaster to flow toward the base. If the plaster is too thin, it will run off the model and build up at the base of the work area. This is not uncommon for beginning mold makers. Simply scoop it up and reapply. A back underhand flip is the usual way to apply plaster to most models. With experience you will learn to do this without splattering the plaster all over the room.

Remember, always clean the base area of the work table and smooth the outer surface of the mold with wet fingers to even the surface. You do not want pieces of set plaster lying around that may cause problems. Place all excess plaster in a trash container and all utensils in the water container. Let the water drain off and discard the "sludge plaster" into the trash receptacle. **DO NOT** wash liquid plaster down the sink or drain, since it will clog the drain as it builds up and hardens. When using bare hands to mix plaster, the skin can become sensitive and dry, and plaster almost always remains in the finger nails and cuticles. Wash with warm soap and water and apply a small amount of hand or skin cream. Mix plaster in a well ventilated or open area and a dust mask is a good safety measure. Mix the plaster with one hand only and keep a container of fresh water handy for cleanup. The use of an inexpensive dust mask is always recommended while mixing plaster.

You may also wear rubber gloves or use a spoon or spatula to mix the plaster and apply it. The rule of thumb for mixing plaster is: 5 pounds of plaster to 2 quarts of water or a ratio of just under 50-50 plaster to water. A more accurate measurement can be found on the weights and measures chart in Appendix E. When the plaster is ready to be applied, tap the container on the work area base to free any air bubbles that may have gotten into the mix. Remove these with your fingers or a tool before applying the plaster to the model.

After the plaster container has been opened and resealed lumps will sometimes show in the plaster. This is due to natural condensation and if the container is stored in a damp area will occur more frequently. The shelf life of plaster is between 6 to 9 months.

PICTORIAL OVERVIEW

Steps in Proper Mixing of Plaster

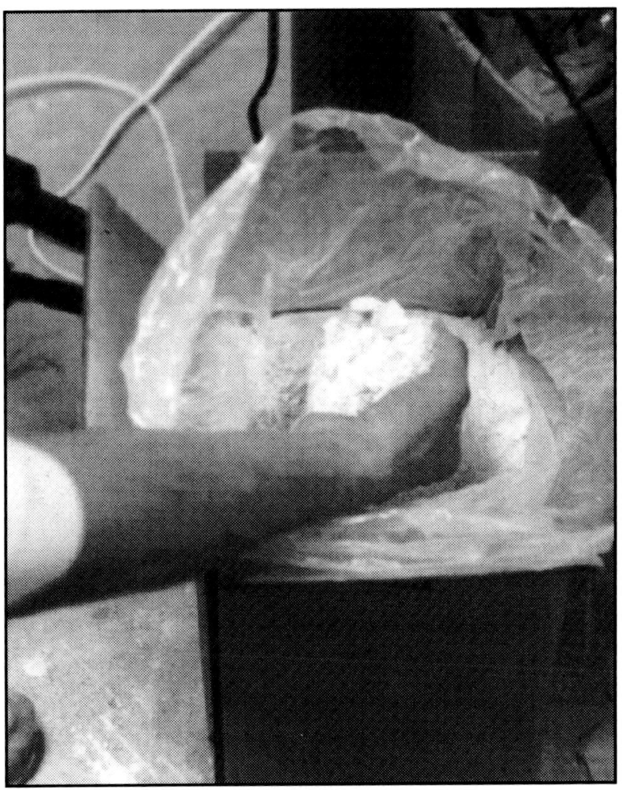

1. Scoop plaster powder from container.

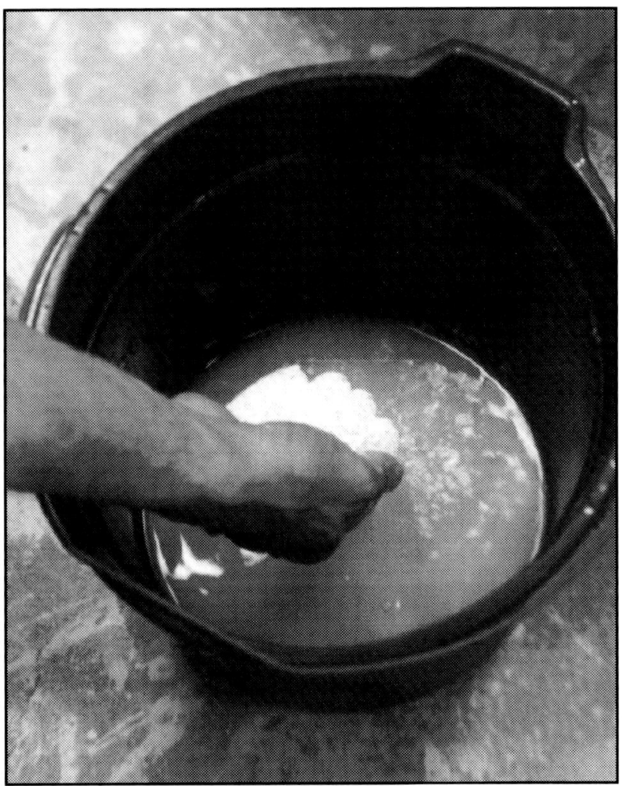

2. Sprinkle lightly through fingers into prepoured water, in a circular motion.

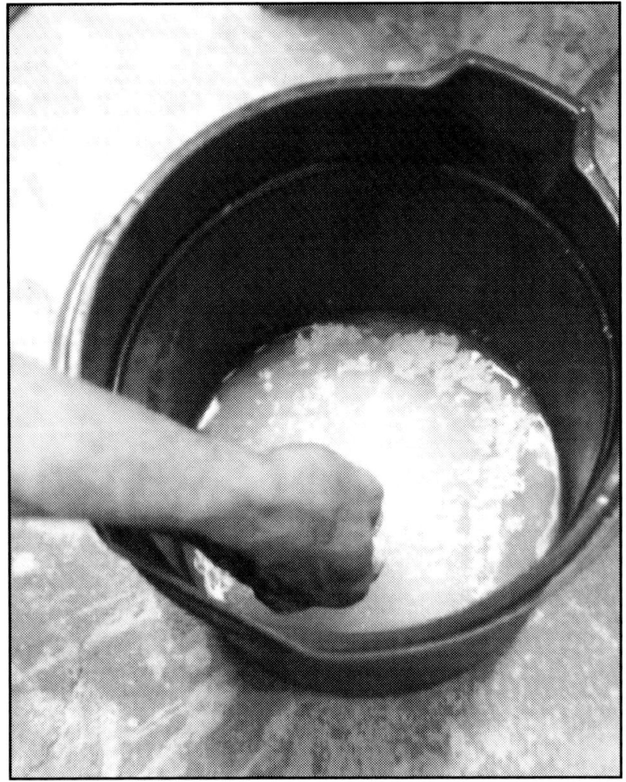

3. Let plaster settle to the bottom of container.

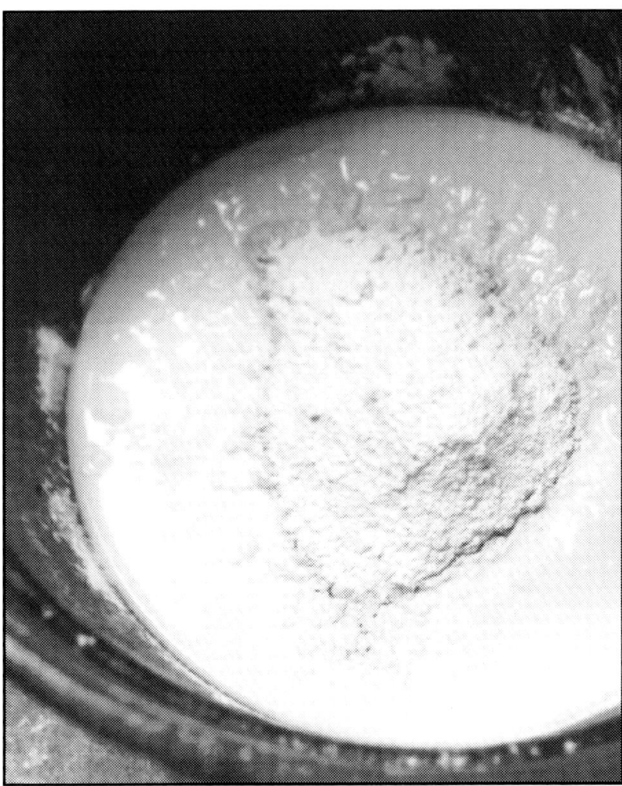

4. Plaster should form a mound about an inch above the water level.

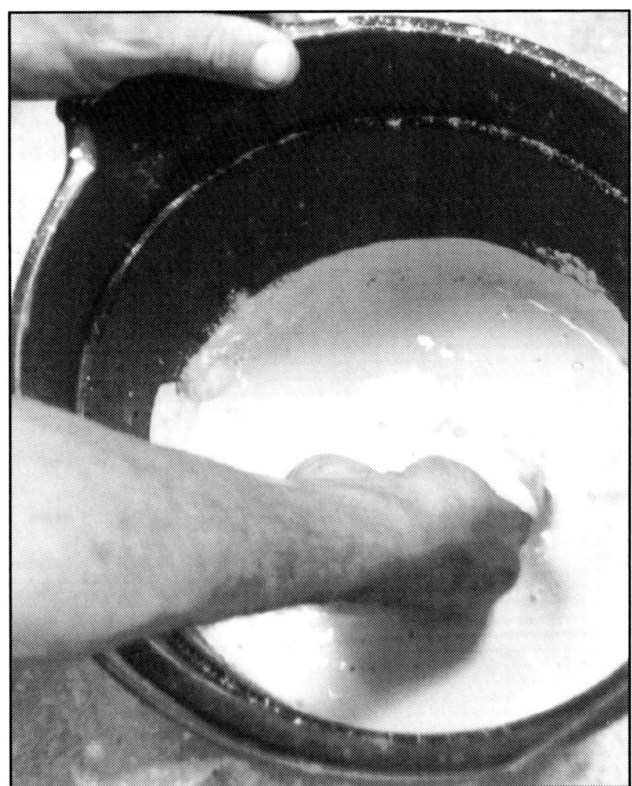

5. Let the water absorb into the plaster mound for about three minutes, then gently begin to mix.

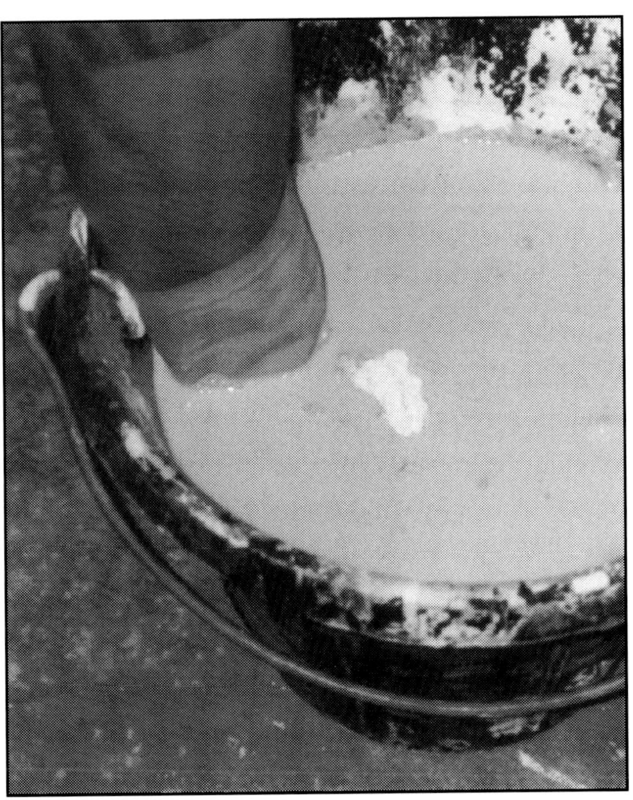

6. Mix the plaster and water from the bottom with the fingers open, scraping down the sides until the mix has the consistency of heavy cream.

MIXING PROCEDURES FOR CASTING

PRISTINE CASTING PLASTER

Casting plaster and hydrocal are considered in the same category where mixing is concerned, though hydrocal is the harder of the two. They are both white powders and are added to water in a circular motion. Sifting the powder through your fingers, breaking up any lumps that may have formed. It is particularly important that no hard pieces of material get into the mix, since we are now making the cast. The mix ratio of powder to water is a little less than when we were making the plaster for the mold. As a general rule, mix 2 1/2 pounds of casting plaster or hydrocal to 1 quart of water to powder weight. These measurements are not necessarily exact, but do not water the material down so much that it will weaken the gypsum.

The powder will settle to the bottom of the container and peak to about 1 inch above the surface level. Let the material settle for 3 minutes to absorb the water. Mixing the plaster for the mold, we will gently stir the mix from the bottom with the fingers open. Move the hand slowly back and forth, so as not to get air into the mix. When the mix becomes heavy cream, it is time to pour.

Initially, we will fill the mold quarter full. Rotating the mold, return the mix to the container; and repeat. All sides of the interior of the mold should now be coated with the liquid mixture. Now fill the mold to the top with the liquid plaster and tap it on the table top or work area. Any air bubbles that have been trapped in the mold will release and rise to the top. Scrape them off with a block scraper. Check to be sure that the level of the cast remains even. Always pour the mixed material slowly, so that air will not get into the casting material.

If there is a leak in the seams of the mold, the level of the plaster will obviously go down. Plug any leaks with lumps of moist clay, and refill the mold.

VATICAN ART CASTING MATERIAL

This material is a powder mix of the base colors. It consists primarily of casting plaster, hydrocal, marble aggregate, and water based pigments. The colors are only meant as base colors and a patina most often will be applied to the material in its final state.

Vatican Art Casting Stone, although very hard like stone, is still a gypsum based product and cannot be exposed to the elements as an outdoor piece.

The colors of Vatican Art Casting Stone in base form are white, terra cotta, grey-green, black (dark grey), and brown. As the material settles in its container, the components may separate and the powder should be mixed by hand before adding to the water. This will ensure an even blend of powder, pigment, and aggregate. Unless the pigments are well mixed into the powder, they will cause an uneven coloring of the cast. This will happen to some degree in any case. When the cast is demolded, **DO NOT** expect a finished colored piece. The base colors will in most cases be pale, washed, and uneven, but this is the effect desired for a good patina. See Chapter 8 for the procedures on patina, which is a separate art unto itself.

The component characteristics of the material in the Vatican Stone and the addition of the marble aggregate make it extremely difficult to mend, join, and repair. The seam lines have always been very hard to repair and cover, even for the professional caster. Take extra care when placing the dividing shims or line on the model. Try to reduce the seam as much as possible and place it in the least conspicuous area possible.

Vatican as a casting material should be in a more liquid form for pouring than the plaster used in the mold making process. We will therefore use more water. When added to water Vatican Stone forms material of a gritty texture. This is a natural characteristic; unlike casting plaster and hydrocal, it will not be smooth and creamy. The mix ratio is 5 pounds of Stone to 3 quarts of water.

As the Vatican powder begins to settle in the bottom of the container, let a small mound form above the water line. Allow the powder to absorb the water for about 3 minutes.

Next, stir from the bottom with the fingers spread and in a gentle manner scrape the sides as the material begins to thicken. Pour the liquid quickly, since the Vatican tends to set faster than plaster once the material is mixed. Pour the casting material as described on page __ and let set. Demold the cast and repair as needed. Apply the final patina as shown in Chapter 8. You may like to buff the cast with a 00 steel wool, to bring out the glitter of the marble aggregate. Be forewarned, when casting Vatican in the different colors, they tend to stain the mold's interior surface and this may carry over to other castings in other colors. This will happen with almost all molds, but especially with plaster molds. The surfaces of these molds can be cleaned thoroughly or several casts of the next color can be drawn from the mold until the color has corrected itself. Remember, Vatican Art Casting Stone is a gypsum based material and though it gives a stone like effect the material is not meant for outdoor use.

HYDROSTONE

This is also a white powder and is mixed with water. This material is extremely hard, the least porous of the gypsum products that we will be using. It is also the most difficult to work with.

The mix ratio is somewhat different than that of the more porous materials: 2 1/2 pounds Hydrostone to 1 pint of water.

Sprinkle the powder into the appropriate amount of water until the settled material forms a peak 1 inch above the water line. Let the material set and absorb the water for only 3 minutes before gently stirring from the bottom until a heavy cream consistency is achieved.

This material can first be applied with a brush, but when pouring, it is a good idea to fill the mold a quarter full and empty it back into the mixing container. Using a rotating motion to cover the entire interior surface of the mold. Then fill the mold to the top. Once full, tap the sides of the mold and tap it on the work table to release any air trapped in the mold. Scrape away any air bubbles that have risen to the surface. If any loss of material occurs due to leakage, plug the areas with moist clay and refill the mold.

HYDROCAL

Hydrocal is the second hardest of the casting materials we will be dealing with, Hydrostone being the hardest. It is a white powder, packaged in 5, 25, and 50 pound containers. Hydrocal is sprinkled into the appropriate amount of water, settling to the bottom of the container until a small mound is formed to about 1 inch above the water line. Allow the powder to settle in the water and absorb for 3 to 4 minutes. The rule of thumb ratio of powder to water is 5 pounds Hydrocal to 1 1/2 quarts of water.

Mix from the bottom with fingers open in a gentle circular motion, folding the material into itself, and scraping down the container's sides until a heavy, smooth cream is formed. Tap the container on the work surface before pouring to release any air bubbles and remove them with the fingers or a block scraper. Then pour the casting material into the mold slowly and evenly.

When the mold has been filled, tap it on the work base to dislodge any air that may have been trapped when pouring; remove the air bubbles. Let the Hydrocal set up for at least 1 hour before demolding. Once the cast has been removed, it can be repaired and the seams finished. Since the Hydrocal is such a hard material, the seam or flashing may be brittle. Use a sharp steel tool or knife to remove this. Once repaired and sanded, the cast can be finished with the desired patina.

APPENDIX B

TROUBLE SHOOTING - MISCELLANEOUS

After making a mold and preparing your casting material, it would seem a simple task to just pour and produce a perfect cast every time, right? No such luck! This is rarely the case. You will be dealing with air bubbles and pockets in the cast, adhesion of the cast to the mold halves, not enough casting material to fill the mold leaving striated sections on the cast, molds that are too thin, molds that break on separation from the model or cast, and last but not least, casts that break in thin areas on demolding. Not to mention a myriad of problems that will pop up when least expected.

Novice mold makers and casters have dealt with all or most of these difficulties at some time or other. Although the masters will look at you as though they were born to greatness, in friendly conversation the stories tend to come out and you will find that have trod the same ground as you. You may even find yourself rolling on the floor with laughter. When you have finished your first few castings, you will have your own stories to tell and I trust they will all be positive in the end. This section is to help you avoid the most common mishaps, relieve pain, and reassure you that all is not lost. I will proceed at random as problems come to mind, so bear with me.

1. When casting plaster into plaster molds, remember to **SOAP** and **SOAK**! Failure to do this is the most common cause of the cast bonding to the mold. Once the plaster mold is set, sealed, and soaped, thoroughly soak it in water for at least 15 minutes, well before the casting plaster is poured. I can never get anyone to believe this until the cast has stuck to the mold and been ruined.
2. Another common error is to pour the casting material directly into the mold without precoating. The result all too often is air pockets in the cast and whole sections that are not there when the cast is removed. With a waste mold, this is really upsetting.

   When pouring a mixed casting material into a mold, fill the mold partially full and rotate it, coating the inner sides, and then return the casting material to the mixing container. This should be done several times to ensure an even surface coating and that all areas of the mold are covered.
3. When mixing the plaster or gypsum material for a mold, do not apply the material too soon; it will only flow onto the floor. Let it become thick enough to adhere to the model. If necessary, mix a fresh batch of plaster and continue. This applies only to mold making, **NOT** the pouring of the cast.
4. When working with plaster, remain cool and collected at all times. Always keep going, **DON'T STOP** for a coffee break. The plaster will start setting once it is added to the water and you will have only a limited amount of working time.
5. Follow the instructions as closely as possible but remember, no book can give you the experience required to make good molds and casts. That will have to come with time and practice. Try playing a round of golf after learning from a book with no prior experience. I'll bet you won't make the pro tour.
6. When they are in use, keep the containers open so you will have easy access to the powder. Fold the plastic cover completely back so your hand will not catch and spill plaster on the floor.

7. Keep your work areas clean. Set pieces of plaster will be troublesome if not removed early on. Discard into the trash receptacle not the drain.

8. Have a container of clean rinse water handy for cleaning tools and hands. Let any residue settle, remove the water on top, and discard the "sludge" into the trash.

9. Dry your tools when clean so they will not rust. Apply a small amount of oil or vaseline if necessary.

10. Have everything you will be needing in front of you before you begin. Once you begin you can't use your mixing hand for anything else since plaster will get all over everything.

11. Try to keep one hand clean and free to handle items as needed.

12. When cleaning seams, scrape even to the contour of the cast and sand. Do not remove more material than necessary.

13. When repairing air holes in the cast or mold, fill and level quickly so the plaster in the smaller container does not set up. You can always sand any excess off the mold or cast later.

14. Inspect all surfaces for damage or repair before casting or finishing. This extra time is preventative and will save time later.

15. Secure the mold tightly and have lumps of moist clay handy for plugging any drainage leaks that occur.

16. Be sure to have a key groove and notches in the molds so they will align properly and not shift when the casting is poured.

17. Do not be afraid to tap the filled mold on the counter top or with a mallet to release air bubbles.

18. Remove a mold with care, using a chisel. Do not break the walls of the mold. Take enough time so that the mold can be removed without breaking.

19. Be careful to apply enough plaster evenly to all areas of the mold. Sections that are too thin will break.

20. After your first casting, you should be very proud and happy. When applying the patina, relax and be creative, don't expect the material to create for you. Use your imagination and have fun. Do a few tests tiles or "pancakes" of set plaster pieces before tackling your finished pieces. Keep a record of the test pieces, materials used, and the procedures followed.

APPENDIX C

Gypsum Product - Plaster General Information

Shelf life ....9 months
Mix ratio ....5 pounds to 2 quarts water.
Setting-up time .... 1 hour
Shore A hardness .... At set plus 600

CAUTION: Heats when setting-up. May cause reaction when skin is directly exposed to liquid.

Plaster is a powder, gypsum based product, a natural material mined in different areas throughout the world, and refined through a heat cured process. In the United States plaster powder is found primarily in the South, Midwest and Northern West Coast. The material is most commonly used in the production of plaster board for the housing industry but there are more than 50 grades that are also used in other forms commercially.

In its powder form plaster is activated by the addition of an amount of water. The generic name most commonly used is plaster of Paris.

The basic grades of plaster are commercial (hardware store), art plaster, Pristine White Casting Plaster, Number 1 Casting Plaster, Hydrocal, Hydrostone, and Ultra-Cal 30. There are other types and grades of gypsum, but since they are not applicable in the sculpture field, we will not discuss them here.

Of these types and grades, we will eliminate the commercial grade as too porous and not suitable, and the art plaster which is normally used for making molds in the ceramic industry, where liquid clay or slip is poured into the mold to make castings known as greenware or bisqueware that are then fired and glazed. The Ultra-Cal 30 we can also eliminate since it is on the edge of being and industrial grade and is too hard for most of the applications in sculpture. Some sculptors however, do sometimes use this product for their casts.

None of the gypsum based products are produced for outdoor use, no matter what the hardness. There are no shortcuts enabling you to produce outdoor casts from plaster. Plaster casts are intended for indoor use only.

This leaves us with the primary group most commonly used in the sculpture field: Pristine White Casting Plaster, Hydrocal, and Hydrostone*.

Pristine White Casting Plaster

Pristine White Casting Plaster is the best all around material for use in the sculpture field. It can be used for the mold making process and is also ideal for casting. This eliminates the need for several types of materials to make the mold and casting. Other plasters can be used for casting only.

Hydrocal

Hydrocal is a gypsum based product in the next highest hardness category of gypsum products. It is used for stronger, more durable casts, but is still easily mixed and poured. This material is **ONLY** recommended for casting. It is not meant for the mold making process.

Hydrostone

Hydrostone is the **hardest** of the gypsum or plaster family members that will suit our applications. The material is somewhat harder in its strength and porosity, but is somewhat more difficult to mix and cast in the proper proportions. It is only intended for use in casting, not for mold making application.

*These are trademarks of the U.S. Gypsum Co., U.S.A.

CUBIC AREA

To find the cubic area or total area, to determine the proper amount of water and plaster needed for a given area, refer to the weights and measures chart on page __.

MENDING - JOINING

For mending and joining, mix in the plaster at the same proportions as for casting. Rough up or scratch the surfaces with crossmarks using a pointed tool. Apply the plaster to both sections at the mend. Place the pieces together and secure firmly until the plaster sets. Any cleaning can then be done as necessary.

MIX RATIO

Although the mixing of plaster is an acquired feel that most of the old time mold makers and casters just seem to know after years of experience, I have come up with a rule of thumb, at least a general idea, for the amounts of material that will be required. It is hoped that with these mix ratios you will have more than enough material rather than not quite enough.

5 lbs. of plaster to 2 qts. water

ALWAYS mix the plaster powder into the water. **DO NOT** pour the water onto the plaster.

RETARD, DELAY SETTING TIME

To delay or retard the setting time of gypsum based products you may add a small amount of lemon juice to the mix. A few drops will generally be enough but you can judge for yourself the exact amount needed. Always try a test batch so you can gauge properly.

RETOUCHING

For retouching a mold or cats. Mix 1 part plaster and 2 parts water (1:2) in a small rubber flexible mixing bowl and stir. When the plaster thickens, apply with a flexible spatula.

TO HARDEN PLASTER

To strengthen or harden plaster, you may add a product called Bone Emulsion. This material is a liquid. When added to the water of the mix, it will make the plaster bone hard. It will not waterproof the plaster.

For best results:

1 pint Bone Emulsion to 25 pounds of plaster to the mix

(a test batch for other amounts is always advisable)

TO INCREASE SETTING TIME

To increase the setting time, add common household salt to the mix. A few pinches will usually suffice, but you be the judge.

WEATHERPROOFING

On of the older and lesser known methods of preservation is to impregnate the cast with boiled linseed oil. Or boil the cast in a mixture of 85% pure beeswax and 15% paraffin. You may also impregnate the plaster with modern day plastic compounds or with weatherproofing materials available at the local hardware store.

Although these methods will not make your product an outdoor piece or enable it to withstand the elements for an extended period, it will seal the plaster against the basic elements for a short period and protect the plaster from normal moisture and temperature change erosion.

MISCELLANEOUS

All the mix ratios are based on a personal use preference and you should conduct individual tests to find the exact amounts most suitable for your applications. Most mold makers and casters do not follow exact mix ratios of weight and volume when mixing and casting plasters. They mix by sight, feel, touch, and most of all, experience. If you should ask mold makers how to mix plaster, you could probably write a book on their responses alone.

The weights and measures chart is therefore meant only as a guide for those not familiar with the product or who are using the material for the first time.

Plaster is generally packaged in 50 pound double walled bags. In most cases, it is then repackaged into 25 pound and 5 pound plastic wrapped bags. The 50 pound units are not handy for the consumer, because of their weight, but they can be purchased in some lumber yards. In art supply stores and sculpture material outlets, you will usually find only the 25 pound and 5 pound units, and occasionally 50 pound bags.

APPENDIX D

BRONZE CASTING

Many people do not realize the variety of steps and difficulties present when casting bronze. Some believe that bronze is modeled directly, but this is not the case. I thought it might be helpful to go over the basics of the bronze casting process. This will be done in extreme short form.

All bronze pieces are cast from a wax model regardless of the material the original model was sculpted in. A rubber mold is made and a hollow wax cast is drawn from this mold. The wax is then repaired, reworked, and finished to the sculptor's satisfaction. Vents are attached within the wax model, in difficult areas where gas may accumulate such as hip area, limbs, and neck. These vents will allow the gas to escape when the molten bronze is poured and will prevent air pockets from forming and exploding the ceramic shell. (We're coming to that.) The ceramic shell is one of the few materials that can withstand the heat of the molten bronze.

When the wax cast is hardened and the vents are in place a ceramic shell is formed over the wax, usually by dipping. After the ceramic shell has set, the wax is melted and the ceramic shell is left intact. Molten bronze is poured into the ceramic shell. When the bronze has cooled, the shell is chipped away using a hammer and chisel.

The bronze must then be repaired and finished. This is called chasing and is a difficult process since the metal is involved. Any air pockets or pits must be brazed with a bronze rod, as in welding. Seams and spurs must be removed by grinding and rasping, then sanding.

The final step is to chase or hammer the vents off the mold with special tools. The natural bronze exterior has a dull finish. A final patina is applied and the bronze can be left matte or polished. Chemicals, pigments, much skill, and a lot of safety equipment are involved.

Note that bronze comes in a variety of alloys. Each will use different chemicals and techniques for patina.

If you want a bronze cast I would suggest that you contact a professional mold maker and/or bronze foundry to have the work done safely and professionally.

COLD CAST BRONZE - BONDED BRONZE

Cold cast bronze or bonded bronze is a name given to plastic resins that have bronze powder added to the mix. It creates the effect of bronze but is less expensive, because it is not the real thing. (Bronze cannot be cast cold.)

To reduce the cost of a real bronze cast, consider modeling directly into wax, eliminating the first mold making cost. However, if anything goes wrong with the casting, you will be left with nothing, instead of a mold that another wax model can be drawn from.

APPENDIX E

ENLARGING

Most large pieces of sculpture over 24 inches have been modeled directly. Some sculptors do work in life size or larger but generally work from models of about 12 to 18 inches. They are enlarged on a pantograph machine by "pointing." Pointing by the pantograph machine can enlarge the model up to 4 times the size of the original. A 12 foot statue was probably a 14 inch model, taken up over several enlargements to the finished size. Only a very few in the world can enlarge by eye.

The pantograph machine must be set properly and the model must be reproduced in exact proportions. As an example, think of a button. Now enlarge the button 5 times, from 1 inch in diameter to 5 inches. Mistakes in proportion become somewhat more noticeable, wouldn't you say?

Without going into every detail here are the basic steps in enlarging. The model is taken from the original mold, then cast into plaster.

Place small x's over the entire model very close together. Set an armature at the other end of the machine, proportional in size to the enlargement desired. Build up plastilina to the general configuration of the armature and model. The small point, is then placed on one of the marks and the arm at the other end of the enlarging machine is then placed on the larger plastilina model and a toothpick is placed in the plastilina. This process is done on every mark of the small model, until there is a general likeness in the original model.

The piece is then turned on a table at both ends. At the larger end, the table is usually a heavy steel fifth wheel, which can hold thousands of pounds. When the process has been done over several times, the piece is then ready to have the sculptor come in and complete the final details, because the enlarging will not give the exact likeness.

A piece mold is then made and sections are cast in wax, then bronze, then fused together. The finishing touches are completed and the bronze is placed for display.

Reducing is done in the same manner, but in reverse.

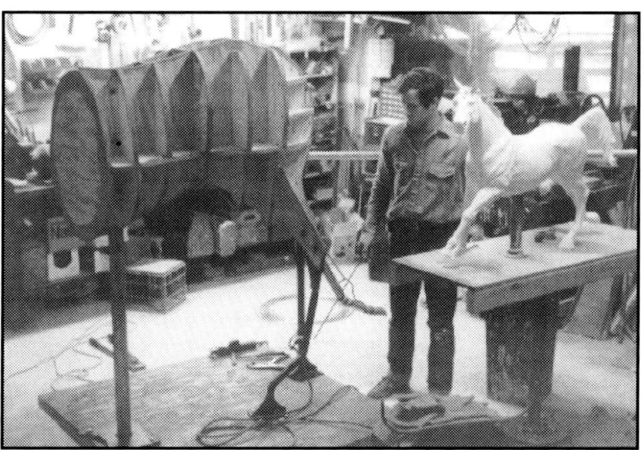

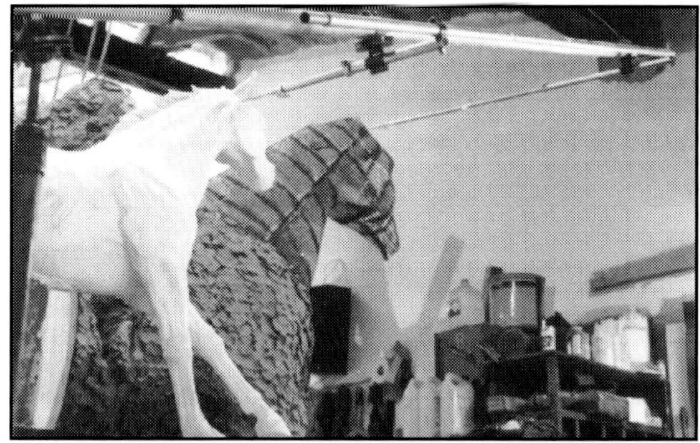

Two stages of a "horse" enlargement being done by Sculpture House Casting, N.Y., N.Y.

APPENDIX F

EQUIVALENCY CHARTS

WEIGHTS

Mold Rubber	1 qt.	=	30 cu. in.
Casting Rubber	1 qt.	=	30 cu. in.
Moulage	1 lb.	=	15 cu. in.
Pos-Moulage	1 lb.	=	10 cu. in.
Moist Clay	1 lb.	=	16 cu. in.
Plastilina	1 lb.	=	16 cu. in.
Plaster Powder	5 lb.	=	150 cu. in.
Hydrocal Powder	5 lb.	=	130 cu. in.
Hydrostone Powder	5 lbs.	=	100 cu. in.
Vatican Art Casting Stone	5 lbs.	=	100 cu. in.
Gallon Water		=	8 lbs.
Gallon Rubber - mold or casting		=	9 lbs.
Gallon Casting Filler		=	11 lbs.

MEASURES

16 oz.	=	1 pt.
4 qts.	=	1 gallon

MATERIAL REQUIREMENTS USAGE CHART

Model Size	Plastilina per/lb.	Moist Clay per/lb.	Plaster Powder for Mold Plaster	Water	Plaster Powder for Cast Plaster	Water	Latex Rubber	Paste-maker	Casting Rubber	Casting Fillers Soft	Medium	Hard	White Rubber	Vatican Art Cast.Stone	Moulage
HEAD & BUST															
HA-2 13" (1/2 Life)	25 lbs.	25 lbs.	15 lbs.	1 gal.	25 lbs.	2 gal.	1 pt.	1 lb.	2 qt.	0	2 - 1	1 - 1	gal.	25 lbs.	2 lbs.
HA-3 15" (5/8 Life)	30 lbs.	30 lbs.	25 lbs.	2 gal.	25 lbs.	2 gal.	1 qt.	1 lb.	2 qt.	0	2 - 1	1 - 1	gal.	25 lbs.	5 lbs.
HA-4 20" (Life Size)	35 lbs.	35 lbs.	40 lbs.	3 gal.	75 lbs.	3 gal.	2 qts.	2 lbs.	1 gal.	0	2 - 1	1 - 1	2 gal.	75 lbs.	10 lbs.
FIGURE															
FA-1 6"	8 lbs.	8 lbs.	10 lbs.	2 qts.	15 lbs.	3	1 pt.	1 lb.	1 qt.	0	2 - 1	1 - 1	qt.	10 lbs.	2 lbs.
FA-3 12"	12 lbs.	12 lbs.	15 lbs.	1 gal.	25 lbs.	2 gal.	1 qt.	1 1 lb.	1 qt.	0	2 - 1	1 - 1	2 qts.	15 lbs.	5 lbs.
FA-4 15"	15 lbs.	15 lbs.	25 lbs.	2 gal.	40 lbs.	2 gal.	1 qt.	1 lb.	2 qts.	0	2 - 1	1 - 1	1 gal.	25 lbs.	10lbs.
FA-5 18"	20 lbs.	20 lbs.	25 lbs.	2 gal.	50 lbs.	4 gal.	2 qts.	3 lbs.	3 qts.	0	2 - 1	1 - 1	1 gal.	50 lbs.	10 lbs.
FA-30 30"	60 lbs.	60 lbs.	50 lbs.	4 gal.	100 lbs.	8 gal.	1 gal.	5 lbs.	2	0	2 - 1	1 - 1	2 gal.	100 lbs.	20 lbs.
ANIMAL															
AA-6 6"	3 lbs.	3 lbs.	10 lbs.	4 qts.	10 lbs.	4 qts.	1 pt.	1 lb.	1 qt.	0	2 - 1	1 - 1	qt.	10 lbs.	2 lbs.
AA-8 8"	8 lbs.	8 lbs.	10 lbs.	4 qts.	10 lbs.	4 qts.	1 qt.	2 lbs.	2 qts.	0	2 - 1	1 - 1	qt.	10 lbs.	21 lbs.
AA-10 10"	14 lbs.	14 lbs.	20 lbs.	8 qts.	20 lbs.	8 qts.	2 qts.	5 lbs.	3 qts.	0	2 - 1	1 - 1	2 qts.	25 lbs.	5 lbs.
FREE FORM use formula L x W (depth) x H apply below amounts															

1. To calculate cubic inches - take height times length times width: H x L x W = cu. in.
2. Plaster powder to water ratio will be approximately two pounds of plaster to one pint of water (H2O)
3. One gallon of water weighs 8 lbs., one gallon of rubber weighs 9lbs., one gallon of casting filler weighs 11 lbs.
4. one cbic inch of plastilina weighs 1 oz., one cubic inch of moist clay weighs 1 oz., all weights are approximate to the ounce.
5. All figures and measurements are based on Sculpture House Inc. materials.

GLOSSARY OF TERMS

Armature - An internal support structure to hold modeling material in a preformed position. Could be made of wood, wire, wax or paper.

Air Bubbles - Holes formed either in the cast or mold when a casting material, plaster, is applied or poured.

Appendages - A raised area or extremity that must be removed prior to making a mold due to the sever undercuts. A separate mold should be made and the piece attached later upon completion of the cast. Example: An Outstretched arm as in waving good-bye to a friend.

Bluing - A water soluble dye used in making the color of a casting material first coat identifiable. Used to color the first coat of a waste mold to show that the cast is close to being chipped.

Block Scraper - A rectangular steel rigged piece of metal, with or without teeth, that is used to remove plaster and level and clean up areas of the mold.

Base - Can be referred to as the bottom of a piece of sculpture. More commonly referred to as the display item that a piece of sculpture is mounted on for display. Usually made of micarta, wood, stone, or marble.

Batch - New or freshly mixed plaster. Commonly referred to when an amount is made up for a certain project or part there of.

Case Mold - A plaster mold primarily used to cast ceramic slip.

Cast - The positive derived from the negative mold.

Ceramic Shell - Used in bronze casting. This material covers the wax model prior to the wax being burned out and the bronze being poured into the ceramic shell mold. The shell is then removed by chipping, leaving the cast bronze piece. Ceramic shell molds are one of the few that can withstand the heat of the bronze without breaking.

Chasing - Hammering or working bronze after casting, to conceal seam lines, etc.

De-Molding - Removing the mold from a piece of sculpture by prying or chipping.

Dead Plaster - Plaster that has been placed in water and has not been mixed but has set up. Also, plaster that has had more water added to it after it has already begun to set up, preventing it from hardening properly.

Digging Out - Removing excess material of the model that was left in the mold when the mold was removed.

Drawn - Taking a piece or cast from the mold.

Fence - Parting material that separates specific areas of the model, making mold sections for easy removal possible.

Flange - Base or seam area of a mold. Area that extends from the base of a model when making rubber molds to help keep the rubber intact while casting. Usually extends three inches from the base of the piece.

Flashing - Seepage when pouring a liquid or molten material into a mold with seam the excess is referred to as the flashing and should be trimmed before completion of the cast.

Gate - Generally known as a system of spurs or vents to let air escape when pouring molten metal and at times resin or plaster. This venting or gating reduces air pockets in joint areas.

Green - When a material has not cured completely or set up to it's final state.

Head - The head is usually considered the face, back of head, and neck, that does not extend below the adams apple on a male.

Head-Bust - The head and bust includes the head with adams apple and also the shoulders extending just below the clavicle.

Investment - A material used to coat a wax or other model prior to bronze casting or hollowing for the inclusion of a molten material.

In the Round - A three dimensional work or sculpture.

Key - A locking devices grooved or cut into the walls of a mold to inhibit shifting or movement when casting material is being poured. May also be referred to as a key groove or key locks.

Key Knife - A knife specifically designed to cut a groove in rubber molds after the rubber has been pour into a hollow cavity. The groove is approximately 1/2 inch thick from the tip of the cutting edge.

Killed Plaster - See Dead Plaster above.

Lost Wax - A process where a wax model has been made of a piece of sculpture from a rubber mold for multiple castings, generally in bronze. The wax is melted out leaving a hollow cavity in which the molten bronze is poured. Thus the wax is lost.

Mother Mold - This is a plaster shell or mold constructed around a rubber inner mold or used as a backing for support of flexible materials. Rubber molds are generally stored in the mother mold.

Mold - A structure that will capture the exact likeness and detail for reproduction of the original. These are most commonly made of plaster, latex rubber, polyurethane rubber, or silicon rubber.

Mold Solution - The material that coast the interior surface of the mold to assist in easier separation of a cast from the mold.

Negative - Is understood as the hollow cavity of the mold in which a cast or positive is drawn.

Notch - This is a round or square indentation cut into the mold wall to act as a locking device in conjunction with key grooves. They are usually placed every three or four inches along the mold wall, depending on the size of the mold.

Notch Knife - See Key Knife above.

Oil Clay - A wax and oil based modeling material that will remain pliable indefinitely. Grades will vary from childrens to professional quality. Some will have a sulphur and some will not depending on the manufacturer.

Pedestal - A display stand for sculpture, not to be confused with a modeling stand which is used as a work table in creating sculpture. Pedestals are usually four feet high and have fourteen inch square sides to the floor. They can also be any size that is required for the display of the sculpture. Pedestals are generally made of either black or white micarta.

Plastilina - Oil based modeling material also known by the names, Plasticum, and plasticine. This material will not harden, can not be fired in a ceramic kiln, and is generally used in model construction that will require a mold to be made.

Patina - This is the coloring of a piece of sculpture with artificial or natural materials to resemble an aging process found on bronze outdoor statues. The patina of plaster is accomplished with pigments and powders. Bronze patination is done with chemicals and pigments.

Parting Agent - Soap, oil or liquid used in the interior of a mold to assist in the separation of the cast or model from the mold. Different rubber molds may require special types of release agents for specific casting materials.

Plug - Is usually placed at the top of a mold on the model of a pliable material that can be easily removed after the construction of the mold so that water may be poured into the mold, between the mold and model for easier separation of the mold.

Positive - A piece or cast taken from a negative mold. A positive is cast into a negative to create the final piece.

Retaining Wall - A wall constructed around a relief panel or small sculpture or medal that will retain plaster to a confined area that will become the mold or section of the mold. This is at times called or referred to as a fence or shim.

Relief - Is a one sided panel with raised positions that make a sculpture. Also known as a bas-relief.

Release Agent - A parting or release agent is applied to a mold or piece of sculpture in order to facilitate the separation of mold from model or cast from mold. Usually soap or oil. Specific separators are required for certain types of rubber molds.

Setting Time - The time a material takes to set up or cure. The time between mixing and final use.

Seam Line - The line that is made between the mold sections when pouring a cast, either in plaster or molten metal or resin.

Shelf Life - The time that a material will be kept before it's effectiveness is no longer available.

Shim - A material that separates or divides a model for different areas of a mold. Generally a clay or metal material placed on the model to be cast.

Sludge - The residue of settled plaster or clay at the bottom of a work pail when cleaning utensils or hands.

Spurs - A system of veins or gating that as vents to release air when a piece is being cast in resin or bronze.

Surface Lumps - Lumps or protrusions caused by improper mold construction that are greater than the original surface contour.

Slip - A ceramic material that is used in casting greenware for ceramic pieces. A material that acts as a binder when mending joints or broken pieces of sculpture.

Slurry - A liquid material that wax casts are dipped into to form a coating or shell prior to the casting of bronze. Also called ceramic slurry.

Under Cuts - Those areas of a modal or sculpture that have exaggerated protrusions or overhangs that will not enable an easy release of a section or part of a mold.

Vents - Channels placed on the model to the exterior of the mold enabling gas and captured air to escape reducing pockets within the cast.

Waste Mold - A mold made of plaster that will be used once and be destroyed by chipping the original mold from the subsequent cast. Thus being wasted or destroyed.

Water Clay - A ceramic or water base clay that is generally used with the intent that the piece will be fired to vitrification in a ceramic kiln. Usually to temperatures of at least 2,000 degrees F. Water base clays are also used to plug leaks in mold walls when casting and for shim or separating material due to their soft and flexible consistency.

RECOMMENDED READING

"Terra Cotta," "Modeling the Head in Clay,"
and "Modeling the Figure in Clay"
by Bruno Lucchesi and Margit Malmstrom.
Watson-Guptill Publications, 1515 Broadway,
N.Y., N.Y. 10036.
These are three great books on modeling with fantastic photos by Margit Malmstrom, including the origin of sculpture shown through the eyes of sculptor Bruno Lucchesi.

"Methods for Modern Sculptor's"
by Ronald D. Young and Robert A. Fennell.
Gives in depth knowledge of the more advanced mold making methods for bronze casting. An exciting book covering spurs, gates, and bronze casting.

"Patination" Available through Sculpt-Nouveau,
21 Redwood Dr., San Rafael, Ca., 94901
Everything needed for those who want to learn the most advanced styles of bronze coloring. This work contains color photos, formulas and just about everything possible on patina of metals.

SOURCES OF SUPPLY

Chemicals for bronze patina:
- Bryant Laboratory, 1101 Fifth St.,
  Berkley, Ca. 94710 Phone 415-526-3141
- City Chemical, 132 W. 22nd St.,
  N.Y., N.Y. 10019 Phone 212-929-2723

Casting resins:
- Industrial Plastics, 309 Canal St.,
  N.Y., N.Y. 10009 Phone 212-226-2010

Bases and pedestals for displaying sculpture:
- Sculpture House Casting, 155 W. 26th St., N.Y.,
  N.Y. 10001 Phone 212-645-9430

Tools materials and accessories for sculpture, mold making and casting:
- Your local Art Supply Store
- Sculpture House Inc., 30 E. 30th St.,
  N.Y., N.Y. 10016 Phone 212-679-7474